NEW YORK
ADMINISTRATIVE LAW,
EXECUTIVE AGENCIES, AND
THE ADMINISTRATIVE LAW JUDICIARY

FELIX NEALS

Published under the title

**NEW YORK
ADMINISTRATIVE LAW,
EXECUTIVE AGENCIES, AND
THE ADMINISTRATIVE LAW JUDICIARY**

PRINTED IN THE UNITED STATES OF AMERICA

2nd Edition.

ISBN: 978-0-692-38807-5.

Cover Design by JACOB VU.

TRIBUTES

A few among the many individuals who underwrote my life:

Dr. Huerta Cortez Neals, patriarch and redeemer.

Judge Seymour Margulies, ultimate teacher, mentor, and friend.

People who shepherded me through mazes of knowledge in the institutions – Stanton School; US Army; Idaho State University; Washburn University School of Law; Menninger Foundation; New York State government.

To All, I am very grateful. Thank you.

Felix.

fneals@gmail.com

THE AUTHOR

Felix Neals, a retired New York State civil servant, worked in various jobs: Agency attorney and Chief Counsel, Office of Economic Opportunity; Administrative Law Judge, Supervising Administrative Law Judge, and Special Deputy Secretary of State, Department of State. Before government service, Felix worked for ITT Corporation (NJ), as legal counsel and administrator of education; and for RCA, as administrator, computer applications early-education (NYC, Pala Alto), a joint venture with Dr. Patrick Suppes of Stanford University's Institute for Mathematical Research in the Social Sciences.

Born in Jacksonville and reared in Jacksonville and Miami, Florida, Felix, when a youth, was considered "mentally slow" by the public and explained as "touched" by the family. Education and medical resources were scarce in the racially segregated communities in which he lived. His childhood was deriding, his early education derisive, and his mental health care indigenous.

At an underage, Felix enlisted in military service and served in racially segregated Army units. After an honorable discharge from military service (WW II, Pacific Theater), he attended and received a B.S. from Idaho State University. He was elected to Who's Who in American Colleges and Universities, won a U.S. National Intercollegiate Oratory Championship, and awarded the Degree of Special Distinction in Pi Kappa Delta Honor Society. He was a finalist in an annual competition of Yale University Series for Younger Poets. Felix obtained a J.D. from Washburn University School of Law, Topeka, Kansas.

In Kansas at the Menninger Foundation (psychiatric treatment and research center), Felix, an employee and outpatient, first learned of "autism." Prior psychiatric diagnoses of "mental retardation" and "schizophrenia" in his life were displaced by the word, "autism," at that time, a relatively new medical categorization.

Felix has been a member of New York State and national, administrative law judge associations. His writings include articles on *Psychosystematics* (Felix's method of forging conceptual mental networks to subjugate autism to his life); two books of essays, short stories, and poetry – *Autistic Reflections in a Steel Mirror Reflected; Autism in Black Matter.*

PREFACE

Law is a science. Law interpretation is an art. Lawmaking, rulemaking, law administration, and law management are scientific procedures. A law or rule carefully crafted to fit a human need inclines both to treat a social condition and to be socially accepted.

Judicial judgment is an art form. The interpretation and application of law to fact to formulate decision are artistic activities. Law grows, ages, and gains legal weight from the artistry of the interpretation and application of law to fact.

Government intends that the services of administrative agencies be efficient economically, proficient politically, and strategic socially. In the implementation of its legislative mission, government balances the services it provides as needed for human advancement through government's regulation of a rational social order.

The power of administrative law is humbling. A decisionmaker in a quasi-judicial, regulatory action acts both as judge and jury. One decision by one New York State, executive, administrative agency may affect the lives of more people and more money than are affected by the total of all decisions made in one year by all New York State judicial courts.

A decision of an executive, administrative agency may impact an industry, a market, a profession, every birth, and every death in New York, and, in effect, express a magisterial sovereignty that parallels that of a decision of the New York State Court of Appeals.

The just dispensation of legislative mandates by quasi-judicial, administrative agencies both to the regulated and to the regulators is imperative to the health, safety, and welfare of the state.

Felix Neals.
Rock City Falls, NY; Long Island City, NY; East Orange, NJ.

CONTENTS

TABLE OF AUTHORITIES.

CHAPTER 1. FUNDAMENTALS OF NEW YORK ADMINISTRATIVE LAW.

§ 1.1. Administrative Law Made in New York. A New York State administrative law begins as a concept compressed into a legislative proposal and chronologically becomes a bill, a chapter law, a session law, and a consolidated or unconsolidated law.

1. Session law is an annual volume of chapter laws published by chapter number. Each year at the end of a legislative session, chapter laws enacted are accumulated consecutively as laws of a session and published as New York State consolidated or unconsolidated laws.

2. The chapter number of a law indicates the numerical position of the law in a legislative session. Chapter 487 of the laws of 2012 (2012 NY Laws 487) illustrates a numerical position of an agency law in the 2012 legislative session. The chapter number 487 denotes the 487th law passed in the 2012 legislative session. The law amends the Vehicle and Traffic Law, §§ 490, 502, and 504; it directs the commissioner of motor vehicles to provide a space on the forms of identification cards and licenses for veterans' notation.

3. New York State organizes state laws into consolidated laws and unconsolidated laws.

A. Consolidated Laws. Ordinarily, a law with statewide effect is codified; the law is classified according to the subject matter (education, insurance, labor, and so forth) and structured into a statute or code. New York does not publish an official text of its code. Statutory law is a compilation of the public, general, and permanent laws of New York. New York State laws are predominantly consolidated laws. Statutes that create executive administrative agencies are consolidated laws.

B. Unconsolidated Laws. Local, regional or laws otherwise limited in application and laws that do not fit within consolidated law chapters are not codified and are published as unconsolidated laws. Examples are: NY wine/grape, Chapter 80 of the laws of 1985; Boxing Sparring and Wrestling, Chapter 912 of the laws of 1920; Port of New York Authority, Chapter 154 of the laws of 1921; Port of Albany, Chapter 192 of the laws of 1925; Emergency Tenant Protection Act, chapter 576 of the laws of 1974.

§ 1.2. Introduction to New York State Administrative Law. New York State administrative law expresses the legal relationships between a state administrative agency and the individuals and entities regulated by the agency, between and among state administrative agencies, and between a state administrative agency and the state.

1. New York State administrative law evolves and develops from a maturation of legal, social, economic, and political systems into a structure of justice that addresses expeditiously compelling public concerns and social needs. Administrative law is a progeny of the redefinition of "public general welfare" in recognition of new civil rights requiring protection by government and from government and of the political abandonment of "laissez-faire," the natural economic order of individual activity free from all government regulation.

2. With enactment of an administrative law, the state creates a

government agency, grants to that agency purposeful, permissive, regulatory authority over designated government functions, and assigns the agency to a branch of state government.

3. The state governs through administrative law. Within federal and state constitutional constraints, New York administrative law strives to acclimatize human behavior to a structured social environment governed by the state; it mandates conduct (shall or must), permits pursuits (may or might) and forbids acts (prohibits or proscribes).

§ 1.3. Structure of New York State Administrative Law. New York State administrative law is the compilation of all statutes, codes, rules, and regulations, and judicial and administrative orders and decisions applicable to State administrative agencies. New York State Administrative law is part of New York State public law.

1. New York State Public Law. New York Public law regulates public relationships – the relationships between and among the state and individuals and the relationships between and among the executive, the legislative, and the judiciary branches of state government. New York public law consists of constitutional public law and statutory public law. Procedural administrative law and substantive administrative law derive from public law.

A. Constitutional Law. The New York State constitution forms the system of state government, limits the powers of state government, and prescribes the fundamental rights of citizens.

(1). The state constitution assigns to and distributes powers among the three branches of state government: The legislative, the executive and the judiciary.

(a). The legislature enacts laws (NY Const art III, § 1).

(b). The executive administers laws (NY Const art IV, § 1).

(c). The judiciary assures the fair and objective administration of laws (NY Const art VI, § 1).

(2). The New York Constitution circumscribes the power of the state in the state's relationship with people. NY Const art I, § 6 forbids the state from taking a person's life, liberty or property without due process of law. NY Const art I, § 8 guarantees freedom of speech and press. NY Const art I, § 12, prohibits unreasonable searches and seizures by government.

B. Statutory Public Law. A statutory public law is a formal, written, legislative enactment that enumerates rights and regulates activities typical to the welfare of people. Illustrations of New York public law statutes are General Business Law art 22 A, Environmental Conservation Law, Vehicle and Traffic Law, Public Authorities Law (bridges, tunnels, parks, parkways), and Public Service Law (gas, electric, steam, telecom, cable television). Statutory public law includes two essential components of New York administrative law, substantive administrative law and procedural administrative law.

(1). Substantive administrative law encompasses:

(a). Laws that form and define executive administrative agencies.

(b). Rules, regulations, orders, and decisions issued by administrative agencies.

(c). The specialized policies created by administrative agencies as consequences of agencies' efforts to implement substantive due process principles through rulemaking and adjudication processes

(d). Judicial interpretations of laws, codes, rules, regulations, orders, and decisions that govern administrative agencies.

(2). Procedural administrative law imposes specific procedures on administrative agencies. Those procedures outline the practices that an agency must follow when enacting and administering substantive administrative laws and rules.

2. Administrative Law as Public Law. Administrative law creates and implements methods through which government may efficiently and expeditiously manage and manipulate human behavior into governmentally constructed social orders. Government control through regulation of economic interests and social benefits is a primary characteristic of administrative law.

CHAPTER II. INTRODUCTION TO ADMINISTRATIVE AGENCIES.

§ 2.1. State Administrative Agencies. A New York State administrative agency is a state government unit statutorily empowered to implement a delegated legislative act. The State Administrative Procedure Act (SAPA) defines "agency" as a government entity that fulfills at least two of three elements: At least one person appointed by the governor must head the entity, and the entity must be empowered by law either to promulgate rules or to make final decisions in administrative adjudications. SAPA § 102 (1).

§ 2.2. Major Classifications of Agencies. The two primary classifications of New York State administrative agencies are executive agencies and independent agencies.

1. Executive Administrative Agencies. An executive administrative agency is a civil department of New York State government (NY Const art V, § 2) statutorily empowered to implement delegated missions. A New York State civil department is directed by an official appointed (and may be removed without cause) by the state's chief executive, the governor. The executive agency is the traditional agency model in New York State, and principal, state administrative agencies are executive agencies. Central command of state executive agencies rests with the governor.

2. Independent Administrative Agencies. Officially, independent agencies are part of the executive branch; but by design and identity, independent agencies are not directly answerable to the governor. A board of members who serve for a limited duration of time manages an archetypal, independent regulatory agency. The governor appoints the board chair and members and fills board vacancies. Law protects board members from arbitrary removal during a term of office. The governor may remove a member only for cause (inefficiency, neglect of duty or misconduct in office). The limitation on the gubernatorial power of removal is real; however, the power to appoint and fill board vacancies influence agency actions. An example of an independent regulatory agency is the New York State Energy Research and Development Authority, a public benefit corporation (Public Authorities Law § 1852).

§ 2.3. Creation and Mission of Executive Agencies. Legislation begets agencies.

1. Creation – Organic Act. The state legislature enacts a law that concurrently creates and empowers an agency to perform a particular governmental task affecting specific persons and activities. The statute is termed an "organic act" or an "enabling statute." Customarily, agencies created by organic acts are

designated as executive administrative agencies and assigned as departments of the executive branch of state government.

A. Limitation on Legislative Delegation. The US Constitution neither restricts nor prohibits a state legislature in the delegation of its powers to a state agency. A New York State constitutional limitation exists (NY Const art III, § 1).

(1). The New York State Legislature cannot delegate all of its law-making power to the executive branch. "Because of the constitutional provision that '[t]he legislative power of this State shall be vested in the Senate and the Assembly' (NY Const art III, § 1), the Legislature cannot pass on its law-making functions to other bodies (citation omitted) but there is no constitutional prohibition against the delegation of power, with reasonable safeguards and standards, to an agency or commission to administer the law as enacted by the Legislature (citations omitted)." *Matter of Levine v Whalen*, 39 NY2d 510 (1976).

(2). "While the separation of powers doctrine gives the Legislature considerable leeway in delegating its regulatory powers, enactments conferring authority on administrative agencies in broad or general terms must be interpreted in light of the limitations that the Constitution imposes (NY Const, art III, § 1)." See *Boreali v Axelrod*, 71 NY2d 1, 523 NYS2d 464 (1987). In *Boreali*, New York State, Department of Health, Public Health Council, acting under its enabling statute, Public Health Law § 225 (5) (a), adopted a regulation that prohibited smoking in most public indoor areas and sharply restricted smoking in restaurants and workplaces. The Court of Appeals found that the agency "overstepped" the line between administrative rule-making and legislative policy-making and held the regulation to be "unconstitutional."

B. Skeleton Organic Statutes. Traditionally, an enabling law broadly formats an agency's mission and latitude of power. Organic acts do not contain the level of administrative and operating specificity required for an agency to function efficiently and effectively. The statutes vest agencies with extensive discretion and expansive power to augment an organic act by implementing regulations compatible with the emancipating legislation. (*General Elec. Capital Corp. v NY St. Div. of Tax Appeals, Tax Appeals Trib.*, 2 NY3d 249, 778 NYS2d 412 [2004]). Simplistic legislation initiates complex regulation.

2. Mission of Agencies. A mission is a specific assignment delegated legislatively to an agency and embodied in a mission statement that delineates the agency's purpose, functions, and goals.

A. Mission Statement of Agencies. A mission statement is an agency's operation roadmap. A mission statement expresses an agency's job in congruence with the agency's skills, resources, and legislative mandate.

B. Dual Attribute of Mission. The mission of an executive agency is inherently twofold, specific and directorial. The specific mission of an executive agency is to efficiently fulfill the legislative mandate imposed by the agency's enabling statute; the directorial mission of an agency is to faithfully implement the applicable laws and policies of the executive branch of state government.

§ 2.4. Rationale of Agencies. Principally, to maintain, to protect, and to advance a proficient, regulatory social order, administrative law administers complex government matters that exceed the expertise of the three branches of state government – of legislators (who write law), of jurists (who interpret law), and of the executive (that executes law).

1. Administrative Tasks of State Government. New York State government is the sovereign administrator of human activity within New York State. The proficient direction, protection, and regulation of a social and political hierarchy of racial, religious, political, educational, and economic strata require state government to manipulate simultaneously three tasks:

A. The state operates within two mandates that often compete. The state's constitutional obligation to safeguard the inalienable rights of individuals and the state's duty to protect and advance the public health, safety, and welfare.

B. The State manages the accelerating challenges of an ever-expanding, ever-evolving, ever-demanding society.

C. The state accumulates, manages, and allocates the vast power and enormous capital needed to pragmatically govern the infinite variables of the social order and to maintain the state's sovereign power.

2. Performance of State Government. The effectiveness of state government mirrors the efficiency of executive agencies. Theoretically, "Practice makes perfect." Experience and expertness go together; the more an agency obtains of the first, the more likely the agency attains the latter. Optimistically, as an agency gains experience in the repetitive performance of the functions of its mission, it develops expertise continuously, improves operating efficiency consistently, and with increasing effectiveness regulates human conduct and serves perspicuous human needs.

§ 2.5. Power and Authority of Executive Agencies.

1. Power. The power of an executive agency derives statutorily as "legitimate," "position," or "official" power. The power of an

executive agency is political; it is the sum of the agency's inherent right, duty, liability (responsibility) and legal capacity (authority) conferred legislatively to enable an agency to legally fulfill the agency's enabling law by acting or not acting (discretion).

2. Authority. Authority enables the use of power by an agency to legally attain the legislative objectives of the agency. Executive agencies possess rational-legal authority. Rational-legal authority derives from the agency's conferred power, is founded on legal rationality and legal legitimacy, and consists of all agency-pertinent laws, rules, regulations, and policies. An agency leader may delegate authority to agency personnel.

3. Tripartite Powers. The legislature delegates tripartite powers (quasi-executive, quasi-legislative, and quasi-judicial) to the executive department through executive administrative agencies. *Cf Dorst v Pataki*, 90 NY2d 296, 665 NYS2d 65 (1997).

A. "Quasi" is a fictional description of a functional distinction in administrative law; "quasi" lacks an assigned legal value or an exact legal reference.

B. Executive administrative agencies formulate, enact, interpret, implement, and enforce critical policies, decisions, and regulations without ratification by the state legislature, the state's constitutional lawmaking branch of government.

4. Quasi-executive Power. Executive magisterial powers delegated to the leaders of executive agencies include:

A. Organization of an agency's resources.

B. Appointment and employment of officers and other employees required to perform the agency functions.

C. Approval of proposed agency policies, rules, and regulations.

D. Enforcement of the agency laws, rules, and regulations.

E. Appointment of public officers. New York State, Secretary of State, appoints and commissions notaries public who are public officers. Executive Law § 130; Public Officers Law § 8; *NY St. Dept. of St., Div. of Lic. Servs. v Del Guidice*, 763 DOS 01 (2001).

5. Quasi-legislative Power. An executive agency's quasi-legislative power is a lawmaking power; it empowers an agency to complete the skeletal organic legislation by implementing within the agency's discretion: (A) Policies, protocols and strategies; (B) intra-agency units; and (C) rules and regulations essential to achieve both the specific and the directorial aspects of the mission of the agency.

6. Quasi-judicial Power. Organic acts confer quasi-judicial power to executive agencies. Possessing the power to perform prosecutorial acts and judicial functions is vital to an executive agency's existence. To successfully execute its legislatively mandated mission, an agency must be able legally to demand obedience to and to enforce compliance with the agency's administrative laws, rules, regulations, and policies.

A. Doctrine of Primary Jurisdiction of Executive Agencies. Enabling statutes confer to executive agencies explicit authority over designated administrative tasks (*Sohn v Calderon*, 78 NY2d 755, 579 NYS2d 940 [1991]). In administrative functions over which an agency has statutory authority, the agency possesses exclusive, original jurisdiction (initial, decisional power) to the exclusion of all other judicial and quasi-judicial entities. " 'The doctrine of primary jurisdiction provides that where the courts and an administrative agency have concurrent jurisdiction over a dispute involving issues beyond the conventional experience of judges the court will stay its hand until the agency has applied its expertise to the salient questions.' " *Matter of Schwartz v East Ramapo Central School District,* 2015 NY Slip Op 02769 (2nd Dept 2015). [1]

B. Limited Jurisdiction of Supreme Court of New York. The Supreme Court of New York is a court of general original jurisdiction with the concurrent jurisdiction of certain classes of actions began in other courts (NY Const art VI, § 7). The power of the Supreme Court to review quasi-judicial determinations is limited to CPLR article 78 evaluations, except where the applicability or constitutionality of a regulatory statute, or other such question, is an issue. *Sohn v Calderon, supra.*

§ 2.6. New York State Executive Agencies. SAPA defines the following units of New York State government as agencies (SAPA § 102 [1]):

1. Agriculture and Markets. Appointed by the governor, a Commissioner leads the agency (Agriculture and Markets Law § 5). The agency enacts, amends, and repeals necessary rules (Agriculture and Markets Law § 1); implements and enforces the laws, rules, and orders that relate to functions, powers, and duties assigned to the agency (Agriculture and Markets Law § 5); regulate the conduct of investigations, inquiries, and hearings (Agriculture and Markets Law § 18.3). Title 1 NYCRR 367 contains procedures governing adjudication and appeals.

2. Alcoholic Beverage Control. The State Liquor Authority supervises the agency. The Authority consists of three members

---

[1] See Haseltine, William B., *Primary Jurisdiction and State Courts: A Modern Proposal for Uniformity,* 3 J. Nat'l Assoc. Admin. L Judges (1983).

(commissioners), citizens and residents of the state and appointed by the governor. The governor designates one member as chairperson (Alcoholic Beverage Control Law § 11). Agency rules need not be uniform (Alcoholic Beverage Control Law § 115). Procedures for revocation, cancellation, suspension or monetary penalty appear in Alcoholic Beverage Control Law § 119. Disciplinary proceedings are stated in 9 NYCRR 54.

3. Civil Service Commission. Three commissioners compose the commission, two of whom may be members of the same political party. The governor designates one of the commissioners as president of the commission (Civil Service Law § 5.2 [a]). The president of the commission directs the agency and prescribes and amends agency rules (Civil Service Law § 6) and hears and determines appeals (Civil Service Law § 6.5). 4 NYCRR 212 contains conference and hearings rules.

4. Department of Corrections and Community Supervision. A Commissioner appointed by the governor heads the department (Correction Law § 5.1). The Commissioner issues and enforces subpoenas and administers oaths, and examines persons under oath. A person examined under oath has the right to be accompanied by counsel (Correction Law § 46.2). 7 NYCRR prescribe agency rules.

5. Department of Environmental Conservation. The governor appoints a commissioner who manages the department (Environmental Conservation Law § 3-0103). The Commissioner promulgates, adopts, amends or repeals any standard, rule, and regulation (Environmental Conservation Law § 3-0301.2 [a]) and conducts investigations, holds hearings, and issues subpoenas (Environmental Conservation Law § 3-0301.2 [h]). 6 NYCRR 622 states uniform enforcement hearing procedures.

6. Department of Financial Services. A gubernatorial appointee, the Superintendent of Financial Services, leads the department (Financial Services Law § 202 [a]). The Superintendent establishes systems of rules, rulemaking, and adjudication responsive to the needs of the banking and insurance industries and the needs of the state's consumers and residents. (Financial Services Law § 102 [b]). The regulations of the Superintendent are in 23 NYCRR ch I.

7. Department of Health. A Commissioner appointed by the governor (Public Health Law § 204) supervises the department, establishes rules (Public Health Law § 206), and institutes formal hearings and procedures (Public Health Law § 12-a). Title 10 NYCRR ch II expresses agency administrative rules and regulations.

8. Homes and Community Renewal. A Commissioner appointed by the governor manages the agency. The appointee also heads the Division of Housing and Community Renewal (Public Housing Law § 11). The agency makes, promulgates, modifies, amends, and repeals rules and regulations. Public Housing Law § 19; 9 NYCRR 1500.

9. Division of Human Rights. The governor appoints a commissioner who establishes, consolidates, reorganizes or abolishes organizational units within the division (Human Rights Law § 293). The commissioner also adopts, promulgates, amends and rescinds rules, policies, and practices, and conducts investigations and hearings (Human Rights Law § 295). 9 NYCRR 465 assembles agency's rules of practice.

10. Department of Labor. Appointed by the governor (Labor Law § 10), the Commissioner of Labor may issue regulations (Labor Law § 21.11), hold hearings, issue subpoenas (Labor Law § 39, and set hearing procedures (Labor Law § 41). Agency rules

are outlined in 12 NYCRR.

11. Workmen's Compensation Board in the Department of Labor. The governor appoints a board of thirteen members and designates one member as chairperson and another as vice-chairperson (Workers' Compensation Law § 140). The board enacts administrative hearing rules (Workers' Compensation Law § 141) and hears and determines all claims for benefits (Workers' Compensation Law § 142.1; 12 NYCRR).

12. Department of Mental Hygiene, Office of Mental Health. The leader of the Office of Mental Health is the Commissioner of mental health. Appointed by the governor (Mental Hygiene Law, § 5.03), the Commissioner must adopt necessary and proper hearing rules. Mental Hygiene Law § 7.09 (b); 14 NYCRR.

13. Department of Motor Vehicles. A Commissioner appointed by the governor (Vehicle & Traffic Law § 200) supervises the agency and enacts, amends, and repeals rules and regulations (Vehicle & Traffic Law § 215 [rules and regulations]; Vehicle & Traffic Law § 227 [traffic infractions]; Vehicle & Traffic Law § 236 [parking infractions]; Vehicle & Traffic Law § 260 [administrative appeals]. Provisions of 15 NYCRR govern the agency.

14. Department of Public Service. A five-member commission manages the department. The governor appoints the commission and designates one member both as chairperson of the commission and as chief executive officer of the department (Public Service Law §§ 3, 4). Provisions of Public Service Law § 20 and 16 NYCRR govern hearings.

15. Department of Social Services. A Commissioner appointed by the governor both commands Social Services (Social Services Law § 11) and is chief administrative officer of the Department

of Social Welfare (Social Services Law, § 34). Social Services Law § 22.8 and 18 NYCRR specify procedures for adjudications and judicial review. [2]

16. Department of State. The Secretary of State appointed by the governor (Executive Law § 90) adopts and promulgates agency rules (Executive Law § 91). Agency adjudicatory proceedings, rules, and guidelines appear in 19 NYCRR 400.

17. Department of Taxation and Finance. Appointed by the governor (Tax Law § 170), a Commissioner heads the agency and makes rules and regulations (Tax Law § 171). Tax Law § 2002 and 20 NYCRR state the rules of Division of Tax Appeals.

18. Department of Transportation. A Commissioner, appointed by the governor, supervises the department and dictates agency rules and regulations. Transportation Law §§ 14.18, 84; 17 NYCRR.

---

[2] Note. Executive Law § 553 correlates the powers and duties of the Justice Center with the Department of Social Services and other state agencies.

CHAPTER III. ENVIRONMENTS OF ADMINISTRATIVE LAW AND AGENCIES.

§ 3.1. Human Events Effect on Administrative Law and Agencies. Legal equations in human existence - historical, social, economic, and political changes – determine redefinition of old legal interests and recognition of new legal rights. The state controls the creation, expansion, modification, and decline of administrative agencies as government search for inventive and resourceful solutions to manage mutable human conditions and developments. Federal and state histories document the effects of human events on the creation, existence, and termination of executive administrative agencies.

1. Federal Events. Historically, the US Congress founded agencies to cope with various human circumstances, relationships, and potentialities. Government formed agencies to cope with military conflicts (Revolutionary War, World Wars I and II, Korea, Vietnam, Iraq, Afghanistan), domestic and foreign social upheavals and economic changes (recessions, depressions, bull and bear markets), terrorist attacks (World Trade Center), and to protect the Homeland.

2. New York State Events. In the New York Constitutional Convention of 1938 (Great Depression and New Deal Era), legislators introduced over thirty amendments that raised issues concerning judicial review of the decision-making power

of agencies and the reform of agencies' procedures. [3]

A. Human events prompted New York to enact: The Division of Veterans' Affairs; Department of Environmental Conservation; New York State Energy Research and Development Authority (a public benefit corporation created through the reconstitution of the New York State Atomic and Space Development Authority); Office for Technology (a New York State agency that provides statewide technology direction and centralized technology policies and services to other New York State governmental entities); Division of Homeland Security and Emergency Services with five offices - Counter Terrorism, Cyber Security, Emergency Management, Fire Prevention and Control, and Interoperable and Emergency Communications.

B. Health epidemics evoke regulatory law enactment. [4] "Public health law was the first administrative law." Communicable diseases such as cholera, yellow fever, and smallpox ravaged the colonies. "Early state governments carried out Draconian measures to control" those diseases. [5] New York City used its police power to close gay bathhouses. In an emergency resolution, the City added a new regulation to the State Sanitary Code (10 NYCRR § 24.2). City *of New York v New St. Mark's Baths,* 130 Misc 2d 911, 497 NYS2d 979 (1986); *New York v New St. Mark's Baths,* 168 AD2d 311, 562 NYS2d 642 (1st Dept 1990).

---

[3] Ernst, Daniel R., The Politics of Administrative Law: New York's *Anti-Bureaucracy Clause and the O'Brian-Wagner Campaign of 1938,* 27 Law & Hist Rev 331-372 (2009).

[4] Jorge E. Galva, Christopher Atchison, and Samuel Levey, *Public Health Strategy and the Police Powers of the State,* Public Health Rep. 2005; 120 (Suppl 1): 20–27.

[5] Richards, Edward P., *Public Health Law as Administrative Law: Example Lessons,* 10 J. Health Care L. & Poly 61 (2007).

C. Economic, political, and social transformations in New York trigger merger, consolidation, reorganization, modification, and abolishment of administrative agencies. Illustrations are:

(1). The Department of Correctional Services and the Division of Parole merged into the Department of Corrections and Community Supervision.

(2). The Department of Banking and the Department of Insurance were consolidated into the Department of Financial Services.

(3). Under a single leadership and management structure, the Division of Homes and Community Renewal, the following agencies were unified: Affordable Housing Corporation, Division of Housing & Community Renewal, Housing Finance Agency, Housing Trust Fund Corporation, State of New York Municipal Bond Bank Agency, SONYMA's Mortgage Insurance Fund, State of New York Mortgage Agency, and Tobacco Settlement Financing Corporation.

(4). During the year 2010, the Office of Mental Retardation and Developmental Disabilities became the New York State Office for People with Developmental Disabilities. The new title eliminated the term "mental retardation" (removed a stigmatization) and included autism in its services (recognized a medical need).

(5). In the year 2011, the Governor's Office of Regulatory Reform was abolished.

(6). On June 17, 2012, Governor A. Cuomo announced the structure of a new agency, the Justice Center for the Protection of People with Special Needs. The agency has criminal jurisdiction and administers administrative investigations previously performed by six state agencies (Office for People with Developmental Disabilities, Office of Mental Health, Office of Alcoholism and Substance Abuse Services, Health Department, Education Department, and Office of Children and Family Services). The Justice Center also absorbed the functions and responsibilities of the Commission on Quality of Care and Advocacy for Persons with Disabilities (except for Federal Protection and Advocacy and Client Assistance Programs designated to non-profit organizations).

§ 3.2. Public Effect of Administrative Law and Agencies. The extent of the public presence of governmental agencies in New York State was estimated in 1986. "Government services in New York . . . (were) provided by 56 federal agencies, 133 state departments and agencies, 62 counties, 62 districts, 5383 special districts, 2202 public authorities, 122 urban renewal agencies, and 104 industrial development agencies . . . " with specialized functions and with regulatory and adjudicative authority. [6]

1. Effect of Administrative Law on People. Administrative law affects people in New York from the cradle to the grave, conception, birth, life, and death. Administrative law guide activities of agriculture, cemeteries, commerce, education, elections, employment, environment, ethics, financial services (banking and insurance), food, health, housing, human rights, information, labor, law enforcement, natural resources, pets (sales and treatment when alive, cemeteries when dead), public assistance, recreation, religion, revenue, technology, and utilities.

---

[6] Carlisle, Jay, *Getting a Full Bite of the Apple: When Should the Doctrine of Issue Preclusion Make an Administrative or Arbitral Determination Binding in a Court of Law*? 55 Fordham L Rev 95 (1986).

2. The Impact of Administrative Law on Industry. State administrative agencies regulate traditional activities:

A. Business. Commerce and industry agencies: Economic Development (Economic Development Law § 10), Office of Business Permits (Executive Law § 877), Agriculture and Markets (Agriculture and Markets Law § 16), and Alcoholic Beverage Control (Alcoholic Beverage Control Law § 2).

B. Finance. State financial agencies: Department of Audit and Control, Division of Budget (Executive Law article 8), Department of Financial Services (Financial Services Law § 201), Office of General Services (Executive Law § 200), Office of General Services (Public Lands Law § 2), and Department of Taxation and Finance (Tax Law § 170).

C. Public Service. Public service agencies: Office of Children and Family Services (Executive Law § 501), Department of Education (Education Law § 101), Department of Environmental Conservation (Environmental Conservation Law § 3-0301), Department of Health (Public Health Law § 201), Highway Safety (Executive Law § 332), Division of Housing (Executive Law § 260), Homes and Community Renewal (Public Housing Law § 10), Division of Human Rights, Department of Mental Hygiene (Mental Hygiene Law § 5.01), Department of Motor Vehicles (Vehicle & Traffic Law § 200), Office of Parks, Recreation and Historic Preservation (Parks, Recreation and Historic Preservation Law § 3.01), Public Authorities Control Board (Public Authorities Law § 50), Board of Social Welfare (Executive Law § 740), Board of Transportation (Rapid Transit Law § 10), Department of Transportation (Transportation Law § 11 and Highway Law § 10), Department and State Board of Social Welfare (Social Services Law § 5).

D. Labor. Labor-related agencies: Department of Civil Service

(Civil Service Law § 5), Department of Labor (Labor Law § 10), Department of Public Service (Public Service Law § 3), and New York State Employees' Retirement System (Retirement and Social Security Law § 10).

E. Law and Military. Agencies with police and military functions: Division of Veterans' Affairs (Executive Law § 351); Department of Law (Executive Law § 60); Office of Fire Prevention and Control (Executive Law § 155); Division of Military and Naval Affairs (Executive Law § 190); Division of State Police (Executive Law § 210); Division of Homeland Security and Emergency Services (Executive Law § 709); Division of Criminal Justice Services (Executive Law § 836), with a witness protection program (Executive Law § 837); Commission on Forensic Science (Executive Law § 995-a), with DNA Identification Index (Executive Law § 995-c); Department of Corrections and Community Supervision (Correction Law § 5); State Militia (Military Law § 2).

CHAPTER IV. GOVERNMENT OVERSIGHT OF EXECUTIVE AGENCIES.

§ 4.1. Government Oversight. Constitutional and statutory laws establish procedures to assist state government to oversee the actions of state administrative agencies. Oversight laws serve as the state's auxiliary eyes and ears and aid government to make informed decisions relating to administrative agencies. The sphere of political persuasion of government oversight entities over agencies become apparent when agency leaders appear before or appeal to branches of state government for appointments, sanctions, preferences, and money (NY Const art VII, § 1).

§ 4.2. Legislative Oversight. Legislature oversight of agencies is constitutionally established. The legislature's lawmaking, appropriation, and confirmation powers sway agencies' actions. Legislation is the source and span of the power both of state administrative law and of executive agencies.

1. State Constitutional Provisions. Eight provisions of the state

constitution relate to state government and state agencies:

A. NY Const art 1, § 18 vests in the legislature the power to enact laws to protect the life, health, and safety of employees (workers' compensation).

B. NY Const art IV, § 7 empowers the governor to approve or to veto proposed legislation. A vote of two-thirds of the members elected to each legislative house overrides a governor's veto.

C. NY Const art 1V, § 8 enumerates the filing requirements to which a rule or regulation of a state agency must comply to become effective.

D. NY Const art V, § 2 limits the number of civil departments in state government to 20 and allows the legislature to change the name of any civil department.

E. The legislature controls the powers and functions of departments, offices, boards, commissions, and executive offices of the governor and may assign, increase, diminish, and modify those entities. NY Const art V, § 3.

F. NY Const art V §, 4 designates the state officials who "shall" head the four departments of agriculture and markets, audit and control, education, and law.

G. The confirmation process of "advise and consent" (NY Const art V, § 4) gives the legislature a measure of political control over the governor's appointments of agency leaders.

H. The power of the purse can be a "blunt tool" that shapes agency behavior. The governor submits the state budget to the legislature (NY Const art VII, § 3) that may strike or reduce an agency's funding (NY Const art VII, § 4).

2. State Statutes. Legislative Law article 5-B charges the Administrative Regulations Review Commission to exert continuous oversight of the process of rulemaking by agencies.

A. Specifically, the statute instructs the commission "to exercise continuous oversight of the process of rule making and examine rules adopted or proposed by each agency . . . with respect to (i) statutory power, (ii) compliance with legislative intent, (iii) impact on the economy and on the government operations of the state and its local governments, and (iv) impact on affected parties; and . . . may examine other issues it deems appropriate." Legislative Law § 87 (1).

B. Definition of "agency" in legislative law is less restrictive than the SAPA 102 (1) definition of "agency." Legislative Law § 87 (1) defines the term agency as "any department, board, bureau, commission, division, office, council, committee or officer of the state or a public benefit corporation or public authority at least one of whose members is appointed by the governor." Legislative Law § 87 (1) does not require an entity to be "authorized by law to make rules or to make final decisions in adjudicatory proceedings" as does SAPA 102 (1).

C. Notification to the legislature is a restricted prerequisite to the implementing of a proposed adoption, amendment, suspension or repeal of an agency's rule (Executive Law § 101-a). Within four months from the effective date of a rule, the temporary president of the senate or the speaker of the assembly may bring an action to invalidate a rule for noncompliance with the procedural requirement of Executive Law § 101-a. The law permits extenuation. An inadvertent failure to comply with the statute does not invalidate a rule.

§ 4.3. Executive Oversight. The defined interests of a trade or industry regulated by an agency narrowly limit the agency's operational viewpoint and area of influence. Antithetically, as the state's chief executive officer, the governor's responsibility is statewide. The effectiveness of statewide administrative policies depends on the tractable advocacy of state executive agencies. Subsequently, critical concerns of the Executive Department are effective oversight of executive agencies and the agencies' compliance with executive policies. State constitution and statutes confer considerable power to the governor to supervise and manage the operations of executive agencies. *Rapp v Carey*, 44 NY2d 157404 NYS2d 565 (1978).

1. State Constitutional Provisions. The state constitution directs the governor to ensure the operational competence of executive agencies. Executive agencies exponentially both extend a governor's powers and expand the political reach of the executive office.

A. NY Const art IV, § 1 vests in the governor the executive power of the state. The constitutional executive power of the governor is direct and independent of legislative ratification.

B. NY Const art IV, § 3 imposes on the governor the duty to assure the faithful execution of the laws of the state.

C. NY Const art IV, § 7 empowers the governor to approve or to reject proposed legislation by veto. A vote of two-thirds of the members elected to each legislative house overrides the governor's veto.

D. NY Const art V, § 4 enables the governor to appoint and to remove executive officers, and, with confirmation of the senate (advice and consent), appoint all department heads (except the departments of agriculture and markets, audit and control, law, and education)

E. NY Const art VII, § 1 directs department heads to provide financial information to the governor in the preparation of the state budget.

F. The governor submits the state budget to the legislature (NY Const art VII, § 3).

2. State Statutes. The Executive Law continues the Executive Department of state government (Executive Law § 30) and the governor's power to establish, consolidate or abolish divisions and bureaus in the Department of State (Executive Law § 31).

A. In addition to designated executive administrative agencies, state divisions, and offices, the Executive Department includes the following offices and divisions: Office of General Services, Office of Information Technology Services, Division of Alcoholic Beverage Control, Division of the budget, Division of Homeland Security and Emergency Services, Division of Housing, Division of Human Rights, Division of Military and Naval Affairs, Division of State Police, and Division of Veterans' Affairs (Executive Law § 31).

B. Executive Law § 6 empowers the governor, at any time, either in person or by appointees, to examine and investigate the management and affairs of any department, board, bureau or commission of the state, to subpoena and enforce the attendance of witnesses, to administer oaths and examine witnesses under oath, and to require the production of any relevant books or papers.

C. Executive Law § 34 commands the governor to examine agencies and to determine the changes necessary to promote (1) improved execution of the laws, (2) more effective management of state government, its agencies and functions, and (3) expeditious administration of public business.

D. Executive Law § 51 defines agencies as executive branch agencies, departments, divisions, offices, boards and commissions, public authorities (except multi-state and multinational public authorities), and public benefit corporations that are headed by appointees of the governor and that do not have a statutorily-designated inspector general.

E. Executive Law § 52 establishes the Office of the State Inspector General in the Executive Department and assigns to the Office the task to investigate, to prevent and to eliminate corruption, fraud, criminal activity, conflicts of interest, and abuse by agencies (as defined in and regulated by Executive Law § 51).

F. The New York Constitution and state statutes instruct the governor to oversee, "but again not necessarily to direct, the administration of the various entities in the executive branch." *Rapp v Carey*, 44 NY2d 157, 404 NYS2d 565 (1978).

3. Executive Orders and Proclamations. Executive orders and proclamations are formal statements issued unilaterally by the governor to execute the delegated powers of the executive office. Executive orders and proclamations take effect without any action by the state legislature.

A. Power Enabling Executive Orders and Proclamations. New York State Constitution and state statutes grant powers to the governor to issue executive orders and proclamations.

(1). Constitutional Power. Two provisions of New York State Constitution vest in the governor (a)the exclusive grant of executive power (NY Const art IV, § 1) and (b) "to take care that the laws are faithfully executed" (NY Const art IV, § 3).

(2). Statutory Power. The statutory power of the governor to issue executive orders and proclamations is an implied power inferred from Executive Law § 34. An expressed statutory grant of power to the governor is an indirect (implied) power; an indirect power is subordinate to the granting statute.

B. Proclamations. A proclamation is a formal public statement issued by the proper authority to proclaim policy, express criteria, or to implement a law or rule. The two classifications of proclamations are ceremonial and official announcements.

(1). A ceremonial proclamation is without legal effect. A ceremonial proclamation commemorates an event or person, is ritualistic, is issued under the governor's constitutional power, and does not have the force and effect of law. For example, in a proclamation issued November 8, 2013, Governor A. Cuomo proclaimed November 2013 as "Military Family Month."

(2). Official proclamations are formal announcements of official government actions. Official proclamations are issued as declarations under specific constitutional or statutory provisions with an intended legal effect. Federal examples are: Proclamation 3, *Enjoining Neutrality as to War against France,* 11 Stat 753, George Washington, April 22, 1793; *Emancipation Proclamation,* Abraham Lincoln, January 1, 1863; Proclamation 157, *Declaring that Peace, Order, Tranquillity, and Civil Authority Now Exists in and Throughout the Whole of the United States of America,* Andrew Johnson, August 20, 1866 (declared an end to the insurrection that existed in the State of Texas).

C. Executive Orders. Executive orders enforce the legislative administrative, and political agendas of the executive office.

(1). Policy Statements and Directives. Through policy and directive statements, the executive office states preferences. Policy statements and directives are issued under the

Governor's direct constitutional power and express general policy, instructions, and interpretations of guidelines. An executive order that directs (not informs or requests) units or employees of the executive office to conduct a designated program has the force and effect of law only as to those units and employees identified in the order.

(a). By public announcement, a governor may make a policy statement that orders executive government entities to adopt and to follow a certain course of action (Executive Order (Cuomo, M.) No. 19 NYCRR 4.19 (May 31, 1983), *New York State Policy Statement on Sexual Harassment in the Workplace*. The executive order ordered every state executive agency to implement the policy of sexual harassment prevention outlined in the order. The policy was extended by Executive Order (Cuomo, A.) No. 2, 9 NYCRR 8.2 (January 1, 2011), *Review, Continuation and Expiration of Prior Executive Orders*.

(b). A directive directs executive agencies to perform specified administrative actions. Executive Order (Cuomo, A) No. 34, 9 NYCRR 8.34 (November 10, 2011), *Continuing the New York State Council on Returning Veterans and Their Families*, is a general directive. The order instructs every executive agency of New York to review paths into the civilian workforce and identify ways that the State may better recognize the skills, education, training, experience, and credentials acquired by veterans while in military service.

(2). Operational Statements. An operational executive order is equivalent to a legislative enactment. Gubernatorial, operational, executive orders based on existing statutes have the force and effect of law. The text of an operational statement serves as the source of authority for an agency to execute the order. (*Cf Clark v Cuomo*, 66 NY2d 185, 495 NYS2d 936 [1985]). Executive orders statutorily founded may define legal rights, order agency action, demand compliance, and impose penalties. Operational executive statements may frame the following actions:

(a). Reorganize state agencies and departments;

(b). establish positions, offices, regulatory commissions, advisory boards, councils or task forces;

(c). make appointments to state executive positions;

(d). provide methods of enforcing existing law;

(e). impose obligations and responsibilities;

(f). apply conditions or processes; and

(g). develop enforcement and penalty obligations.

(3). Governor Andrew Cuomo issued an operational, executive order on January 18, 2012, to executive agencies (Executive Order No. 38 [9 NYCRR 8.38]) directing agencies to enact regulations to limit compensation and administrative expenses to state-funded service providers. Order No. 38 was continued by Executive Order (Cuomo, A.) No. 43 (9 NYCRR 8.43), April 23, 2012.[7]

D. Validity of Executive Order. A valid executive order complies with an implied power to enforce the laws or conforms to either an expressed constitutional or statutory provision. A judicial determination of the validity of an executive order requires an analysis of four issues:

---

[7] Business Council of New York State, Inc., *Comments on Draft Executive Order 38 Implementation Rules* (July 16, 2012).

(1). What is the category of the executive order? A policy statement, a directive, or an operational statement?

(2). Under what power was the order issued? An implied power or an expressed state constitutional or statutory power?

(3). Does the order violate the separation of powers doctrine by interfering with the lawmaking power vested in the legislature?

(4). Does existing legislation refer to the subject addressed in the executive order?

E. Judicial Review of Executive Orders. A judicial review of an executive order is limited to determining if the governor's action conforms either to the state constitution or to a state statute. Judicial review does not consider the way the Governor exercises power (*Mulroy v Carey*, 58 AD2d 207, *affd* 43 NY2d 819 [1979]). "For abuse of lawful discretionary authority, the remedy, as a rule, lies . . . at the polls, or with a constitutional amendment, or with corrective legislation." (*Johnson & C v Pataki*, 91 NY2d 214, 668 NYS2d 978]). On point are the following decisions:

(1). In *Clark v Cuomo*, 66 NY2d 185, 495 NYS2d 936 (1985), the Court of Appeals reviewed an executive order issued under Election Law § 5-211 by Governor M. Cuomo. The order activated a voter registration program for state agencies to distribute, to render assistance in completing, and to collect voter registration forms. The Court held sections of the executive order valid and held a component invalid.

(a). The Court held that the distribution and the assistance-in-completion sections of the order valid and legally based on a prior, legislative policy directive to the State Board of Elections to encourage the broadest, possible voter participation in elections. Election Law § 3-102 (14).

(b). The Court rendered invalid the section of the order that authorized agencies to collect completed, voter registration forms. The collection function too closely approximated "voter registration" then restricted constitutionally to a bipartisan board.

(c). Subsequently, an amendment to the state constitution removed the bi-partisan board restriction (NY Const art II, § 6). An amendment to the Election Law (Election Law § 5-211) authorized agencies to receive and transmit completed, voter registration applications to the appropriate Board of Elections.

(2). Executive Order (Carey) No. 45 (9 NYCRR 3.45), January 7, 1977, ordered state agencies to institute affirmative action programs. The Supreme Court held that the order violated the separation of powers doctrine. "Where an executive order extends and expands requirements of statutes, it does not serve the enforcement function and therefore constitutes an unwarranted exercise of legislative power." *Fullilove v Carey*, 91 Misc2d 531, 398, NYS2d 226 (Sup Ct 1977).

(3). Governor Carey issued an executive order under NY Const art IV, § 3 and Public Officers Law § 74, requiring specified state employees to file extensive, personal, financial statements and to abstain from various activities. The Appellant Division declared the order unconstitutional for lack of statutory authority (*Rapp v Carey*, 58 AD2d 918 [3rd Dept 1977]). The Court of Appeals affirmed and concluded that the order represented an unconstitutional encroachment on the powers of the legislative branch. A statute is required to compel the financial disclosure demanded by the executive order (*Rapp v Carey*, 44 NY2d 157, 404 NYS2d 565 [1978]).

(4). The legislative legislates legislative policy into law. The executive branch implements those laws. The creation of a new, procedural, administrative mechanism by the executive branch to better implement a legislative policy "does not offend" the New York State Constitution. "In other words, '[i]t is only when the Executive acts inconsistently with the Legislature, or usurps its prerogatives, that the doctrine of separation is violated.' " *Bourquin v Cuomo*, 85 NY2d 781, 628 NYS2d 618 (1995).

§ 4.4. Judicial Oversight. Judicial oversight of agencies occurs through the New York State Supreme Court's limited power to review the actions and decisions of executive agencies.

1. New York State Constitution and state statutes empower the New York State Supreme Court to review agency actions to ensure that agencies observe constitutional and statutory dictates in the execution of government mandates.

2. The New York Supreme Court reviews administrative actions that do not involve the applicability or constitutionality of a regulatory statute. NY Const art VI, § 8; CPLR 7801; *Sohn v Calderon*, 78 NY2d 755, 579 NYS2d 940 (1991).[8]

§ 4.5. Public Oversight. Government is public business, and laws bestow to the people procedures by which the public may oversee the governmental actions of executive agencies.

1. Government – The Public Business. Public accountability laws (PALs) give visibility to government's conduct of the people's business and keeps government responsible through exposure to multilevel public scrutiny. "Publicity is justly commended as a remedy for social and industrial diseases. Sunlight is said to be

---

[8] Chapter XV §15.4. Judicial Review of Administrative Proceedings.

the best of disinfectants; electric light the most efficient policeman." Brandeis, Louis, *Other People's Money And How the Bankers Use It* (1914).

2. Freedom of Information Law (FOIL). FOIL offers a view of government to people by granting public access to agency records. Public Officers Law § 87 (2) gives members of the public (any person) access to records of agencies (on request without reason) and provides a process by which members of the public may review and copy an agency's records. "Full disclosure by public agencies is, under FOIL, a public right and in the public interest, irrespective of the status or need of the person making the request." *M. Farbman & Sons v NY City*, 62 NY2d 75, 476 NYS2d 69 (1984).

A. The Committee on Open Government, a state unit housed in New York State, Department of State, adopts regulations that integrate procedures for accessing, inspecting, and copying an agency's records. The Committee gives advice, conducts training classes, and provides advisory opinions to the public, to governments, and to news media about FOIL, Open Meetings Law (OML), and Personal Privacy Protection Law (PPPL).

B. Administrative agencies must promulgate rules and regulations that conform with prescriptions of both Public Officers Law § 87 (2) and the Committee on Open Government.

C. State government records are subject presumptively to inspection and copying unless exempted statutorily by FOIL. *Capital Newspapers Division of Hearst Corp. v Burns*, 67 NY2d 562, 505 NYS2d 576 (1986).

(1). An agency must make all agency records available for public inspection and copying in accord with published agency regulations. Public Officers Law § 87 (2).

(2). A record is defined as "any information kept, held, filed, produced or reproduced by, with or for an agency or the state legislature, in any physical form whatsoever . . . (such as) reports, statements, examinations, memoranda, opinions, folders, files, books, manuals, pamphlets, forms, papers, designs, drawings, maps, photos, letters, microfilms, computer tapes or discs, rules, regulations or codes." Public Officers Law § 86 (4).

D. An agency may deny public access to the following categories of records:

(1). Records that would constitute an unwarranted invasion of personal privacy, such as:

(a). Employment, medical, credit, or personal references of applicants for employment.

(b) Medical or personal records of a client or a patient in a medical facility.

(c). Information concerning the interest of surviving family members in the affairs of deceased persons. "Surviving relatives have an interest protected by FOIL in keeping private the affairs of the dead...." *NY Times Co. v City of NY Fire Dept.*, 4 NY3d 477, 796 NYS2d 302 (2005). The matter involved 911 tapes recordings of persons who died in the terrorist attack on the World Trade Center on September 11, 2001. [9]

(d). Personal information that would cause a party economic or personal hardship and the subject information is not

[9] Justice Rosenblatt's dissent in *NY Times v NY City Fire Dept.*, 4 NY3d 477, 493 (2005), argues that granting access to the 9-11 tape recordings with concomitant adherence to strict ethical standards would serve the public's good.

pertinent to the ordinary work of the agency requesting or maintaining the information.

(e). Personal information reported in confidence to an agency and not relevant to the regular work of the agency.

(f). Sale or release of lists of names and addresses for solicitation or fund-raising. A digital list of the names and addresses of all pistol licensees in New York City is exempt from disclosure where the materials are requested for fundraising or commercial gain. *NY State Rifle and Pistol Assn. Inc. v. Kelly*, 55 AD3d 222, 863 NYS2d 439 (1st Dept 2008).

(g). Employee's personal information in an employer's file. Workers' Compensation Law § 110-a.

(h). Electronic contact information (e-mail address or a social network username) collected under Real Property Tax Law from a taxpayer.

(2). Records that could impair contract awards or collective bargaining negotiations.

(3). Records containing trade secrets or documents submitted to an agency by, or derived from an agency by a commercial enterprise, or derived from information obtained from a commercial enterprise that if disclosed would cause substantial injury to the competitive position of the business.

(4). Records compiled for law enforcement and if disclosed:

(a). Would interfere with law enforcement investigations or judicial proceedings;

(b). would deprive a person of a right to an impartial hearing;

(c). would identify a confidential source or disclose confidential information related to an investigation;

(d). would reveal non-routine investigative techniques or procedures.

(5). Records if disclosed could endanger the life or safety of a person.

(6). Interagency or intra-agency memoranda regarded as part of an agency's deliberative process.

(a). Inter or intra-agency deliberative process memoranda: (i) statistical or factual tabulations or data, (ii) staff instructions that affect the public, (iii) final agency policy or determinations, and (iv) external audits performed by the state comptroller or by the federal government.

(b). Written communications made within or between agencies may constitute intra-agency or interagency memoranda within the statutory exemption of statements made in an employment relationship between agencies.

(i). An employment relationship did not exist, and the exemption did not apply in a situation where two agencies were involved jointly in a project to achieve a common goal; each agency had statutory responsibility for the project site; and the enforcement efforts of the two agencies were coordinated through written cooperative agreements. *Matter of Town of Waterford v NY St. Dept. of Envtl. Conservation, appeal dismissed* 15 NY3d 906 (2010), *mod and affd* 18 NY3d 652 (Ct App 2012).

(ii). The ruling in Waterford was upheld on appeal by the Court of Appeals. The Court rejected the argument that the EPA was the equivalent of an outside consultant and held:

"Moreover, unlike typical consultants, these agencies represent different constituencies and their interests may diverge. We note that this interpretation is consistent with that of the Committee on Open Government, which has determined both that the EPA cannot be characterized as a consultant 'retained' by DEC (*see* Comm on Open Govt FOIL-AO-11985 [2000]) and that the definition of 'agency' does not include federal agencies (*see* Comm on Open Govt FOIL-AO-12034 [2000])." *Matter of Town of Waterford v NY St. Dept. of Envtl. Conservation, supra.*

(c). Interagency or intra-agency memoranda exclusions also apply to communications between an agency and a consultant firm employed by the agency. *Id.*

(7). Records of examination questions or answers requested before the final administration of the test questions.

(8). Records if disclosed would jeopardize the capacity of an agency or an entity that has shared information with an agency to guarantee the security of its information technology assets that encompass both electronic information systems and infrastructures (for example, computer access codes).

(9). Records of photographs, microphotographs, videotape or other recorded images prepared under authority of Vehicle and Traffic Law, §§ 1111-a, 1111-b.

E. The list of exemptions in Public Officers Law § 87 (2) is not exclusive. A determination of whether disclosure of the information demanded under FOIL would be an unwarranted invasion of personal property requires balancing the private interests against the public interest in allowing access to the information. In *NY Times Co. v City of NY Fire Dept.*, 4 NY3d 477, 796 NYS2d 302 (2005), the Court decided, "The desire to preserve the dignity of human existence even when life has passed is the sort of interest to which legal protection is given under the name of privacy. We thus hold that surviving relatives have an interest protected by FOIL in keeping private the affairs of the dead . . . ."

F. Duplicate agency records may be open to public access. A statute exempting from public disclosure agency records in possession of a particular agency may not exempt from disclosure copies of those records in possession of another agency.

(1). "There are a variety of instances in which records sought from one agency are exempt from disclosure, but . . . the same records in possession of a different agency are accessible. . . . In short, although records may be exempt from disclosure when in possession of an agency that is the subject of a specific statute that confers confidentiality, that restriction does not render duplicate records maintained by other agencies confidential, unless there is statutory direction to do so." *NY St. Dept. of St., Comm. on Open Govt.,* FOIL-AO-13559 (2008).

(2). Mental Hygiene Law §33.13 requires confidentiality by third-party recipients of confidential information. Clinical records about patients or clients maintained by a mental health facility are confidential, and Mental Hygiene Law § 33.13 (f) directs that confidential information disclosed to third parties "shall be kept confidential by the party receiving such information and the limitations on disclosure in this section shall apply to such party."

G. Disclosure of records does not constitute an unwarranted invasion of personal privacy in four circumstances under Public Officers Law §§ 89 (2) (a) and 89 (2) (b):

(1). Identifying details are deleted before disclosure.

(2). The person to whom a record pertains consents in writing to the disclosure.

(3). A person seeks access to his or her records.

(4). A record or group of documents relates to a right, title or interest in real property, or refers to inventory, status, or characteristics of real property.

H. An agency's denial of a FOIL request for access to records is appealable. A denial of a FOIL request for access to records must be in writing, state the reason for the denial, and inform of the right to and the process of an appeal of the denial.

(1). Appeal to Agency. A party has thirty days from the date of an agency's denial of a FOIL request to appeal to the agency. Within ten business days of receipt of the document of appeal, the agency must either grant access to the information sought or fully explain in writing the reason for further denial. An agency must provide a copy of all appeal and determination documents to the Committee on Open Government. Public Officers Law § 89 (4) (a).

(2). Judicial Appeal. CPLR article 78 sets the procedure for judicial review of an agency's final denial of a FOIL demand. A denial of record access based on an exception listed in Public Officers Law § 87 (2) must prove that the record sought fits within the statutory exemption. Public Officers Law § 89 (4) (b).

3. Open Meetings Law. Public Officers Law article 7 requires every session of a public body to be open to the public (except executive session meetings held under Public Officers Law § 105).

CHAPTER V. LEGISLATIVE LIMITATIONS ON TRIPARTITE POWERS.

§ 5.1. Fundamental Functions of Executive Agencies. Executive administrative agencies perform three primary functions: Rulemaking, enforcement, and adjudication operations. Administrative agencies of the executive branch are the only New York State agencies legislatively conferred with rulemaking and enforcement powers. [10]

§ 5.2. Regulation of Agency Rulemaking Power. The New York State Constitution and state statutes place conditions on a state agency's rulemaking power.

1. New York State Constitution. NY Const art IV, § 8 mandates that a proposed rule or regulation of a state agency must be filed in the office of the Division of Administrative Rules (DAR) of the Department of State.

2. New York State Law. State Administrative Procedure Act (SAPA), Civil Practice Law and Rules (CPLR), and New York Codes, Rules and Regulations (NYCRR) prescribe the administrative procedures that govern executive agencies. [11]

---

[10] Chapter II § 2.5. Power and Authority of Executive Agencies.
[11] *Rule Making in New York Manual*, New York State, Department of State, Division of Administrative Rules.

A. Agencies Regulated by SAPA. The application of SAPA's regulations to state agencies is restricted. Consequently, SAPA is not a standardization of administrative procedures applicable to all state administrative agencies. Administrative procedures of agencies differ. Each agency adapts procedures suitable to the strategies and objectives governing that agency. SAPA applies only to agencies as defined within the act. SAPA 102 (1) defines an "Agency" as "any department, board, bureau, commission, division, office, council, committee or officer of the state, or a public benefit corporation or public authority at least one of whose members is appointed by the governor, authorized by law to make rules or to make final decisions in adjudicatory proceedings."

B. Agencies Excluded from SAPA. The following agencies operate under procedural regulations other than SAPA and are excluded from some or all provisions of SAPA: Executive Department (Governor); legislative and judicial agencies; agencies created by interstate compact or international agreement; Department of Labor; Division of Military and Naval Affairs to the extent it exercises responsibility for military and naval affairs; Division of State Police; Identification and Intelligence Unit of the Division of Criminal Justice Services; State Division of Parole (SAPA article 2, rulemaking provisions applicable); Department of Corrections and Community Supervision (SAPA article 2, rulemaking provisions applicable); Court Administration; Judiciary (NY Const art VI, Judiciary Law); State Insurance Fund (Workers' Compensation Law article 6); and Workers' Compensation Board (Workers' Compensation Law articles 7 and 8; Workers' Compensation Law § 117 [2] requires the Board to publish a Regulatory Agenda in accordance with the "Notice of proposed rule making" provided in SAPA 202 [1]).

C. Adjudicatory Procedures Omitted from SAPA. SAPA 102 (3)

limits the definition of "Adjudicatory proceeding" by excluding employee disciplinary actions and administrative determinations of traffic offenses. " 'Adjudicatory proceeding' means any activity which is not a rule making proceeding or an employee disciplinary action before an agency, except an administrative tribunal created by statute to hear or determine allegations of traffic infractions which may also be heard in a court of appropriate jurisdiction, in which a determination of the legal rights, duties or privileges of named parties thereto is required by law to be made only on a record and after an opportunity for a hearing."

D. Rules Excluded from SAPA. SAPA 102 (2) (b) is not applicable to the following types of rules:

(1). Rules controlling the internal management procedures of an agency but do not directly and significantly affect the rights of the public to legal proceedings and practices.

(2). Rules governing day-to-day staff procedures and operations of an agency.

(3). Rules that relate to public works, including streets and highways, such as signs and signals that communicate the data of the rules to the public. Traffic signs and pavement markings are the primary communication devices placed by a highway agency to inform the traveling public of laws and regulations, traffic and roadway conditions, destinations, and other directorial information.

(4). Declaratory rulings issued under SAPA 204 and the right to a judicial review of agency rules under CPLR 7801 (SAPA 205).

(5). Rules implementing contracts between public employer-employee organizations regulated by the Taylor Act, Public Employees Fair Employment Act (Civil Service Law § 204-a).

(6). Non-legislative rules such as forms and instructions, interpretive statements, and statements of general policy that are explanatory and without legal effect. [12]

(7). Rates of interest prescribed by the superintendent of banks. Banking Law § 14-a.

(8). Rules relating to the approval or disapproval of subscriber rates contained in an application to the Public Service Commission after a public hearing and approval by a municipality for a certificate of confirmation or an amendment to a franchise agreement.

(9). State equalization rates, class ratios, special equalization rates and special equalization ratios calculated under the Real Property Tax Law.

(10). Rates subject to approval by the superintendent of insurance or to flexible rate limitations in problem markets. Insurance Law § 2344.

(11). Any regulation declaring an interim price and any final marketing order made by the commissioner of Agriculture and Markets fixing prices for milk and marketing agreements. Agriculture and Markets Law, § 258-m. See *Nebbia v New York*, 291 US 502, 54 S Ct 505. [13]

(12). Rules enacting specific fees. Fees set by statute; fees of

---

[12] Chapter VI § 6.7. Non-legislative Rulemaking.
[13] Chapter XI § 11.9.2. (A). State Price Regulation for the Public Welfare.

less than one hundred dollars; fees of one hundred dollars or more reasonably expected to result in a one-thousand dollar annual aggregate collection; fees established through negotiation, written agreement or competitive bidding, including, but not limited to, contracts, leases, charges, permits for space use, prices, royalties or commissions; a fee, charge or an assessment levied by an agency upon another agency or by an agency upon another unit of state government.

(13). Changes in a schedule filed by a telephone corporation subject to the jurisdiction of the Public Service Commission.

(14). Rules relating to requests for authority by a telephone corporation subject to the jurisdiction of the Public Service Commission under Public Service Law §§ 99, and 101, and by a public utility subject to the jurisdiction of the Public Service Commission under Public Service Law § 107.

E. Minimum Standards of Procedures. SAPA 201 sets minimum rulemaking procedures for agencies and allows the adoption of additional procedures by agencies.

F. Civil Practice Law and Rules (CPLR). CPLR contains provisions that apply to agency administrative proceeding (1) by direct reference in the statute or (2) through incorporation by reference in an agency's rule, as allowed by SAPA 201.

G. New York Codes, Rules and Regulations (NYCRR). NYCRR is the official body of substantive administrative law; it is the compilation of titles of codes, rules, and regulations adopted by administrative agencies through the administrative process of rulemaking. NYCRR consists of 23 Titles. Titles 1–20 and Title 23 of NYCRR record the codes, rules, and regulations promulgated by administrative agencies. Each title is unique to an administrative agency.

§ 5.3. Regulation of Agency Enforcement Power. Federal and state constitutions, state statutes, and agency rules prescribe the way and the extent to which an agency may exercise its investigative power. Replicate federal and state constitutional provisions (US Const Amend IV and NY Const art I, § 12), protect the privacy rights of citizens by restricting administrative searches.

1. The Fourth Amendment to the US Constitution extends the application of the precepts of the due process of law clause of the Fourteenth Amendment to New York State agencies. *Mapp v Ohio*, 367 US 643, 81 S Ct 1684 (1961).

2. NY Const art I, § 12 governs state agencies.

3. The text of the Fourth Amendment to the US Constitution and the text of art I §12 to the NY Constitution are linguistically identical and are legally analogous.

A. Both provisions prohibit unreasonable searches and seizures. "The right of the people to be secure in their persons, houses, papers, and effects, against unreasonable searches and seizures, shall not be violated . . ." and

B. both provisions prescribe that a search warrant should issue only after judicial approval based on evidence of probable cause. "[N]o Warrants shall issue, but upon probable cause, supported by oath or affirmation, and particularly describing the place to be searched, and the persons or things to be seized." The Fourth Amendment protects privacy, not property (*Warden v Hayden,* 387 US 294, 87 S Ct 1642 [1967]). "The Fourth Amendment protects people, not places." *Katz v United States*, 389 US 347, 88 S Ct 507 (1967).

C. NY Const art VI, § 1 assigns the issuing of warrants to courts in the unified court system of New York State. Warrants are served and executed in the state by the Court of Appeals, by the Supreme Court, by the Court of Claims, by the County Court, by the Surrogate's Court, and by the Family Court.

§ 5.4. Laws Governing Agency Adjudications. US and NY Constitutions, state statutes, and specific agency rules governing agency adjudication include:

1. US Const Amend V and Amend XIV (due process).

2. NY Const art I, § 6 (due process, self-incrimination).

3. Enabling or organic legislation (statutes that create and define executive agencies).

4. SAPA 301 (hearings), SAPA 302 (hearing record), SAPA 303 (presiding officer), SAPA 304 (powers of presiding officers), SAPA 305 (disclosure), SAPA 306 (evidence), SAPA 307 (decisions, determinations and orders), SAPA 401 (licenses), and SAPA 501 (representation of parties).

5. CPLR 7801 (judicial review of an agency's final decision); CPLR 2301-2308 (nonjudicial subpoenas); CPLR 2310 (provisions of CPLR article 23 are not applicable to subpoenas issued in proceedings before the New York State Labor Relations Board).

6. NYCRR (compilation of specific agency rules).

7. Real Property Law § 441-e (revocation, suspension, reprimands, fines of real estate brokers and salespersons), Real Property Law § 441-I (denial of license, complaints, notice of hearing of home inspection professionals), and Real Property Law § 446-F (revocation, suspension, reprimands, and fines of

apartment information vendors).

8. General Business Law § 800 (complaint, notice of hearing, and denial of registration of hearing aid dispensers).

CHAPTER VI. AGENCY IMPLEMENTATION OF RULEMAKING POWER.

§ 6.1. Agency Rulemaking Power. The Legislature delegated to executive agencies lawmaking power in the form of rulemaking power within the confines of the state constitution. Organic laws prescribe discretionary and mandatory rulemaking procedures for agencies. Discretionary legal provisions permit agencies to issue rules and regulations as may be necessary to administer the legislation. Mandatory laws order agencies to implement prescribed procedures Agencies use the administrative process of rulemaking to formulate, implement, monitor, enforce, amend, and repeal regulations for efficient program administration.

§ 6.2. Administrative Rules and Regulations. Rules and regulations act as an agency's operating principles. The terms "rule" and "regulation" often used interchangeably have specific meanings. Rules restrict. Regulations control.

1. Rule. A rule states principles or instructions that restrict or

explain conduct within an activity and imposes an authoritative, general standard of order. Rules structure routine operating processes to govern performance in designated operations. A rule may form, implement, interpret, monitor, and enforce an agency law or policy affecting a regulated activity. Rules are part of regulation.

2. Regulation. A regulation prescribes procedures or directives to control conduct within an activity and imposes penalties as a consequence of a breach of the regulation. Regulations may form, implement, interpret, monitor, and enforce an agency rule, law or policy affecting a regulated activity. A regulation may be a legal rule or consist of a set of rules with legal connotations

3. Legal Differentiation of Rule and Regulation. An agency may differentiate between a rule and a regulation.

A. Workers' Compensation Law § 152 states that a regulation directing the administration of the agency's board and employees "[S]hall not be deemed a rule within the meaning of the Labor Law."

B. SAPA 102 (2) exempts from coverage "rules" governing an agency's internal affairs, internal management procedures, and the day-to-day staff procedures and operations.

§ 6.3. Rulemaking Procedures and Practices. Agencies promulgate rules by using five administrative proceedings: Formal rulemaking, informal rulemaking, consensus rulemaking, non-legislative rulemaking, and retroactive rulemaking.

§ 6.4. Formal Rulemaking. Formal rulemaking by an agency is legislative rulemaking. An agency enacts, implements and publishes rules in NYCRR as prescribed in applicable provisions of NY Const art IV and SAPA 201.

1. NY Const art IV, §8 mandates that a public rule or regulation enacted by a state department, board, bureau, officer, authority or commission must be filed in the office of the Department of State to become legally valid.

2. SAPA 201 enunciates a three-step process (publication, public comment, and filing) that regulates an agency's adoption, amendment or repeal of a rule:

A. Publication. Commonly called "accountability rationale," the publication of a proposed rule informs the regulated community of the why, what, where, and how of the proposed rule. Compulsory publication forces an agency to document the terms and issues of the proposed rule and to create a record of the processes of rulemaking and decision making.

B. Public Comment. The public feedback mechanism of public comment encourages public participation and consultation in an agency's rulemaking procedure. An agency solicits information from regulated and interested entities regarding concerns about and potential consequences of a proposed rule.

C. Filing of Public Comments. An agency files with DAR an evaluation of public comments received by the agency and the agency's final version of the proposed rule. DAR reviews and determines first, whether the rule filed is a logical outgrowth of the initial proposed rule and in character with the original scheme (there should not be a meaningful difference between the initial and final versions of the rule) and second, whether the agency assessed and responded correctly to the public comments received by the agency.

3. A legislative rule imposes a duty with the force and effect of law on and demands compliance by the regulated community within an agency's jurisdiction.

§ 6.5. Informal Rulemaking. Informal rulemaking is termed idiomatically as "notice and comment" rulemaking.

1. An agency adopts a rule after publication and public comment. An informal rulemaking procedure does not require a public hearing.

2. Before adopting an informal rule, agencies regularly ask for and receive advice and comment from interested parties. Agencies "often communicate with affected interests as they develop notices of proposed rulemaking, and . . . input can occur through a wide variety of mechanisms . . . letters, informal conversations between agency staff and affected interests, the appointment of advisory committees, hearings, and even focus groups." West, William, *Administrative Rulemaking: An Old and Emerging Literature*, Public Administration Review, Nov/Dec 2005, Vol. 65, No. 6, p. 663.

§ 6.6. Consensus Rulemaking. " 'Consensus rule' means a rule proposed by an agency for adoption on an expedited basis in anticipation that an objection to the rule's adoption is improbable." A consensus rule eliminates a rule no longer applicable to any person, implements or conforms a rule as required by law, makes technical changes, or is otherwise uncontroversial. SAPA § 102 (11).

§ 6.7. Non-legislative Rulemaking. Non-legislative rules are informal guidance documents issued by an agency. A new rule made to clarify an uncertain or confusing phrase or provision formulated in a prior rule is an act of clarification; it is not considered retroactive rulemaking.

1. SAPA 102 defines a guidance document as "any guideline, memorandum or similar document prepared by an agency that provides general information or guidance to assist regulated parties in complying with any statute, rule or other legal requirement, but shall not include documents that concern only the internal management of the agency or declaratory rulings issued pursuant to... (SAPA 202)."

2. A non-legislative statement explains either an existing rule or how an agency intends to act in future practices. Non-legislative rules do not have the force and effect of law; however, the regulated population must comply with an unchallenged, implemented, non-legislative rule.

3. Two enactments of non-legislative rulemaking are interpretive rules and policy statements.

A. Interpretive Rules. An agency's interpretive rule explains a duty imposed by an existing statute or a rule (*Shalala v Guernsey Memorial Hospital*, 514 US 87, 115 S Ct 1232 [1995]). In *Shalala*, Health and Human Services issued properly an interpretive rule determining that "defeasance losses" are amortizable. The rule is a prototypical example of an interpretive rule: (a) that advises the public of the agency's construction of statutes and rules it administers, (b) that does not require notice-and-comment before issuance, and (c) that does not have force and effect of law. However, the unchallenged, implemented interpretive rule's explanation of amortization of defeasance losses affects the regulated community. Interpretive rules are forbidden retroactive application. *Lehman v Burnley*, 866 F2d 33 (2nd Cir 1989).

B. Policy Statement. A policy statement establishes direction. An agency uses a policy statement to explain how the agency intends to exercise a discretionary power in subsequent rulemaking or adjudication processes. Agencies make policy statements in guides, guidelines, manuals, opinion letters, employees' directives or similar documents. Policy statements give general or guidance information to assist regulated parties to comply with statutes, rules, or other legal obligations. An illustration: The New York State Office of Information Technology issued the New York State Information Technology Policy, NYS-P08-001 (PTP Policy) NYS-PO8-002, *Authority to Establish State Enterprise Information (IT) Policy, Standards and Guidelines.* The PTC Policy applies to every state entity over which the Governor has executive power. [14]

4. Non-legislative rulemaking by an agency is without legal force; the usual constraints imposed on substantive rulemaking do not apply in non-legislative rulemaking.

§ 6.8. Retroactive Rulemaking. Retroactive rulemaking occurs when an agency implements a rule that enforces a new regulatory policy to past activity (imposes new legal standards to acts that occurred before the rule was enacted).

1. Methods of Retroactive Rulemaking. The two methods of retroactive rulemaking are primary and secondary rulemaking.

A. Primary Retroactivity Rulemaking. Enactment of a rule that changes the past legal consequences of past actions that occurred before the enactment of the rule is classified as primary retroactive rulemaking.

B. Secondary Retroactivity Rulemaking. Secondary retroactive

---

[14] A statute may express a policy. Public Service Law, § 30 declares the continued provision of utility services to residential customers necessary for public health and general welfare as a policy of the state.

rulemaking changes future legal consequences of past transactions that occurred before the rule is adopted.

2. Retroactive Rulemaking Restraints. There is a statutory presumption against retroactive rulemaking. *Bowen v Georgetown University Hospital*, 488 US 204 (1988); *General Motors Corp. v National Highway Traffic Safety Administration*, 898 F2d 165 (DC Cir 1990).

A. Statutory Authorization. Law prohibits primary retroactivity rulemaking unless authority is granted in explicit, statutory terms.

B. Rational Analysis. The end justifies the means (Machiavellian philosophy).

(1). An agency may change an enforcement policy retroactively with proof by the agency that the retroactive change serves a legitimate need to achieve statutory mandates. A reviewing court evaluates an agency's rationale for a retroactive change of a practice to determine whether an agency's decision justified the retroactive change of an enforcement policy. See Chapter XIV §14.6. Policy Effects on Final Decisions.

(2). An agency's retroactive change of a practice based on a matter involving the agency's expertise is judicially persuasive. Additionally, agency behavior that exhibits public welfare virtuosity is judicially supported.

§ 6.9. Proclamations. An executive agency may enforce a law by proclamation if statutorily authorized. Business Corporation Law § 1014 and Tax Law § 203-a empower the Secretary of State to dissolve corporations by proclamations for delinquent tax payments (except Public cemetery corporations).

CHAPTER VII. AGENCY IMPLEMENTATION OF ENFORCEMENT POWER.

§ 7.1. Agency Enforcement Power. An agency's implementation of its legislative mission depends principally on the power of an agency to compel compliance with its laws, rules, and regulations.

§ 7.2. Agency Investigation Authority. The authority of investigation is part of the enforcement power granted legislatively to agencies. An agency exerts its enforcement power through its investigative and prosecutorial authorities.

1. Purpose of Administrative Investigations. Investigations impact agency operations. Agencies conduct administrative investigations to monitor regulated entities, to obtain

information, to uncover unlawful activity, to determine culpability, and, ultimately, to increase regulatory effectiveness.

2. Parameters of Administrative Investigations. State statutes and agency rules proclaim the method and the scope of an agency's exercise of its investigative authority. The conduct of an administrative investigation must be for a legitimate purpose, must seek relevant information, must reasonably relate to the accomplishment of an agency's statutory mandate, and must not be unreasonably oppressive in execution.

§ 7.3. Standard Methods of Investigation. Standard methods of investigation used by agencies to obtain information are compulsory record keeping and reports, investigative subpoena, grant of immunity, and administrative inspection and search.

1. Records and Reports. Routinely, agency rules demand regulated entities to maintain and to file with the agency extensive business and financial records and reports. Agencies impose severe penalties for failure to comply with required filing procedures of specified documents.

2. Investigative Administrative Subpoenas. During an investigation and before an adjudicatory action begins, an agency may serve an administrative subpoena to discover information relevant to a legitimate inquiry.

3. Grant of Immunity. [15] A grant of immunity by an agency must be authorized by statute or rule. Immunity is granted to obtain testimony not otherwise obtainable; a witness's unimmunized

---

[15] Typical statutes authorizing the grant of immunity by an agency are Executive Law § 295.7, Public Service Law § 20.2, Real Property Law §442-e (7), and Transportation Law § 84.2.

testimony would expose the testifying witness to criminal proceedings or administrative penalties.

§ 7.4. Administrative Search by Warrant. Administrative search by warrant is a search authorized by a written, lawfully issued, judicial order (warrant). A valid warrant legalizes an invasion of privacy; it permits and directs the search and the seizure of property, person, place, or thing. [16]

1. An agency's use of administrative search is a law enforcement technique that challenges an individual's right to privacy. An administrative search intrudes on an individual's right to privacy; the agency is looking for something in a privately-owned location.

2. *Camara v Municipal Court of San Francisco*, 387 US 523, 87 S Ct 1727 (1967), is the first case in which the US Supreme Court held that specific administrative inspection programs must obey the probable-cause warrant requisite of the Fourth Amendment. "(E)xcept in certain carefully defined classes of cases, a search of private property without proper consent is unreasonable unless . . . authorized by a valid search warrant."

3. Administrative searches of business and residential premises are subject to the search-warrant prerequisite of the Fourth Amendment. "Administrative entry without consent upon the portions of commercial premises that are not open to the public may only be compelled through prosecution or physical force within the framework of a warrant procedure." *See v City of Seattle*, 387 US 541, 87 S Ct 1737 (1967).

---

[16] See Rosenblatt, Albert M., *The Complete Search Warrant, Annotated*, "Administrative Searches" at 91, New York State Unified Court System (consol. ed. November 2004).

4. Constitutional restraints on an administrative search restrict both an inspection and a search as logical equivalents. Search means to look for; inspect means to look at. "To say that the people, in requiring adoption of the Fourth Amendment to restrict invasion of homes if government officials are looking for something, but not to restrict it if the officials were merely looking, is to ascribe to the electorate of that day and to the several legislatures and the Congress a degree of irrationality not otherwise observable in their dealings with tyranny." *District of Columbia v Little,* 85 US App DC 242, 78 F2d 13 (DC Cir 1949), *affd on other grounds* 339 US 1, 70 S Ct 468 (1950).

§ 7.5. Criteria for Lawful Administrative Search by Warrant. A lawful administrative search by warrant fulfills four criteria, the three criteria fixed by US and New York State Constitutions and the criterion established by a US Supreme Court decision.

1. Constitutional Criteria. US and New York State constitutions demand that an administrative search by warrant meet three criteria: Reasonableness, search warrant, and probable cause.

A. Reasonableness. The search is reasonable. The evaluation of the reasonableness of a search balances the significance of the government interest fulfilled by the search against the extent to which the search intrudes on an individual's privacy right.

B. Valid Search Warrant. The search is performed as directed by a valid search warrant, A valid search warrant defines and limits the discretion of inspecting officers to the time, place, and scope of the search.

C. Probable Cause. The issuance of a search warrant is based on evidence of probable cause. Probable cause deals with probabilities. Probable cause exists where the known facts cause a reasonable person to believe that a violation of law has been or is being committed. (*Draper v United States*, 358 US 307, 79 S Ct 329 [1959]). Probable cause for an administrative search is analogous to reasonable cause. Probable cause justifying the issuance of an administrative search warrant is founded on one of two evidential justifications: Either there is evidence of an existing violation of agency law or rule; or there is evidence that the inspection is in accord with a legally authorized, reasonable legislative or administrative program of inspection derived from a neutral source. (*Marshall v Barlow's Inc.*, 436 US 307, 98 S Ct 1816 [1978]). [17] Effective regulation of the monitored activity requires systematic and recurrent inspection.

(1). Probable Cause Based on Evidence of Violation of Agency Law. Evidence of a violation of agency law constitutes probable cause for issuance of an administrative warrant. Administrative searches sanctioned on explicit evidence of violations of agency law strengthen an agency's ability to enforce its laws and regulations and protect public health, safety, and welfare. *Cf Camara v Municipal Court of San Francisco*, 387 US 523, 87 S Ct 1727 (1967).

(2). Probable Cause and An Agency's Inspection Program. An application for an administrative search warrant based on an agency's general inspection program "must describe the program in sufficient detail to enable the 'neutral and detached magistrate' to determine that 'there is a reasonable legislative or administrative inspection program (the agency's program is reasonable) and . . . that the desired inspection fits within that program.' (inspections enable an agency to proficiently enforce regulations)" (*City of Seattle v Leach*, 29 Wn App 81, 627 P2d

---

17. Also see Civil Rights Law § 8. "no warrants can issue but upon probable cause supported by oath or affirmation, and particularly describing the place to be searched, and the persons or things to be seized."

159 [1981]). An agency's need for inspections corroborates the agency's general inspection program where the behavior of a regulated industry implores scheduled general inspections to assure compliance with agency rules. Examples of markedly regulated industries are food, alcohol, and firearms.

(3). Grounds Justifying Probable Cause. A judicial determination of probable cause to issue an administrative search warrant must be based on justifying grounds that exist both at the time the warrant is issued and at the time the warrant is executed. *Mitchell v United States*, 258 F2d 435 (DC Cir 1958).

2. Judicial Criterion for Lawful Search. The US Supreme Court added a fourth criterion to the constitutional three-factor criteria for a lawful search. A "neutral and detached magistrate" must determine probable cause (*Johnson v United States*, 333 US 10, 68 S Ct 367 [1948]). The magistrate must be impartial and not a member of the "competitive enterprise" of law enforcement (*California v Acevedo*, 500 U.S. 565, 111 S Ct 1982 [1991]). Judges, lawyers, and court clerks potentially qualify as "neutral and detached" and may become magistrates.

A. A magistrate is an officer empowered to issue warrants. Courts have used the term "judicial officer" interchangeably with that of "magistrate." *Katz v United States*, 389 US 347, 88 S Ct 507 (1967).

B. A judge or magistrate must be neutral, detached, and capable of determining whether probable cause exists for the requested search (*Johnson v United States*, 333 US 10, 68 S Ct 367 [1948]). An unsalaried justice of the peace who received a sum of money for each warrant issued, but received nothing for reviewing and denying a warrant, is not sufficiently detached (*Connally v Georgia*, 429 US 245, 97 S Ct 546 [1977]). Persons engaged in law enforcement activities are not viewed as neutral and detached parties. Police officers and prosecutors do not qualify ordinarily as neutral and detached magistrates. (*Coolidge v New Hampshire*, 403 US 443, 91 S Ct 2022 [1971]).

C. The Supreme Court extended a Fourth Amendment protection to corporations by requiring federal inspectors to obtain a search warrant before conducting a safety inspection of corporate property. *Marshall v Barlow's Inc.*, 436 US 307, 98 S Ct 1816 (1978).

3. New York State Statutory Authorization. State statutes grant to agencies the authority to obtain administrative search warrants. Two, typical, authorizing statutes are Environmental Conservation Law § 71-0911 and Public Health Law § 309 (e).

§ 7.6. Warrantless Administrative Searches. Warrantless administrative searches may be performed only where statutorily prescribed. A statute structuring a warrantless, administrative search must provide legal parameters for the conduct of the search. Lack of legal guidelines in a statute authorizing a warrantless, administrative search may invalidate a search conducted under the statute. *Id.*

1. Statutory Prerequisites. A statute granting a warrantless search power to an agency must meet three prerequisites: The law must serve an existing compelling, substantial or urgent agency interest, must further the agency's legislative mandate, and must provide a protection equivalent to the constitutional safeguards designated to administrative search warrants (concise, comprehensive, and reasonable).

A. Law Serves Vital Government Interest. The law granting a search power to an agency must fulfill an existing, substantial, compelling, or urgent government interest. A substantial interest, a compelling interest, and an urgent interest are equivalent and are legally interchangeable. Compelling state interests are "interests of the highest order." *Church of the LukumiBabalu Aye Inc. v City of Hialeah*, 508 US 520, 113 S Ct 2217 (1993).

(1). Substantial Government Interest.

(a). Government has substantial interests in maintaining public parks (*Clark v Community for Creative Non-Violence,* 468 US 288 [1984]).

(b). New York State has a substantial interest in regulating the right of nonresident attorneys to practice law in New York.

(i). In *Schoenefeld v New York*, 907 F Supp 2d 252, 266 (ND NY 2011), the district court determined that the Judicial Law § 470 office requirement involved nonresident attorneys' fundamental right to practice law in New York, and the statute did not bear a substantial relationship to the interests asserted because there were less restrictive means of accomplishing those interests.

(ii). In *Schoenefeld v New York*, 748 F3d 464, 467 (2d Cir 2014), the United States Court of Appeals stated that the statutory requirements that must be met by nonresident attorneys in order to practice law in New York reflect an important state interest and implicate significant policy issues; and the constitutionality of the statute was dependent upon New York's interpretation of the law office requirement, a determinative question of New York law without a controlling precedent by the New York Court of Appeals. Subsequently, the Court of Appeals for the 2d Circuit certified the question to the New York Court of Appeals. (Fed Rules App Pro, 2d Circuit Local Rule 27.2 [a]).

(iii). In *Schoenefeld v. State*, 25 NY3d 22 (2015), the Court of Appeals held that the state does have an interest in ensuring that personal service can be accomplished on nonresident attorneys admitted to practice in New York. "CPLR currently authorizes several means of service upon a nonresident attorney, including mail, overnight delivery, fax and (where permitted) email (see CPLR 2103 [b]). Under our own Court rules, the admission of attorneys who neither reside nor have full-time employment in the State is conditioned upon designating the clerk of the Appellate Division in their department of admission as their agent for the service of process for actions or proceedings brought against them relating to legal services offered or rendered (see Rules of the Court of Appeals [22 NYCRR] § 520.13 [a]). Therefore, there would appear to be adequate measures in place relating to service upon nonresident attorneys . . . ."

(iv). The US Court of Appeals determined in *Schoenefeld v Scheiderman COPS* ___ F3d _ (2nd Cir April. 22, 2016), (Raggie, J dissenting and Hall, J dissenting in a different opinion), that Judicial Law § 470, requiring non-resident members of the New York bar to maintain an office in New York was not enacted for a protectionist purpose. Consequently, the "state need not demonstrate that . . . (Judicial Law § 470 is) narrowly tailored to a legitimate purpose."

(2). Compelling Government Interest. The right of a competent adult to refuse medical treatment, even if premised upon fervently held religious beliefs, may be overridden by a compelling state interest. State interests judicially identified as compelling in cases involving medical treatment are: (a) preservation of life, (b) prevention of suicide, (c) protection of innocent third parties, and (d) maintenance of the ethical integrity of the medical profession. *Matter of Delio v Westchester County Med. Center*, 129 AD2d 1, 516 NYS2d 677 (1987).

(3). Urgent Government Interest. Government's regulation of interstate transport of firearms furthers an urgent government interest. *United States v Biswell,* 406 US 311, 92 S Ct 1593 (1972).

B. Statutory Support of An Agency's Mandate. A statute granting warrantless search authority to an agency must promote the agency's legislative, regulatory mandate. Specific regulated business activities are subject to warrantless inspection intrusions to accomplish regulatory goals. The state constricts offensive social issues with administrative rule. An example is the automobile vehicle-dismantling and junkyard industry with which motor vehicle theft, a significant social problem, is associated. New York State has a substantial interest in and confronts that industry with regulations (Vehicle & Traffic Law § 415-a 5).

C. Enabling Law Provides Constitutional Safeguards. A statute granting authority for a warrantless search must provide the constitutional safeguards that regulate administrative search warrants. The conferring statute must be concise, comprehensive, and sanction reasonable action.

(1). The authorizing statute is concise. The law should not be so voluminous that it cannot be read or so incoherent that it cannot be understood (Madison, James, *The Federalist No 62* [February 27, 1877]). "a statute which either forbids or requires the doing of an act in terms so vague that men of common intelligence must necessarily guess at its meaning and differ as to its application violates the first essential of due process of law." *Connally v General Construction Co.*, 269 US 385, 391, 46 S Ct 126 (1926).

(2). The enabling statute is comprehensive. From the language of the enabling law, a reasonable person perceives or should be able to perceive (a) that the property is subject to periodic inspections conducted by an agency for specific purposes (*Donovan v Dewey,* 452 US 594, 101 S Ct 2534 [1981]); (b) that the search is subject to law and has an adequately defined scope; and (c) that the discretion of inspecting officers is limited carefully to the time, place, and scope of the search (*New York v Burger,* 482 US 691, 107 S Ct 2636 [1987]). Fundamentally, the law must be sufficiently explicit to give adequate information and notice to regulated persons and to provide clear criteria to enforcement agents.

(3). The conferring statute confines a search agent's conduct to reasonable action. The authority of a search agent begins and ends with the performance of a lawful search. During a warrantless search or inspection, agency personnel may demand and examine records, conduct tests, seize materials and data, and perform all acts allowed by and reasonably necessary to enforce agency's laws relevant to the regulated activity and to protect the public health, safety, and welfare.

(a). Police officers and administrative agents may jointly perform warrantless, administrative searches. Where the ultimate purpose of a regulatory statute is the same as that of a penal law (the deterrence of criminal behavior), a search done under an administrative statute may uncover violations of both regulatory law and penal law. A police officer has the authority to arrest persons during a lawful administrative search that discloses violations of penal law.

(i). If the purpose behind an administrative search is fulfilled during the search, any further search at that time is a search to gather criminal evidence; and such further search is justifiable only upon obtaining a warrant based on criminal probable cause. *Michigan v Clifford,* 464 US 287 (1984).

(ii). Evidence obtained during an administrative search without a warrant is constitutionally prohibited admissibility in a subsequent criminal proceeding. Evidence obtained in a search initially permitted for administrative purposes requires the securing of a warrant to be admitted in a criminal prosecution. *People v Laverne*, 14 NY2d 304, NYS2d 452 (1964).

(b). Warrantless inspections are restrained statutorily (*Finn's Liquor Shop Inc. v State Liq. Auth.*, 31 AD2d 15, 294 NYS2d 592 [1968], *affd* 24 NY2d 647, 301 NYS2d 647 [1969], *cert denied* 396 US 840 [1969]). During an unannounced, warrantless inspection of his liquor shop, Finn produced the book and records requested by and permitted a State Liquor Authority inspector to inspect the licensed premises. The inspector searched and obtained incriminating evidence from the pockets of a coat hanging in a rear room of the premises. The Court held Finn's personal clothing "to be free of a warrantless intrusion by government." *Id.*

2. Unannounced Warrantless Search as Administrative Tool. In unannounced, warrantless searches, privacy rights yield to public health, safety, and welfare precautions. Information collected by agencies during warrantless searches, inspections, tests, and seizure of products and materials assist agencies in discovering, stopping, and preventing unlawful activity, and to increase operational effectiveness. Unannounced, warrantless searches and inspections give an agency the advantage of surprise and the flexibility of time, scope, and frequency essential for a search to be useful as a credible deterrent to unlawful behavior. Government proclaims that to safeguard public health, safety, and welfare in specific industries, there is an urgent need for power to invade clear rights of privacy through regulations. *Marshall v Barlow's Inc.,* 436 US 307, 98 S Ct 1816 (1978).

§ 7.7. Regulated Industries, Commercial Products, and Social Activities Vulnerable to Warrantless Search or Inspection. In government's experience, specific industries, commercial products, and social activities demand rigorous regulation in the interests of the public welfare.

1. Regulated Industries. The following industries are strictly regulated and subject to strict supervision and inspection by regulatory agencies:

A. Automobile junkyards. *New York v Burger,* 482 US 691 (1987).

B. Coal mines. *Youghiogheny and Ohio Coal Co. v Morton,* 364 F Supp 45 (SD Ohio 1973).

C. Drug manufacturing. U*nited States v Jamieson-McKames pharmaceuticals Inc.*, 651 F2d 532 (8th Cir 1981), *cert denied* 455 US 1016 (1982).

D. Electrical and plumbing plants. *Marshall v Barlow's Inc.*, 436 US 307 (1987).

E. Firearms. *United States v Biswell,* 406 US 311 (1972).

F. Food warehouses. *United States v Gel Spice Co. Inc.,* 601 F Supp 1214 (EDNY 1985); *United States v New England Grocers Supply Co.*, 488 F Supp 230 (1980).

G. Liquor. *Colonnade Catering Corp. v United States,* 397 US 72, 90 SC 774 (1970).

H. Mining. *Donovan v Dewey,* 452 US 594, 101 S Ct 2534 (1981).

I. Pawn shops, *We Buy Inc. v Town of Clarkstown NY,* 2006 US

Dis. LEXIS 76792 (SDNY October 20, 2006).

J. Pharmacies. *United States ex. re. Terraciano v Montanye,* 493 F2d 682 (2nd Cir 1974), *cert denied* 419 US 875 (1974).

2. Regulated Commercial Products. Statute and rule subject to routine inspection the manufacture, distribution, and sale of conventional commercial products.

A. General Business Law § 387 permits the Department of State to inspect the manufacture, sale, delivery, and sanitization of all articles of materials, to open and examine contents, and, upon reasonable belief of an existing violation, to seize and hold for evidence any article of bedding.

B. General Business Law article 29 authorizes the Department of Labor, to inspect, examine, place off-sale, and seize and hold for evidence any article of wearing apparel, interior furnishing, sleeping bag, or portable temporary shelter where there is a reason to believe that the product is made, sold or possessed in violation of law.

C. Agriculture & Markets Law § 16.27 sanctions the seizure or destruction of any unwholesome food or food product exposed for sale or sold in markets of New York State.

3. Regulated Social Activities. Warrantless emergency searches manifestly made to protect public health, safety, and welfare are usually upheld judicially. *North American Cold Storage Co. v City of Chicago*, 211 US 306, 29 SC 101 (1908).

A. Emergency Societal-Risk Situations. Home entry and search are permitted in an urgent situation (a circumstance in which exists an imminent, critical societal risk that endangers life, health or property, and time is life-threatening). A social worker may take a child into emergency protective custody when there is reasonable cause to believe the child is in imminent danger, and the condition of the child or the imminent-danger circumstances do not allow time in which to obtain a court order (Social Services Law § 417; Family Court Act § 1024). After a child is taken into emergency protective custody, a petition must be filed forthwith with the court, and a hearing must occur "as soon as practicable." (Family Court Act § 1026). A valid, temporary assertion of custody by the state does not violate due process guarantees. A critical societal risk that endangers life, health, or property justifies both preemptive action and a reasonable postponement of a due process hearing.

B. Home Inspections of Entitlement Recipients. New York courts consistently uphold warrantless visits (regulatory inspections) of private premises occupied by persons receiving welfare benefits and restrict a right of privacy in the interest of compelling public interest.

(1). *Wyman v James*, 400 US 309, 91 S Ct 381 (1971) exemplifies the judicial position that upholds warrantless visits to private dwellings of welfare recipients. James, a beneficiary under the program for Aid to Families with Dependent Children, refused a caseworker's written request for a home visit (then required under Social Services Law § 134, New York Policies Governing the Administration of Public Assistance § 175, and 18 NYCRR §§ 351.10, 351.21). After an administrative hearing, the agency terminated James's benefits, and she appealed the agency's determination. The Supreme Court reasoned that the home visit as designed in New York law is not a "search" within the Fourth Amendment. Even if deemed a "search," it would not violate the standard of reasonableness. "New York's program is reasonable, as it serves the paramount needs of the dependent child; enables the State to determine that the intended objects of its assistance benefit from its aid and that state funds are being properly used; helps attain parallel federal relief objectives; stresses privacy by not unnecessarily intruding on the beneficiary's rights in her home; provides essential information not obtainable through secondary sources; is conducted, not by a law enforcement officer, but by a caseworker; is not a criminal investigation; and (unlike the warrant procedure, which necessarily implies criminal conduct) comports with the objectives of welfare administration." (*Wyman v James*, 400 US at 318).

(2). A recipient's acceptance of state welfare is tantamount to a recipient's consent to the state to conduct warrantless inspections of ("visits" to) the recipient's private dwelling as the state deems reasonably necessary to fulfill the legislative mandate of aid to dependent children.

CHAPTER VIII. ELEMENTS OF QUASI-JUDICIAL POWER.

§ 8.1. Quasi-judicial Administrative Adjudication. The quasi-judicial process adjudicates public legal rights to determine the legal rights of specific persons and entities. In quasi-judicial administrative adjudication, agencies apply existing laws and rules to facts to resolve a legal dispute between an agency and a regulated entity. Quasi-judicial administrative adjudication is intended to be faster and less expensive than trial by jury.

§ 8.2. Delegation of Adjudication Authority. The authority of an executive administrative agency to conduct quasi-judicial adjudications is granted through the quasi-judicial power conferred by the agency's organic act.

1. Delegation of Adjudication Authority to Agency. An executive agency's quasi-judicial power includes an agency leader's authority to initiate and to implement proper procedures to govern an agency's quasi-judicial administrative matters.

2. Delegation of Authority to Administrative Law Judges. An agency leader delegates authority to agency personnel designated to administer adjudicatory proceedings that conform to state law (SAPA 303), executive order (9 NYCRR 4.131), and specific agency rules (NYCRR). Agencies refer to quasi-judicial hearing officials as hearing officers, hearing examiners, hearing masters, administrative law judges or otherwise. In New York, administrative law judge (ALJ) is the title used most often by executive administrative agencies.

§ 8.3. Administrative Law Judiciary. Administrative law judges of executive administrative agencies compose the administrative law judiciary of the executive branch of New York State government. Executive administrative agencies are departments of the executive branch of state government and act with the power conferred by the state. Administrative law judges of executive agencies, regardless of individual agency affiliations, operate exclusively in accord with the laws and policies of the executive branch of state government.

1. Role of Executive Administrative Law Judiciary. In New York State, the executive administrative law judiciary is an agency-aligned judiciary.

A. Functional Independence of quasi-judicial functions. SAPA 303 and specific agency rules (NYCRR) prescribe that within legal constraints, the quasi-judicial function of an executive agency must be conducted impartially and independently of other agency operations; the quasi-judicial function is not conducted autonomously of the agency. Law advocates an ALJ's quasi-judicial decisional independence, not an ALJ's sovereign independence from the rules and policies of the employing administrative agency.

B. Functional Independence and Separation of Quasi-Judicial

and Enforcement Functions. Functional independence and decisional independence of administrative quasi-judicial units and judges are logical and legal consequences of organic statutes. Executive order and agency rules formulate and enforce the functional freedom of a quasi-judicial activity through the operational and physical separation of the quasi-judicial function from the prosecutorial operation. [18]

(1). Executive Order (Cuomo, M.) No. 131 (9 NYCRR 4.131), issued December 4, 1989, demanded executive administrative agencies to file an administrative adjudication plan. The executive order required an agency's written verification that the agency had implemented a church-and-state type of rule ensuring the separation and independence of the quasi-judicial function of the agency from the prosecutorial task of the agency.

(2). 19 NYCRR 400.2 illustrates an agency's enactment of an administrative rule in response to 9 NYCRR 4.131. Within the Department of State, the rule established the Office of Administrative Hearings (OAH). Housed in New York City, the OAH is separate from the offices of the prosecutorial function based in Albany. Administrative law judges conduct adjudicatory proceedings, are licensed to practice law, are forbidden to serve in any other capacity in the agency, and report directly to the agency leader. Decisions and orders of an ALJ are final determinations unless appealed by a proper party. A proper party is any party in an adjudication affected by an ALJ's order or decision, including a unit of the agency.

2. Conduct of Administrative Law Judges. Public Officers Law § 73, SAPA 303, SAPA 304, and 9 NYCRR 4.131 regulate the professional conduct of administrative law judges.

---

[18] Moliterno, James E., *The Administrative Judiciary's Independence Myth*, 41 Wake Forest L. Rev 1191 (2006).

A. ALJ as Impartial Decision-maker. An ALJ should be knowledgeable, proficient, fair, and an impartial decision-maker. SAPA and other pertinent statutes and rules prescribe standards of conduct to govern an ALJ in the exercise of the authority of a presiding officer in quasi-judicial administrative actions. The due process clause of the Fourteenth Amendment of the US Constitution requires recusal of a judge who demonstrates bias, who has an economic interest in the outcome of the action, or where significant facts create a probability of bias. *Caperton v A T Massey Coal Co., Inc.*, 556 US 868, 129 S Ct 2252 (2009).

B. Ex Parte Communications. Ex parte communications between a presiding ALJ and parties to an administrative proceeding are governed by SAPA 307 (2).

(1). Law forbids an ALJ from communicating directly or indirectly with any party or a party's representative about any issue of fact or law involved in a proceeding unless all parties to the proceeding are given an opportunity to participate in the communication. SAPA 307 (2).

(2). An ALJ may communicate with and ask for the aid and advice of agency staff that has not been or is not engaged in investigative or prosecutorial actions associated with the case under deliberation or to any case related factually to the case under consideration. SAPA 307 (2).

(3. The constraints of SAPA 307 (2) are not applicable to applications for initial licenses of public utilities, or of carriers, or to proceedings involving the validity or use of rates, facilities or practices of public utilities or carriers.

3. Authority of ALJ as Decision-maker. The quasi-judicial authority conferred to an ALJ differs among agencies. By agency

specific rules, an agency delegates quasi-judicial authority to a hearing officer. Three typical delegations of quasi-judicial authority by agencies are:

A. An ALJ, as the primary fact-finder in agency adjudications, makes and submits either an initial finding or a recommendation (not a decision) to an agency chief. In deciding, the head of the agency may conduct a de novo review of the litigation, affirm, alter, or completely override the finding of the administrative law judge (Department of Agriculture and Markets, 1 NYCRR 200.4; Department of Environmental Conservation, 6 NYCRR 622).

B. An ALJ issues a final decision appealable by an aggrieved motorist to the agency's appeal unit (Vehicle and Traffic Law § 242, 15 NYCRR 124). The ALJ's decision is not appealable by the agency.

C. An ALJ issues a final decision that is appealable to the agency leader by any party to the action (including a unit of the agency). If not timely appealed to an agency leader by a party to the adjudication, the ALJ's decision becomes the agency's final action. Department of State, 19 NYCRR 400. 2.

4. Authority and Duties of ALJ. In quasi-judicial adjudications of executive agencies, the authority of an ALJ is extensive and atypical of that of a judiciary judge. An ALJ decides adjudicative facts (questions of fact: who, what, where, why, and how) and legislative facts (questions of law, policy, and discretion).

A. The justiciable goal of an ALJ is twofold, to protect the public from untrustworthy and incompetent persons and to assure the regulated community of procedural and substantive due process conduct by government. An ALJ is entrusted to apply sagaciously and equitably an agency's quasi-judicial authority.

B. Administrative law authorizes an ALJ to perform the following acts (SAPA 304):

(1). Consolidate actions. An ALJ may schedule two are more adjudications to be heard simultaneously for the following three reasons: (a) In the interest of justice and fairness; (b) for procedural efficiency (expedite and simplify the issues for consideration); and (c) economy (avoid unnecessary costs and delay). (*NY St. Dept. of St., Div. of Lic. Servs., Application of Friedman*, 19 DOS 95 [1995]). Friedman had two applications pending before the agency: one for renewal of a license as an associate real estate broker and the other for a commission as a notary public. The agency purposed to deny both applications because of the applicant's prior criminal conviction. The tribunal determined, "The two actions at bar involve common questions of law and fact. To avoid the unnecessary duplication of cost and expense and to prevent any injustice that could result from divergent decisions based on the same facts, the matters are consolidated in the interest of justice and administrative economy. Baron v New York State Department of Motor Vehicles, 28 AD2d 993, 284 NYS2d 187 (1st Dept. 1967); NY St. Dept. of St., Div. of Lic. Servs *v* Cosme, 75 DOS 85 (1985)."

(2). Order discovery and disclosures.

(3). Issue subpoenas.

(4). Conduct settlement conferences.

(5). Promote agreement on issues, stipulations of facts, and proofs.

(6). Rule on procedural requests and motions, such as: Adjournments, more explicit statement of charges, failure to state a cause of action, failure of proof of complaint or of specific charges, amendment or supplement to a complaint or an answer, and demands for information (subpoenas, depositions, disclosure, or discovery).

(7). Administer oaths or affirmations.

(8). Examine witnesses when necessary to promote due process, particularly in pro se proceedings.

(9). Make evidentiary rulings on objections, offers of proof, admissibility of documents, and classification of expert witnesses.

(10). Request memoranda or briefs on issues of law and fact.

(11). Issue interim and final orders, decisions, and determinations.

(12). Order restitution of funds unlawfully obtained and retained by a regulated party. As a rule, an executive agency is not statutorily empowered to assess damages (*NY St. Dept. of St., Div. of Lic. Servs. v Cincotta,* 10 DOS 88 [1988]). An exception to the general rule is the Division of Human Rights. Human Rights Law § 297 (4) (c) empowers the agency to award punitive damages and to assess civil fines and penalties in housing cases involving issues of discrimination.

(13). Decide post-hearing proceedings – proposed findings of fact and motions to reargue or to reopen a matter for reasons of fraud, material mistake, or newly discovered evidence.

(14). Decide motions to stay all proceedings to enforce an agency's final order or decision during a pending appeal.

(15). Incorporate a settlement into the record of an action as

"So Ordered" by the tribunal.

(16). Make and preserve a complete record of the proceedings. Exclusiveness of the hearing record is essential in quasi-judicial adjudication. Executive and judicial reviews rely on a formally complied hearing record to determine the legal sufficiency of an agency's decision. SAPA ascribes the components of a complete and accurate record of a quasi-judicial proceedings as follows:

(a). Documents are submitted and accepted into evidence as exhibits.

(b). Findings of fact are based exclusively on the evidence and on matters officially noticed. SAPA 302 (3).

(c). As part of the hearing record, a decision, a determination, or an order should include a ruling on each proposed finding of fact submitted in an adjudication. *Goldberg v Kelly*, 397 US 254, 90 S Ct 1011 (1970)

(d). All aspects of a quasi-judicial hearing not conducted "off the record" are conducted "on the record" and are part of the record to be preserved (SAPA 302 [2]). For clarification and completeness of a hearing record, an ALJ should state the reason for an "Off the record" interval. An ALJ's on-the-record explanation of the reason for an "Off the record" interim should be made by the ALJ immediately and initially at the return to "On the record" status of the hearing.

(e). The record of a quasi-judicial hearing includes all testimony, pleadings, notices, motions, offers of evidence, offers of proof, exhibits, objections, exceptions, rulings, proposed findings of facts, conclusions of law, recommended and final opinions, orders, determinations, and decisions. SAPA 302 (1).

(f). Testimony in an adjudicatory proceeding may be recorded stenographical or electronically. Unless otherwise directed by statute, an agency may use any recordation method the agency considers appropriate. Any adjudication recordation method utilized by an agency must comply with applicable requirements of procedural due process of law.

(17). Confer Immunity. An agency agrees not to charge a witness with a violation of law or rule referred to in the immunized testimony or in the evidence produced by the witness. Immunity enables a witness to provide evidence of illegal activity without exposure to criminal prosecution.

(a). A grant of immunity may be informal (given in a letter from an agency) or formal (requires a hearing to determine the validity of a claim of privilege, the claim of the right to refuse to divulge information). Informal or letter immunity does not impart constitutional protection. *United States v Camp*, 72 F3d 759 (9th Cir 1995), *cert denied* 116 S Ct 1557 (1996).

(b). An agency may grant formally two forms of immunity, transactional immunity and testimonial immunity.

(i). Transactional ("blanket" or "total") immunity confers complete protection to and fully shields a witness from actions by an agency that charge the witness with any violation of law or rule revealed in the witness's immunized testimony or immunized production of evidence before the agency.

(ii). A grant of testimonial ("use and derivative use") immunity precludes an agency from using in an action against a witness either the witness's immunized testimony or any evidence derived from that testimony. Agencies grant testimonial immunity to compel a witness to testify in a proceeding. Evidence obtained independently of a witness's testimony may be used to prove a violation of a law or rule disclosed in the witness's immunized testimony or production of evidence.

5. Appointment of Independent ALJ. A party accused in an adjudication by an agency may request the appointment of an independent hearing officer, a person who is not an employee of the accusatory agency.

A. To obtain the appointment of an independent ALJ, a party must prove by explicit evidence that the hearing officer assigned by the agency to preside over the hearing harbors personal bias or cannot be impartial. *Matter of O'Connor v Ginsberg,* 2011 NY Slip Op 21209 (U) (Sup Ct, Albany County 2011), *mod and affd* 2013 NY Slip Op 03363 (3rd Dept 2013).

B. SAPA 303 provides a statutory procedure for resolving allegations against an ALJ of bias or lack of impartiality. "Hearings shall be conducted in an impartial manner. Upon the filing in good faith by a party of a timely and sufficient affidavit of personal bias or disqualification of a presiding officer, the agency shall determine the matter as part of the record in the case, and its determination shall be a matter subject to judicial review after the adjudicatory proceeding."

§ 8.4. Classification of Quasi-Judicial Adjudications. Executive administrative agencies adjudicate three classes of actions: Regulatory, entitlement, and enforcement proceedings.

1. Regulatory Actions. In a regulatory action, a regulated party challenges the validity of an agency's proposed or adopted administrative rule usually because of a potential industry-wide effect of the rule. For example, a rule may require substantial economic increases to affect a change in physical plants, in product line retooling requirements or to comply with changes

in workplace safety, insurance, wages and benefits, and environmental issues.

A. A regulated party challenges the validity of an agency's proposed or adopted rule by filing a petition in a special proceeding. CPLR 103 (b). [19]

B. Actions challenging the legality of a rule attack both the rule's principal provisions (the substantive application of the rule) and the agency's procedures (the process used to implement the rule). A special proceeding challenging a rule is limited to the following issues: [20]

(1). An agency failed to perform a duty imposed by law.

(2). An agency's action is arbitrary and capricious, an abuse of discretion, and without a rational basis.

(3). The rule conflicts with an agency's enabling statute; the agency exceeded its authority in the subject matter of the rule.

(4). The rule constitutes a deprivation of due process.

C. Courts apply a presumption and the highest standard of evidence in deciding the validity of an administrative rule.

(1). A Court gives an agency the benefit of the presumption that the challenged rule abides by all legal procedures. *NY St. Assoc. of Counties v Axelrod*, 78 NY2d 158, 573 NYS2d 25 (1991).

---

[19] CPLR § 103 (b). Except where otherwise prescribed by law, procedure in special proceedings shall be the same as in actions, and the provisions of the civil practice law and rules applicable to actions shall be applicable to special proceedings.

[20] Chapter XV § 15.7. Scope of Judicial Review.

(2). The party challenging the validity of an agency rule must prove the rule to be illegal or arbitrary and unreasonable beyond a reasonable doubt, and no other logical explanation can be derived from the evidence submitted in the hearing.

(a). The substantial evidence rule applies only to a review of an agency's determination made after a hearing is held in which evidence is taken under law. *Colton v Berman*, 21 NY2d 322 (1967).

(b). "When there is no hearing pursuant to direction by law, then CPLR § 7803, sub. 3 applies . . . the court reviews whether the determination was made in violation of lawful procedure, was affected by an error of law or was arbitrary and capricious or an abuse of discretion, including abuse of discretion as to the measure or mode of penalty imposed (see Felton v. Halperin, 228 AD2d 595 [2nd Dept., 1996])." *Kahn v NY City Dept. of Hous. Preserv. & Dev.*, 28 Misc 3d 1206 (A), 2010 NY Slip Op 51197 (U) (Sup Ct, Kings County 2010).

(3). A proceeding brought under CPLR 7804 (a) to dispute an agency's rule may be converted into a declaratory judgment action if a motion is made to dismiss the article 78 claim (CPLR 103 [c]). [21] In an article 78 proceeding brought against the Department of Health, *NY St. Assoc. of Counties v Axelrod*, 78

---

[21] CPLR 103 (c). If a court has obtained jurisdiction over the parties, a civil judicial proceeding shall not be dismissed solely because it is not brought in the proper form, but the court shall make whatever order is required for its proper prosecution. If the court finds it appropriate in the interests of justice, it can convert a motion into a special proceeding, or vice-versa, upon such terms as may be just, including the payment of fees and costs.

NY2d 158, 573 NYS2d 25 (1991), *Assoc. of Counties* alleged in three causes of action that a DOH regulation: (a) was arbitrary and capricious, an abuse of discretion and without a rational basis, (b) violated Public Health Law §§ 2807 and 2808, and (c) deprived nursing homes of due process of law. The Court denied the agency's motion for an order dismissing the petition and converted the article 78 proceeding into a declaratory judgment action under CPLR 103 (c).

D. A regulated party may challenge an administrative rule in an informal action where an agency's organic act does not contain a statute of limitations that lists the time in which to contest a rule.

2. Entitlement Actions. An entitlement action is a process by which a party disputes an agency's denial, suspension or revocation of a benefit, license, commission, permit or other interest conferred statutorily by government to qualified persons.

A. Entitlement interests are considered judicially as legally protected property interests.

B. Constitutional constraints limit a state's power to terminate an entitlement "whether the entitlement is denominated a 'right' or a 'privilege' Sherbert v. Verner, 374 U.S. 398 (1963) (disqualification for unemployment compensation); Slochower v. Board of Education, 350 U.S. 551 (1956) (discharge from public employment); Speiser v. Randall, 357 U.S. 513 (1958) (denial of a tax exemption); Goldberg v. Kelly, supra (withdrawal of welfare benefits)." *Bell v Burson*, 402 US 535, 91 S Ct 1586 (1971).

3. Enforcement Actions. An executive agency's enabling statute enables and demands the agency's enforcement of the legislated

regulatory program. An enforcement action of an executive agency is a formal, quasi-judicial, administrative action in which an agency charges a regulated party of a violation of law or regulation that the agency is mandated legislatively to enforce.

CHAPTER IX. NONADJUDICATORY ADMINISTRATIVE PROCEDURES.

§ 9.1. Declaratory Rulings. A declaratory ruling is an agency's written determination of the applicability of specific statutes, rules, regulations or orders of the agency to suppositional data submitted in a petition to the agency for a determination.

1. Rationale of Declaratory Rulings. By offering advice to parties in a declaratory ruling of the rights and obligations in a proposed situation, an agency seeks to help the regulated community and the public avoid inadvertent violations of law.

2. State Legislation. SAPA 204 (1) governs agencies' procedures that provide for the submission, review, and disposition of petitions for declaratory rulings.

A. "On petition of any person, an agency may issue a declaratory ruling with respect to (i) the applicability to any person, property, or state of facts of any rule or statute enforceable by it, or (ii) whether any action by it should be taken pursuant to a rule." SAPA 204 (1).

B. An agency "shall prescribe by rule" the form of petition and procedure for the submission, consideration, and disposition of a petition for a declaratory ruling. SAPA 204 (1).

3. Agency Procedure. Each agency adopts procedures for the submission, review, and disposition of petitions for declaratory rulings on the applicability of agency statutes, rules, regulations, and orders. Declaratory ruling procedures unique to an agency are published in an agency-specific title of NYCRR. [22]

A. Within sixty days of receipt of a petition for a declaratory ruling, an agency must issue a declaratory ruling or issue a statement declining to render a declaratory ruling.

B. An ALJ may either adjourn or schedule an administrative hearing pending the resolution by an agency of a petition for a declaratory ruling on an issue raised concurrently in the pending adjudication (*NY St. Dept. of St., Div. of Lic. Servs., Matter of the Application of Rachelle Nacht*, 124 DOS 92 [1992]). After filing a petition for a declaratory ruling (NYS DOS Declaratory Ruling 92-43 [November 6, 1992]), Nacht moved to adjourn a pending quasi-judicial hearing until the agency resolved her petition. The question raised in the petition and in the pending action was whether experience gained by registered mortgage brokers (as governed by Banking Law § 591-a) in the solicitation, processing, negotiation, and placement of residential mortgage loans (as defined in Banking Law § 590) qualifies as equivalent real estate experience as defined in Real Property Law § 441 (1) (b). The ALJ denied the motion for an adjournment or a stay during the pendency of the petition for a declaratory ruling and scheduled the matter for hearing.

---

[22] Examples are 6 NYCRR 619, Department of Environmental Conservation; 8 NYCRR 313.1, Department of Education; 4 NYCRR 210, Department of Civil Service; and 19 NYCRR 264, Department of State.

C. The filing of a petition for a declaratory ruling does not prevent an agency from beginning, continuing, or completing any authorized proceeding against the petitioner.

4. Declaratory Rulings Legally Binding. A declaratory ruling binds an agency to the agency's statement of the applicability of any rule or statute to the facts and the conduct hypothesized in the petition by the petitioner. A declaratory ruling is legally binding until one or more of the following events occur:

A. A court of competent jurisdiction sets aside or modifies the declaratory ruling.

B. The legislature changes the law cited in the declaratory ruling.

C. An agency changes prospectively its interpretation of a law cited in the declaratory ruling (*Matter of Charles A. Field Delivery Serv. [Roberts]),* 66 NY2d 516, 498 NYS2d 111 [1985]). Law forbids an agency from retroactively changing a valid declaratory ruling. SAPA 204 (1). [23]

5. Competing Federal and State Rules. If a federal rule and a state rule impose incompatible obligations on a regulated party, the party may petition the state agency for a declaratory ruling asking if compliance with the federal requirement is acceptable as compliance with the state directive. SAPA 206.

§ 9.2. Alternative Dispute Resolution Programs (ADRP). ADRPs support the efforts of agencies and regulated entities to resolve arguments by agreement and avoid adjudication.

---

[23] See Chapter VI § 6.8.2. (B). Rational Analysis.

1. State ADRP. The Community Dispute Resolution Centers Program (CDRCP) is a component of the New York State Unified Court System's (UCS) Office of Alternative Dispute Resolution Programs. The CDRCP contracts with not-for-profit organizations in all 62 counties of New York State to provide dispute resolution services to individuals, organizations, and communities, including government agencies. The Government Law Center at Albany Law School conducts ADRP workshops and training for state agencies.

2. Agency ADRP. An agency may establish an in-house ADRP. The hearing officer assigned by the agency to conduct the hearing may or may not be the same person who acts as mediator. Practices among agencies vary: An agency may prescribe, prohibit, or urge parties to a proceeding to agree to the assignment of an ALJ to preside over both an ADRP procedure and a subsequent administrative hearing. [24]

§ 9.3. Settlement Procedures. A settlement is the resolution of a dispute by agreement between an agency and a regulated party. Public policy encourages the resolution of disputes to avoid adjudication. Usually, settlement negotiations begin after an agency's notice to a regulated party of alleged violations of law.

1. Customarily, an executive agency's notice of alleged violations to a regulated party orders attendance to an informal conference at a place and time requests the submission of selected documents, advises a party of the right to representation, and may make an offer of settlement.

---

[24] An exemplary ADRP is the ADRP of the Department of Public Service Commission that encourages consumers and utilities to resolve disputes amicably.

2. A settlement agreement may order: A dismissal of part of or all of the charges; an admission or no admission of wrongdoing; a reprimand; a fine; restitution; surrender of a benefit, license, commission or registration; revocation or suspension of a benefit, license, commission or registration; or any lawful combination of any of the above-listed consequences.

3. The signatures of the regulated party and the agency finalize the negotiated settlement agreement. A settlement agreement executed after the start of an administrative hearing should be recorded into the record of the hearing and "So Ordered" by the presiding administrative law judge.

4. A settlement agreement obligates legally only the parties who execute the settlement agreement.

CHAPTER X. ADMINISTRATIVE DISCLOSURE AND DISCOVERY PROCEEDINGS.

§ 10.1. Information Demands in Administrative Actions. An information demand is a written request for access to or for the release, transfer or divulgence of information lawfully obtainable in an administrative action.

§ 10.2. Disclosure and Discovery. A disclosure request is a written demand for legally obtainable information valuable in the discovery of relevant material or facts in an administrative proceeding. Information legally obtainable through depositions or other information-demand procedures may reveal the identity and location of pertinent persons, places, things, or data.

§ 10.3. Purpose and Aim of Information Demands. Knowledge is the purpose of information demands. Preparation is the aim of knowledge. Disclosure procedures permit the collection of as much information as legally allowed to formulate legal strategies. "Mutual knowledge of all the relevant facts gathered by both parties is essential to proper litigation." *Hickman v Taylor*, 329 US 495 (1947).

§ 10.4. State Regulation of Information Demands. The right of access to gather information is not a constitutional right. In administrative actions, there is not a due process right to disclosure and discovery. "The right to speak and publish does not carry with it the unrestrained right to gather information." (*Zemel v Rusk*, 381 US 1 [1965]). There is "no general right to disclosure in a disciplinary proceeding." *Matter of Sinha v Ambach*, 91 AD2d 703 (1982), *affd* 69 AD3d 1080, 2010 NY Slip Op 00340 (3rd Dept 2010).

1. Legislation empowers an agency to implement disclosure procedures. Regulation of information demand procedures balances the preservation of protected secrets (specified privacy interests and privileges) against the right to gather information in pursuit of truth or to promote justice.

2. Provisions of SAPA, CPLR, and FOIL regulate demands for disclosure.

A. SAPA and CPLR enable an agency to enact a scope of disclosure appropriate to the agency's hearing proceedings. *Miller v Schwartz*, 72 NY2d 869, 532 NYS2d 354 (1988).

(1). SAPA disclosure provisions provide:

(a). SAPA 304 authorizes a presiding hearing officer to sign and issue subpoenas in the name of an agency and to provide for taking testimony by deposition at the request of any party to a proceeding before the agency.

(b). SAPA 305 permits agencies to adopt rules to provide for the taking of depositions. The rules adopted by an agency must lawfully fit within the agency's established rules of procedure.

(c). SAPA 401.4 controls information demands made in hearings seeking revocation of a license or a permit previously granted by an agency. Either party to a revocation hearing must "upon demand and at least seven days prior to the hearing, disclose the evidence that the party intends to introduce at the hearing, including documentary evidence and identification of witnesses (except) . . . information or material otherwise protected by law from disclosure, including information and material protected because of privilege or confidentiality."

(2). CPLR disclosure provisions provide:

(a). Disclosure provisions of CPLR may be incorporated into an agency's proceedings by reference in the rules adopted by the agency. SAPA 305.

(b). CPLR 3102 (a) outlines six disclosure methods by which information may be obtained: (i) Depositions by oral questions within the state and by written questions without the state; (ii) interrogatories; (iii) demands for addresses; (iv) discovery and inspection of documents or property; (v) physical and mental examinations of persons; and (vi) requests for admission.

B. FOIL provides a way of public access to agency information. "Full disclosure by public agencies is . . . a public right and in the public interest, irrespective of the status or need of the person making the request." *M. Farbman & Sons v New York City*, 62 NY2d 75, 476 NYS2d 69 (1984).

§ 10.5. Information Demand Procedures. A party makes an information request in writing by letter, by interrogatories, or by subpoena (depositional, testimonial or documentary order).

1. Letter Information Demands. A prehearing disclosure command by letter to an opposing party is a request for information lawfully discoverable, such as documents, names of proposed witnesses, and other appropriate, relevant information.

2. Interrogatories Information Demands. An interrogatory is a written list of questions to which one party asks the opposing party to respond in writing. Interrogatories ask for information lawfully obtainable and admissible as evidence in the underlying action. Interrogatories are permitted in an administrative action only where sanctioned by statute or rule.

A. An agency may by rule allow the use of interrogatories.[25]

B. An agency may incorporate the disclosure provision of CPLR 3102 (a) into the agency's rules to permit the use of interrogatories.

3. Depositions. A deposition is a proceeding in which testimony (oral evidence) of a witness is taken under oath and is subject to cross-examination and limited objections.

A. Commencement of Deposition Proceeding. A subpoena initiates a deposition procedure. Valid service of a subpoena on

---

[25] See 6 NYCRR 622. 7 (b) (2). Department of Environmental Conservation.

a person begins the process. A subpoena orders a person to appear at a time and place to be deposed, or to produce described documents, or to do both.

B. Conduct of Deposition Proceeding. Deposition proceedings are conducted at reasonable times and locations external to an administrative law tribunal and without the presence or supervision of an ALJ. At a deposition proceeding, parties to the administrative action and any party's representative have the right to be present, to ask questions, and to make tactical objections. (See Chapter X § 10.6.4. Objections during Deposition Proceedings).

C. Suspension of Deposition Proceeding. A party to the administrative action or a person from whom discovery is sought in a deposition proceeding may apply by motion for a protective order (CPLR 3103 [a]). During pendency of the motion, the deposition proceeding is suspended. CPLR 3103 (b).

D. Purposes of Depositions. Depositions are conducted:

(1). To preserve the testimony of a witness who may become unavailable for the hearing or who resides a significant distance from the hearing venue.

(2). To simplify the adjudication by narrowing the issues through stipulations of fact or other agreement.

(3). To discover information, such as identification of additional parties, location of exhibits, framing of pleadings, and obtaining of evidence.

E. Conduct of Practitioners During Depositions. Uniform Rules for the Conduct of Depositions, Part 221, enacted under Uniform Rules for Trial Courts,incorporates parts of CPLR article 31.

4. Administrative Subpoenas. An administrative (nonjudicial) subpoena ("under penalty") is a legal document that orders a person to appear at a place and at a given time to provide described information, oral, written, or both.

A. Forms of Subpoenas. Different forms of subpoenas are used for various purposes at various stages of an administrative action.

(1). A subpoena ad testificandum orders a person to appear and give circumscribed testimony.

(2). A subpoena duces tecum ("under penalty to bring with you") demands the production of identified books, papers, records, documents, or other tangible items subject to discovery.

(3). Parties use investigative subpoenas to find and to acquire discoverable relevant information during a lawful inquiry or investigation. An investigative subpoena is served during an investigation and before the commencement of a formal administrative proceeding.

B. Grant of Subpoena Power to Agencies. Subpoena power is granted to an agency by statute and implemented by agency rule. SAPA 304 (2) authorizes an agency to "Sign and issue subpoenas in the name of the agency, at the request of any party, requiring attendance and giving of testimony by witnesses and the production of books, papers, documents and other evidence" and permits attorneys to issue subpoenas under provisions of CPLR.

C. Parties Subject to Subpoena. An agency may subpoena regulated entities, persons not involved directly in adjudication, and individuals not subject to the agency's jurisdiction. Service of an administrative subpoena on a nonparty does not violate due process obligations if law sanctions the process, the evidence sought is of general relevance and reasonable scope, and the agency action is not arbitrary, capricious, an abuse of discretion or otherwise in violation of law. *Cf State ex rel Railroad & Warehouse Com. v Mees*, 235 Minn 42, 49 NW2d 386 (1951).

D. Issuance of Administrative Subpoena. CPLR 2302 (a) and SAPA § 304 (2) authorize an agency leader, a presiding ALJ, and an attorney of record for a party to an administrative action to sign and issue administrative subpoenas.

E. Service of Administrative Subpoena. Provisions of SAPA, NYCRR, and CPLR regulate the service of nonjudicial subpoenas in administrative procedures.

(1). Service of a subpoena on a witness is made in person or by certified or registered mail, return receipt requested, or in the same manner as a summons. CPLR 308; CPLR 2303.

(2). An agency may either prescribe or prohibit payments of travel and witness fees in administrative actions.

(a). CPLR 2303 compels payment of witness fees: "Any person subpoenaed shall be paid or tendered in advance authorized traveling expenses and one day's witness fee."

(b). 12 NYCRR 460.4 (a) (3) illustrates a rule governing the payment of witness's fees "Witnesses subpoenaed for any hearing shall be paid or tendered witness and mileage fees in advance in accordance with the provisions of section 2303 of the Civil Practice Law and Rules of the State of New York." Department of Labor, Division of Unemployment Insurance.

(c). Financial Services Law § 306 (b) forbids payments of witness or mileage fees to regulated persons targeted in an agency's investigation. The law provides, "No person subject to the provisions of this chapter, the insurance law or the banking law whose conduct, condition or practices are being investigated, and no officer, director or employee of any such person, shall be entitled to witness or mileage fees."

§ 10.6. Challenges to Information Demands. Provisions of CPLR and NYCRR assemble procedures that govern challenges to information demands.

1. Challenges by Motion. Any party or person from whom discovery is sought in an administrative action may challenge the discovery request by a motion for a protective order against disclosure or discovery of protected matters. A motion may be made either in the administrative tribunal where the underlying action is pending (if allowed by statute or rule to hear the challenge) or in a court of competent jurisdiction if the administrative tribunal lacks jurisdiction. CPLR 3103 (a). [26]

A. Protective Orders Authorized by Agency Rule. A protective order controls legal access to information. A template of an agency's procedure to obtain a protective order appears in 6 NYCRR 622.7 (c) (1). "A party against whom discovery is demanded may make a motion to the ALJ for a protective order . . . to deny, limit, condition or regulate the use of any disclosure device to prevent unreasonable annoyance, expense, embarrassment, disadvantage, or other prejudice." Department of Environmental Conservation.

B. Protective Orders Authorized by State Statute. A "court may at any time on its own initiative, or on motion of any party or of

[26] Chapter XII § 12.10. Motions in Administrative Actions.

any person from whom discovery is sought, make a protective order denying, limiting, conditioning or regulating the use of any disclosure device. Such order shall be designed to prevent unreasonable annoyance, expense, embarrassment, disadvantage, or other prejudice to any person or the courts." CPLR 3103 (a).

C. Purpose of Protective Orders. The essential objective of a protective order is the just resolution of two competing interests without the unjust subjugation of either interest. A motion for a protective order requires the balancing of privacy rights of an individual against fundamental public rights. An individual's right to privacy and the public's right to information in the interest of the public health, safety, or welfare are juxtaposed.

(1). Privacy. Privacy is a virtual liberty, a freedom.

(a). The right to life embraces the right to privacy. The right to life means the right to enjoy life, the right to be let alone. The right to privacy is the right of a person to be free of unlawful intrusions into life's activities. Warren, Samuel D., and Brandeis, Louis D., *The Right to Privacy*, 4 Harv. L. Rev. 193 (1890).

(b). The US Constitution does not contain explicit-right-to-privacy provisions. Specific privacy rights are judicially determined as conferred by six constitutional provisions: First Amendment (privacy of belief); Third Amendment (privacy of home); Fourth Amendment (privacy of person and possessions); Fifth Amendment (privacy of personal information); Ninth Amendment (privacy general protection); and Fourteenth Amendment (privacy resulting from "liberty" interests [family, marriage]).

(c). Explicit privacy rights are also legislatively granted in state statutes. Legislative codifications and judicial interpretations of the privacy rights of individuals augment the freedom of the individual to refuse to perform specific acts and to decline to disclose information. [27]

(d). The individual has a vital and valid interest in maintaining privacy in personal legal matters.

(e). A party or a witness in an administrative proceeding has a due process right to invoke the power of a privilege in a motion for a protective order to prevent disclosure of confidential or other non-public information obtained in legally sheltered situations. [28]

(2). Compelling Public Rights. Compelling public rights shape state public law. Public laws entrust the state with protecting the exigent quality-of-life rights of people. The state has a legitimate interest in protecting public safety, public health, and public welfare. State enactment of reasonable public safety laws (vehicle and traffic rules, gun control) and public health laws (regulation of health professions and facilities) advance a legitimate interest of the state. Compelling public rights infringe with legal permission on privacy rights.

2. Objections to Interrogatories. An agency's procedure outlines

---

[27]. *Cruzan, by her parents and co-guardians v Director, Missouri Department of Health,* 497 US 261 (1990); *Griswold v Connecticut,* 381 US 479, 85 S Ct 1678 (1965); *Irwin Ravin v State of Alaska*, 537 P2d 494 (1975); *Kelly v Johnson*, 425 US 238 (1976); *Lawrence v Texas,* 593 US 558 (2003); *Meyer v State of Nebraska*, 262 US 390 (1923); *Moore v City of East Cleveland, Ohio*, 431 US 494 (1977); *Stanley v Georgia*, 394 US 557 (1969).
[28] Chapter XIII §§ 13.9.1. Privileges, and 13.9.3 (C). Privilege Communications.

how and where objections to interrogatories are made, whether to the agency (6 NYCRR 633.7[c][2]) or to a court of competent jurisdiction (CPLR 3125). An objection to interrogatories must be in writing under oath and states with "reasonable particularity" the rationale for the objection. CPLR 3133(b).

3. Objections to Deposition Subpoenas. A person served with a deposition subpoena in an administrative action has a due process right to challenge the validity of the subpoena.

A. New York adopted the Uniform Interstate Depositions and Discovery Act as CPLR 3119. The statute provides a process by which a New York resident may be served with an out of state subpoena in an action that is pending in another state or in a territory of the United States.

B. Depositions conducted under CPLR 3119 must comply with the procedures provided in the Uniform Rules for the Conduct of Depositions. Counsel may object, and a witness may decline to answer questions posed during the depositions by claiming the privilege that the answer would divulge confidential information or trade secrets (*Matter of Kapon v Ko*ch, 2012 NY Slip Op 51992 [U] [Sup Ct, NY County 2012]), *affd* 2014 NY Slip Op 02327 [Ct App 2014]). Parties to depositions conducted under CPLR 3119 may make any objection permitted by CPLR 3115.

4. Objections during Deposition Proceedings. Except for specific objections, during depositions objections are reserved until the hearing when an ALJ is present to rule on objections.

A deponent is compelled to answer a question regardless of objection, except for objections asserting the following claims (CPLR 3115):

A. A deponent objects to an improper form of a question.

B. A deponent claims a constitutional right, palpable irrelevance, or to preserve a privilege. [29]

C. A deponent enforces a limitation as outlined in a court order.

D. An improper question asked and if answered would cause significant prejudice to a person.

§ 10.7. Statutory Enforcement of Information Demands. An agency enforces information demands directly through quasi-judicial proceedings or indirectly through judicial interventions. The authority of an agency to enforce information demands derived directly from the agency's conferred power is vastly more proficient and resourceful than the requirement of an agency to enforce information demands indirectly using judicial intervention.

1. Enabling Legislation. All disclosure and discovery procedures in administrative actions originate legislatively. Enabling legislation, other statutes, and rules identify and define differing processes for the enforcement of discovery and disclosure information actions by agencies.

2. Enforcement through Judicial Adjudication. State statutes that authorize agencies to enforce discovery processes through court proceedings usually contain the following provision: A party's failure without reasonable cause to comply with a valid administrative subpoena constitutes a misdemeanor; an action to enforce a discovery demand may be brought in any court of competent criminal jurisdiction, or in the Supreme Court of any

[29] Chapter XIII § 13.10. Constitutional Privileges.

county where venue is proper for an order requiring compliance with the subpoena, or in any court of record in the state.[30]

3. Enforcement through Rulemaking. [31] Executive agencies may adopt procedural rules for the direct implementation of information demands (SAPA 305). The following are exemplary discovery enforcement procedures implemented by agencies through rulemaking proceedings:

A. Department of Environmental Conservation: An ALJ, considering motions for a protective order under CPLR 3103, may: deny, limit, condition or regulate the use of any disclosure device; compel disclosure; order preclusion of material from the hearing for failure to comply with a discovery request without making a timely objection; quash or modify a subpoena under standards in CPLR article 23; draw an inference that material demanded is unfavorable to the noncomplying party. In a subpoena of a non-party witness, the ALJ may quash or modify a subpoena without the request of the non-party. 6 NYCRR 622.7; 6 NYCRR 624.8.

B. Department of Labor. Motions to quash, to fix conditions, or to modify a subpoena are made to the presiding ALJ who may impose reasonable conditions upon the grant or denial of a motion. The ALJ may take or cause depositions to be taken of a witness residing within or without the state. 12 NYCRR 460.4 (a); 12 NYCRR 460.4 (b).

C. State Department of Social Services. Agency rules provide detailed procedures for an ALJ to follow if the agency fails to comply with a lawful disclosure request where documents or

---

[30] See Real Property Law § 442-e (6); Financial Services Law § 306 (c).

[31] Chapter VI § 6.1. Agency Rulemaking Power.

witnesses sought are under the control of the agency. An ALJ may compel the production of witnesses or documents without a subpoena, may fashion a remedy (18 NYCRR 358-3.7 [b] [4]), and recess or adjourn a proceeding to allow time to produce witnesses or documents (18 NYCRR 358-5.6 [b] [8]).

4. Enforcement through Incorporation of CPLR Provisions. An agency may argument its procedure to enforce information demands by adopting CPLR discovery rules through rulemaking proceedings. SAPA 305.

A. A state statute may incorporate provisions of CPLR into an agency's discovery procedures. Examples are:

(1). Agriculture and Markets § 34 (3). A person shall be guilty of a misdemeanor and may be prosecuted therefor in any court of competent criminal jurisdiction if, without reasonable cause, the person fails to obey the command of a subpoena, refuses to be sworn or to be examined or to answer a question or to produce a book or paper when legitimately ordered, or fails to subscribe and swear to a valid deposition. CPLR governs subpoenas.

(2). Alcoholic Beverage Control. Alcoholic Beverage Control Law § 17 (5) authorizes the Authority "To administer oaths, to examine any person under oath and in connection therewith to require the production of any books or papers relative to the inquiry." CPLR regulates any subpoena issued under the law.

(3). Civil Service Commission. The commission may subpoena and require the attendance of witnesses and the production and examination of books and papers material in lawful investigations and inquiries. The commission possesses all the powers conferred by legislative law upon a committee of the legislature or by the CPLR upon a board or a committee.

Subpoenas are issued under Civil Service Law § 6 and are regulated by the CPLR.

(4). Department of Financial Services. The person authorized to conduct hearings or investigations may subpoena witnesses, compel the attendance of witnesses, administer oaths, examine any person under oath, and compel any person to subscribe to his or her testimony after it has been correctly reduced to writing, and to require the production of any books, papers, records, correspondence or other documents deemed relevant (Financial Services Law § 306 [a]). CPLR article 3 regulates subpoenas.

(5). Department of State. CPLR regulates subpoenas issued under Real Property Law § 441-e (1).

B. Provisions of CPLR articles 23 and 31 apply to the enforcement of information demands by agencies.

(1). CPLR article 31 provides, in part, if a person fails to respond to or to comply with any request, notice, interrogatory, demand, question or order, except a notice to admit under CPLR 3123, the party seeking disclosure may move in a court of competent jurisdiction in the county where the action is pending to obtain the following orders:

(a). Under CPLR 3124 for an order to compel compliance with or a response to any request, notice, interrogatory, demand, question or order, except a notice to admit under CPLR 3123.

(b). Under CPLR 3126 for an order that the issues relevant to the demanded information are deemed resolved in accordance with the claims of the party obtaining the order, or that prohibits the disobedient party from introducing any evidence regarding the nondisclosed information, or that strikes the pleadings or parts or staying further proceedings until the order is obeyed, or that dismisses the action or any part thereof, or that renders a judgment by default against the disobedient party.

(2). CPLR 2308 (b) (1) applies to an administrative agency where agency law or rule does not include a penalty for failure of a party to comply with an administrative subpoena.

(a). CPLR 2308 (b) (1) establishes a judicial action to obtain an order of compliance with a disclosure demand. An affected party may move in the Supreme Court to compel compliance with a subpoena. The Court may order compliance, assess costs up to fifty dollars, impose a fifth-dollar maximum penalty and damages, and issue a warrant committing a person to jail to remain until the person performs the act ordered or is discharged.

(b). CPLR 2308 (b) (1) does not include the penalty of preclusion of evidence for disobedience of a nonjudicial subpoena. Consequently, the introduction of evidence cannot be precluded as a penalty for the disobedience of a non-judicial subpoena duces tecum (*Matter of St. Div. of Human Rights v Berler,* 46 AD3d 32 [2nd Dept 2007]). In contrast, CPLR 2308 (a) allows as a penalty the striking of a party's pleading for the party's disobedience of a judicial subpoena.

§ 10.8. Enforcement of Information Demands by Executive Powers. When acting as a sovereign, an executive agency that lacks statutory authority to enforce discovery demands by procedural methods operates with a procedural limitation that robs the agency of administrative efficiency, consumes time impractically, expends money needlessly, and delays the administrative process unnecessarily.

1. Where the specific statutory conditions outlined below in § 10.8.2 exist, an executive agency lacking express statutorily authorization to directly enforce information demands without judicial participation may promulgate rules to implement procedures for the direct enforcement of information demands (SAPA 305), or may use delegated quasi-executive and quasi-judicial powers to directly discipline regulated entities for disobedience of agency-ordered discovery demands.

2. An executive administrative agency without authorization to directly enforce information demands may enforce information demands directly through its executive and judicial powers under the following two conditions:

A. The executive agency's statutory disclosure and discovery provision is not prohibitive. The statute (1) does not prohibit an enforcement action by the agency, (2) is not exclusive or mandatory, (3) does not designate an exclusive penalty (thereby barring any other penalty or procedure), and (4) does not contain a list of remedies (thereby excluding any remedy that is not included in the list).

B. The executive agency's quasi-judicial power authorizes the agency to determine whether a regulated party demonstrates incompetence or untrustworthiness by violating a law or rule either in licensed activities or unlicensed activities. For example:

(1). An abuse of trust by a licensee constitutes untrustworthiness. The issuance of a bad check constitutes untrustworthiness by an apartment information vendor (*NY St. Dept. of St., Div. of Lic. Servs. v Nrekic*, 140 DOS 99 [1999]). Failure to pay a valid judgment without proof of inability to pay demonstrates untrustworthiness by a commissioned notary public and licensed real estate broker (*NY St. Dept. of St., Div. of*

Lic. Servs. v Engles, 30 DOS 98 [1998]). Code of Professionally Responsibility violations by an attorney places in issue his untrustworthiness as a licensed real estate broker (*NY St. Dept. of St., Div. of Lic. Servs., Matter of Pennisi*, 79 DOS 91 [1991]; *Matter of Dowd*, 106 AD2d 78, 559 NYS2d 365 ([1990]).

(2). Unlawful behavior by a licensee in an unlicensed activity pivotal to a public-protection mandate of an agency demonstrates untrustworthiness or incompetence. An example: A licensed private investigator's unlawful actions in unregulated activities were judged to be untrustworthy under the statutory requirements of trustworthiness and competence prescribed for the protection of the public by General Business Law § 72 (*Greenberg v Schaffer*, 139 AD2d 648, 527 NYS2d 287 [2nd Dept 1988]). A license or permit issued or a commission appointed by the New York State Department of State may be suspended or revoked on the grounds of "demonstrated untrustworthiness" by a licensee, permittee, or appointee in any public activity. Untrustworthiness is evidenced by acts or conduct that "would warrant a conclusion of unreliability, and which establishes that any confidence or reasonable expectation of fair dealing to the general public would be misplaced." *In re Chiaino v Lomenzo*, 26 AD2d 469, 474, 275 NYS2d 658 (1st Dept 1966); *In re Diona v Lomenzo*, 26 AD2d 473, 275 NYS2d 663 (1st Dept 1966).

(3). In the exercise of its prosecutorial and enforcement functions, an agency imposes penalties of revocation, suspension, forfeitures, fines, and restitution. *NY St. Dept. of St., Div. of Lic. Servs. v Broojerdpoor*, 1 DOS 94 (1994); Real Property Law § 442-e (6); Board of Social Welfare § 747 (15); Financial Services Law § 306 (c).

3. An executive agency possessing the above circumscribed judicial and executive powers may directly enforce information

demands through the application of its quasi-legislative and quasi-judicial powers.

A. The agency may use its quasi-legislative power to enact a specific enforcement procedure in accord with the rulemaking procedures delineated in SAPA 305. [32]

B. The agency may use its quasi-judicial power to determine whether the disobedience of an agency's information request by a regulated entity constitutes unlawful behavior pivotal to the public-protection mandate of the agency and thereby demonstrates untrustworthiness or incompetence, and if so, determine and impose an appropriate penalty. Although an agency "should not consider evidence of untrustworthiness where the general public would not be adversely affected . . ." (*Matter of Stowell v Cuomo*, 52 NY2d 208 [1981]), the deliberate disobedience of a tribunal's order of disclosure is evidence of untrustworthiness (*cf Eich v Shaffer*, 136 AD2d 701, 523 NYS2d 902 [1998]).

[32] Chapter VI § 6.3. Rulemaking Procedures and Practices.

CHAPTER XI. APPLICATION OF DUE PROCESS OF LAW IN ADMINISTRATIVE ADJUDICATIONS.

§ 11.1. Due Process of Law Concept.
§ 11.2. US Constitutional Due Process of Law Provision.
§ 11.3. New York State Constitutional Due Process of Law Provision.
§ 11.4. Due Process Interests – Right v Privilege.
§ 11.4.1. Rights.
§ 11.4.2. Privileges.
§ 11.5. Procedural and Substantive Due Process.
§ 11.5.1. Emergent Political View of Government.
§ 11.5.2. Emergent Judicial View of Government.
§ 11.5.3. Procedural Due Process of Law.
§ 11.5.4. Substantive Due Process.
§ 11.6. Scope of Judicial Review to Determine Presence of Due Process Issue.
§ 11.7. Scope of Judicial Review to Resolve Due Process Issue.
§ 11.8. Application of Scope of Judicial Review to Resolve Due Process Issue.
§ 11.9. Standards of Judicial Review in Due Process Actions.
§ 11.10. Application of Standards of Judicial Review in Due Process Actions.
§ 11.10.1. Strict Scrutiny Standard of Judicial Review.
§ 11.10.2. Intermediate Scrutiny Standard of Judicial Review.
§ 11.10.3. Rational Scrutiny Standard of Judicial Review.
§ 11.11. Limited Application of Due Process in Administrative Law.
§ 11.12. Due Process Protected Liberty Interests in Administrative Law.
§ 11.12.1. Due Process Protected Liberty Interests Created Legislatively.

§ 11.1. Due Process of Law Concept. The due process of law concept is a constitutional vow vesting in people the legal right to have government provide just laws and fair proceedings when functioning as a sovereign in deprivation actions.

1. Due process of law provisions in both the federal and the New York State Constitutions express a legal relationship in powers between government and the people, between the powers retained by people (individually) from government as a servant and the powers relinquished by people (collectively) to government as a sovereign. The constitutional due process doctrine binds both people and government.

2. The judiciary applies due process concept in determinations to constrain the actions of state government.

§ 11.2. US Constitutional Due Process of Law Provision. A due process of law clause is stated twice in the US Constitution, in Amendments Five and Fourteen.

1. Fifth Amendment. In 1788, New York submitted to the US Congress an amendment to the US Constitution: "That no person ought to be taken imprisoned or disseized of his freehold, or be exiled or deprived of his Privileges, Franchises, Life, Liberty or

Property but by due process of Law."

A. James Madison reworded New York's federal constitutional resolution and presented the restated clause to Congress. Congress adopted Madison's language. Ratified in 1791, Amendment Five declares, in part, "nor shall any person be deprived of life, liberty, or property, without due process of law."

B. In 1833, the Supreme Court ruled that the Fifth Amendment to the Constitution (as part of the Bill of Rights) restricts only the powers of the federal government and is not enforceable against state governments. *Barron v Mayor and City Council of Baltimore,* 32 US 243 (1833).

2. Fourteenth Amendment. Ratified in 1868, the Fourteenth Amendment to the federal constitution extends the due process of law dictates to state governments and subjects state action to federal intervention when a Fourteenth Amendment right is at issue in a state action.

A. "With faithfulness to the constitutional union of the States, we cannot leave to the States the formulation of the authoritative laws, rules, and remedies designed to protect people from infractions by the States of federally guaranteed rights." (*Chapman v California*, 386 US 18, 87 S Ct 824 [1967]). The Fourteenth Amendment exclaims, in part, "nor shall any State deprive any person of life, liberty, or property, without due process of law . . . ."

B. The Fourteenth Amendment defines the minimum level of due process that a state owes to a person in an action to deprive a person of life, liberty or property. A state may provide additional due process rights for its citizens through its constitution and laws. *Cooper v Morin,* 49 NY2d 69 (1979), *cert denied* 446 US 984 (1980).

C. By decisions, the US Supreme Court extented the application of due process guidelines of the Fourteenth Amendment to the constraints of seven of the ten amendments to the Bill of Rights: First Amendment; Second Amendment; Third Amendment (applicable in the US Judiciary Second Circuit, *Engblom v Carey*, 677 F2d 957 [2nd Cir 1982], *in rem* 572 F Supp. 44 [SDNY 1982], *affd per curiam* 724 F2d 28 [2nd Cir 1983]); Fourth Amendment; Fifth Amendment (excluding the grand jury provision); Sixth Amendment; and the Eighth Amendment (the cruel and unusual punishment clause).

3. "Person" as designated in the equal protection clause of the Fourteenth Amendment includes a corporation. "A private corporation is included under the designation of 'person' in the Fourteenth Amendment to the Constitution, section I." (*Pembina Consolidated Silver Mining Co. v Pennsylvania,* 125 US 181 [1888]). Purportedly, the fiction of corporate personhood was introduced jurisprudentially in a Supreme Court Justice's prehearing statement made in *Santa Clara County v Southern Pacific Railroad Co.,* 118 US 394, 6 S Ct 1132 (1886). [33]

A. The Fourteenth Amendment, enacted to protect rights of emancipated, formerly enslaved persons, neglected in its language either to define the term, "person" or to associate it to a concept either of an "artificial" or of a "natural" person. Consequently, the Fourteenth Amendment is cited in actions granting the status of "personhood" to corporations. Of the 307 Fourteenth Amendment cases brought before the Supreme Court between 1890 and 1910, 288 dealt with corporation, and

---

[33] See Chapter VII § 7.4.5. Corporations Protected by Fourth Amendment.

19 involved African-Americans [34] The US Supreme Court further bestowed the constitutional civil rights of a person upon entities possessing perpetual structure and legal immortality.

B. A debated tongue-in-cheek issue is whether a corporation with legal personhood under the Constitution is owned and held in servitude by its stockholders in violation of the Thirteenth Amendment. [35]

4. The two, federal, due process clauses are identical denotatively. The US Supreme Court decided that the due process of law clauses stated separately in Amendments Five and Fourteen have identical meaning: "To suppose that 'due process of law' meant one thing in the Fifth Amendment and another in the Fourteenth is too frivolous to require elaborate rejection." *Malinski v New York*, 324 US 401, 65 S Ct 781 (1945, Frankfurter, J., concurring).

§ 11.3. New York State Constitutional Due Process of Law Provision. New York State enacted a due process of law clause in the state Constitution of 1822. Article VII, § 7 of the Second Constitution of New York prescribes that "No person" shall be deprived of life, liberty or property without due process of law." Currently, article I, § 6, NY Constitution of 1938, as amended.

1. The New York State, constitutional, due process of law provision differs from that of the Fourteenth Amendment to the US Constitution that forbids "any state" from depriving a person of life, liberty, or property, without due process of law. "The

---

[34] Edwards, Jan, *Timeline of Personhood Rights and Powers*, Women's International League for Peace and Freedom [revised June 2002

[35] See Korten, David C., *The Post Corporate World, Life After Capitalism*, San Francisco Berrett-Koehler, 1999, Print.

historical differences between the Federal and State due process clauses make clear that the clauses were adopted to combat entirely different evils." *Sharrock v Dell Buick-Cadillac, Inc.*, 56 AD2d 446 (1977).

2. The New York State Constitution exists and functions independently of the federal constitution. When determining due process issues, the courts of New York make independent interpretations of the differences in the text of the two due process provisions, the federal provision, "any state" from New York's provision of "no person." The US Supreme Court interpretations of the fourteenth amendment are "simply not controlling" of New York's "construction of . . . (its) own Constitution." *Ives v South Buffalo Ry. Co.*, 201 NY 271 (1911).

§ **11.4. Due Process Protected Interests – Right v Privilege.** Well-defined, legal distinctions exist between a right guaranteed to a person and protected by the federal or the New York State Constitution and a privilege granted to a person by a federal or a New York State statute that may or may not include due process benefits. Administrative law actions frequently involve issues of right versus privilege.

1. Rights. A right is a power constitutionally or legislatively vested in a person (person of inheritance) and associated with a correlative, legal duty upon another person (person of incidence). The legal obligations that govern interactions between and among people and government total the power of a right. Classified by origin, a right is fundamental (primary) or non-fundamental (secondary).

A. Fundamental (basic) rights originate from state and federal constitutions. Fundamental rights are inalienable, inherent, and irrevocable entitlements acquired by a person at the legal beginning of the life of the person (personhood). Fundamental rights form part of the legal order of society and cannot be conferred or refused by government. Constitutional dictates to government to protect fundamental rights are "shall" or "must" mandates. Government is commanded, directed, ordered, and obligated without discretion.

B. A right conferred legislatively by the state to a person during life is a non-fundamental (secondary) right that the conferring government may restrict or revoke.

2. Privileges. Privileges are statutorily created. Government legislatively creates, defines, and grants a privilege to a person during life.

A. A privilege may be a benefit, a permit, a license, or other statutory permission or opportunity granted by the state to a person or entity to act in the public sector. A privilege may or may not be a constitutionally protected interest. A law bestowing a privilege may or may not provide procedural safeguards.

(1). A license or permit by law to engage in a profession or to build a building is a privilege. Once granted, a privilege may be limited or taken away by government as prescribed in the granting statute.

(2). License to drive an automobile in New York is a privilege regulated by the state. The grant of the privilege is conditioned upon a person providing "such proof of identity, age, and fitness (and other specifications) as may be required" by law. New York issues a driver's license to a living person who meets the age and other requirements statutorily prescribed for obtaining the types of licenses listed in Vehicle and Traffic Law § 501 (2).

B. The state may impose arbitrary limitations on or withhold a privilege entirely. The precept of privilege is permission. With discretion, government may approve, authorize, certify, consent, permit, sanction, or deny a privilege.

§ 11.5. Procedural and Substantive Due Process. "Let the welfare of the people be the ultimate law." [36] The extent to which due process principles apply to the regulatory legislation of a society typifies the contemporaneous ethnicities of that society.

1. Emergent Political View of Government. Dependency of people on the state increases as public needs increase. The state's control over the private life of individuals proliferates; the state's role in the public sector escalates, and the state's influence in the private sector intensifies.

2. Emergent Judicial View of Government. Judicial tenets confine administrative actions. The judiciary opposes the unbridled growth of the power of state government. Judicial effort to restrain by decision the administrative actions of the state may be measured in degrees of judicial definitions of precepts of procedural and substantive due process. The right-privilege principle and the constitutional due process of law doctrine undergo constant redefinition through judicial treatment of due process obligations to interests not expressly designated as rights either in the federal or the state constitution.

3. Procedural Due Process of Law. The process must be fair. Procedural due process of law forbids a government from taking a person's life, liberty, or property without just procedures. Due process forces fairness in the legal processes used by government to deprive a person of life, liberty, or property interest. "By the law of the land (due process of law) is most

---

[36] Cicero, Marcus, *De Legibus (On the Laws)*, Book III, section 11.

clearly intended the general law; a law which bears before it condemns; which proceeds upon inquiry, and renders judgment only after trial. The meaning is that every citizen shall hold his life, liberty, property, and immunities under the protection of the general rules which govern society." *Trustees of Dartmouth College v Woodward*, 17 US (4 Wheat) 518, 4 L Ed 629 (1819), Oral Arguments of Daniel Webster. The Court determined that Dartmouth College, as a corporate charter, possessed constitutional, due process protection.

A. Minimum Process of Law Due in Administrative Actions. Adequate notice, a fair hearing, and an impartial arbiter are the minimum, due process of law prerequisites owed to a person in an administrative action by the state to deprive the person of a liberty or a property interest. *Cf Goldberg v Kelly*, 397 US 254, 90 S Ct 1011 (1970).

B. Statutory Procedural Due Process of Law. State laws and agency codes, rules, and regulations require that the adjudicatory procedures of executive administrative agencies provide the minimum provisions of an impartial tribunal. Minimal hearing procedures offer sufficient notice, the legal basis of the action, opportunity to be represented by counsel, opportunity to answer allegations, right to present evidence, right to discovery (to obtain legally discoverable opposing or supporting evidence), right to cross-examine adverse witnesses, a complete, accurate and exclusive record of an adjudication, and a decision based solely on the evidence admitted at the hearing.

C. Effect of Administrative Proceedings Providing Due Process. Enactment by an agency of administrative hearing procedures that mandate the minimum procedural due process of law requirements in a hearing renders moot the issue of whether the value of a state-conferred interest raises a procedural due process question in a proceeding. Alternatively, the issue of review then becomes the legitimacy of the state's administration of substantive administrative law in the exercise of police power or the validity of decision – Is the state action arbitrary and capricious, an abuse of discretion, not supported by substantial evidence, or otherwise not in accordance with law. *Barsky v Board of Regents*, 347 US 442, 74 S Ct 650 (1954); *NY St. Dept. of St., Div. of Lic. Servs. v Jemmott*, 58 DOS 93 (1993).

4. Substantive Due Process. Substantive due process forces government to substantiate a sovereign's rule or administrative action regardless of the fairness of the procedure used by government to implement the rule or to enforce the action. In a review of the substance of an administrative rule or government action, courts apply substantial due process principles to "liberty" and "property" interests to determine whether the rule or action impedes a liberty or property right. Judicial decisions construct the body of law of substantive due process.

A. Judicial View of Substantive Due Process. The US Supreme Court applied substantive due process as a concept in two pivotal cases, *Bloomer v McQuewan*, 55 US 539 (1852) and *Dred Scott v Sanford*, 60 US (19 How) 393 (1856).

(1). Citing the Fifth Amendment in *Bloomer v McQuewan, supra,* the Court coupled a substantive standard with the principle of due process by restricting the substantive content of two, special, congressional acts. During the original term of a patent, the licensee purchased two machines and the right to use the machines for the term of the patent from the patentee of the machines. Subsequently, by two special acts, US Congress extended the original patent-term for two, consecutive, seven-year durations of time. The legal issue: Was the license to use the machines unaffected or extended by the legislation? The Court held: The licensee's right to use was "a property right extended by the two congressional acts." A judicial construction that the "acts of Congress terminated the license during the validity of the patent would deprive the licensee of that property right and could not be regarded as due process of law."

(2). In 1856, in *Dred Scott v Sanford, supra,* the Supreme Court applied the substantive due process theory. Dred Scott, an enslaved man who returned to Missouri after traveling to and living in Illinois (a "free territory"), sued for emancipation as a citizen under the laws of Missouri. The case challenged the constitutionality of the Missouri Compromise of 1820, a law passed by the proslavery and the anti-slavery alliance in the United States Congress. The law proclaimed that once an enslaved person entered a free territory, he or she remained free for life. Utilizing the substantive due process concept, the Supreme Court held (in accord with the opinion of many state courts) as follows:

(a). An enslaved person was not entitled to sue as a "citizen." The Court reasoned that the rights of citizens ("the full liberty of speech in public and in private upon all subjects upon which . . . citizens might speak; to hold public meetings upon political affairs, and to keep and carry arms . . .") if given to an enslaved person, would inevitably produce "discontent and insubordination" and endanger the peace and safety of the State.

(b). The fundamental constitutional right of a citizen to possess and to bear arms assisted the Court in determining who was a property owner and free and who was a property and enslaved. The ownership of enslaved persons as "property" became a constitutionally protected due process interest. "Thus, the rights of property are united with the rights of person, and placed on the same ground by the fifth amendment to the Constitution, which provides that no person shall be deprived of life, liberty, and property, without due process of law. And an act of Congress which deprives a citizen of the United States of his liberty or property merely because he came himself or brought his property into a particular Territory of the United States, and who had committed no offense against the laws, could hardly be dignified with the name of due process of law." Ruling that the Missouri Compromise deprive owners of enslaved people of a constitutionally protected liberty interest, the Court declared the act invalid.

(3). "By 1868, a recognizable form of substantive due process had been embraced by courts in at least twenty of the thirty-seven then-existing states." Williams, Ryan C., *The One and Only Substantive Due Process Clause*, 120 Yale L J 408 (2010). Also see Tushnet, Mark, *New Histories of the Private Law of Slavery*, 18 Cardozo L. Rev. 301 (1996); and Wahl, Jenny B., *The Jurisprudence of American Slave Sales*, 56 (1) J. Econ. Hist. 143 (1996).

B. Classification of Substantive Due Process. Substantive due process actions involve three classifications of due process protection: Constitutional, substantive due process, fundamental, substantive due process, and non-fundamental, substantive due process.

(1). Constitutional, substantive due process derives from the judicial application of substantive due process principles stated in Amendments 5 and 14 to rights enumerated as the liberty interests in the Bill of Rights (freedom of speech, press, religion, assembly, and petition).

(2). Fundamental, substantive due process is the application of substantive due process principles to derivative rights, rights derived judicially from constitutional rights and afforded due process protection as "liberty" interests or "property" interests. The federal constitution does not grant derivative rights.

(A). "Liberty" in the due process clause denotes more than mere "freedom from bodily restraint." (*Meyer v Nebraska*, 262 US 390, 43 S Ct 625 [1923]). "In a Constitution for a free people, there can be no doubt that the meaning of 'liberty' must be broad indeed . . . . The meaning embraces '[T]he right of an individual to contract, to engage in any of the common occupations of life, to acquire useful knowledge, to marry, to establish a home and rear children (and freedom of worship), and generally to enjoy those privileges long recognized . . . as essential to the orderly pursuit of happiness by free men.' " (*Board of Regents v Roth*, 408 US 564, 92 S Ct 2701 [1972]).

(b). Government's use of its police power to take or to restrain the rights of individual property owners raises substantial due process issues (*Euclid* v *Ambler Realty Co.*, 272 U.S. 365 [1926]). In *Moore v City of East Cleveland*, 431 US 494 (1977), the Supreme Court declared unconstitutional a zoning ordinance restricting the number of unrelated individuals who could share a home. To be declared unconstitutional, a zoning ordinance "must be shown to be clearly arbitrary and unreasonable as having no substantial relation to the public health, safety, morals, or general welfare; (The City of East Cleveland) . . . failed totally to explain the need for a rule that would allow a homeowner to have grandchildren live with her if they are brothers but not if they are cousins . . . ." Under that standard, the city's ordinance was a taking of property without due process and without just compensation.

(3). Non-fundamental, substantive due process rights in state administrative law evolve judicially from state law. Non-fundamental, substantive due process interests consist primarily of judicial application of principles of substantive due process to state-regulated economic and social benefits.

(a). Statutory permission by the state to qualified persons to practice a profession, to collect unemployment insurance, or to receive welfare benefits are privileges that have been assigned vested interests by the judiciary.

(b). The practice of a profession, receipt of welfare benefits, and the collection of unemployment insurance by qualified persons after the valid grant of the statutory privileges are determined judicially as due-process, protected, non-fundamental substantive rights.

(c). A non-fundamental substantive right arises only from a privilege that has been statutorily created. The due process protected rights created by statute are the right to acquire and the right to exercise the privilege statutorily granted. The obtaining and the retaining of the privilege is afforded protection; the privilege is not converted into an irrevocable right. The statute conferring the privilege offers two conditional rights: The right to obtain and the right to retain the privilege when legal requirements are met. Meet the initial legal conditions, obtain the privilege; comply with the continuing legal conditions, retain the privilege. The law granting the privilege may at any time within constitutional restraints be legislatively modified or repealed by the state.

(d). An agency's action to issue a reprimand, to assess a fine, to order restitution or to deny, restrain, suspend or revoke a person's statutory privilege raises three decisive questions: First, does the agency proceedings involve a protected or an unprotected privilege? Second, if a protected interest is involved in the action, which due-process of law is due (procedural, substantive, or both)? Third, what amount of due-process of law is due?

§ 11.6. Scope of Judicial Review to Determine Presence of Due Process issue. During a judicial review to determine a due process issue, a reviewing court must first conclude as a matter of law whether a due process obligation exists in the administrative action. In making that determination, the reviewing court considers the following three factors. Where the three factors exist, due process obligations coexist. [37]

1. The administrative adjudication is commenced by government acting as a sovereign.

A. The administrative action is commenced by an agency or agent of government or by a party whose conduct is chargeable to government acting as a sovereign. *Lugar v Edmondson Oil Co.*, 457 US 922, 102 SC 2744 (1982).

B. New York judicial interpretation of what constitutes a state action differs with federal court evaluations. "Conspicuously absent from the State Constitution is any language requiring State action before an individual may find refuge in its protections. That is not to say, of course, that the due process clause of the State Constitution eliminates the necessity of any State involvement in the objected to activity (see Stuart v Palmer, 74 NY 183, 188). Rather, the absence of any express State action language simply provides a basis to apply a more flexible State involvement requirement than is currently being imposed by the US Supreme Court with respect to the Federal provision." *Sharrock v Dell Buick-Cadillac, Inc.*, 56 AD2d 446 (1977).

2. The state action is a deprivation proceeding; the proceeding strives to deprive a person of a due process protected right. [38]

---

[37] 36 See Chapter XV § 15.4. Judicial Review of Administrative Proceedings.

[38] Chapter XI § 11.11. Due Process Protected Liberty Interests in Administrative Law.

3. The deprivation action by the state is brought against a person. Due process guarantees protect rights of individuals.

§ 11.7. Scope of Judicial Review to Resolve Due Process Issue. Appellate resolution of a due process of law issue evaluates (A) the fairness and reliability of an agency's procedures and the probable value of any additional procedural protections, and (B) the derivational effect of an agency's action on citizens' liberty or property interests. The judicial review involves a three-part analysis. First, "the private interest that will be affected by the official action . . . " second, "the risk of erroneous deprivation of such interest through the procedures used, and probable value, if any, of additional or substitute procedural safeguards . . . " and third, "the Government's interest, including the function involved and the fiscal and administrative burdens that the additional or substitute procedural requirements would entail." *Mathews v Eldridge,* 424 US 319, 96 S Ct 893 (1976).

§ 11.8. Application of Scope of Judicial Review to Resolve Due Process Issue. The three-factor test initiated in *Mathews v Eldridge, supra.*, was applied by the court with an explanation in *Wayfield v Town of Tisbury*, 925 F Supp 880 (1st Cir 1996).

1. Due Process Issue. Contending that Wayfield was "disruptive" and that a menorah was missing after his visit, the public library suspended Wayfield's library privileges without either a pre-deprivation hearing or a post-deprivation method in which to appeal the suspension. Wayfield sued the town alleging a deprivation of due process of law under the Fourteenth Amendment. In deciding that the town owed Wayfield a due process obligation, the Court concluded:

A. "The first step in determining whether a plaintiff has a due process claim is to identify a specific liberty or property interest affected by the alleged governmental action. Board of Regents v. Roth, 408 U.S. 564, 569, 92 S.Ct. 2701, 2705, 33 L.Ed.2d 548 (1972). The next step, if a liberty or property interest has been affected, is to evaluate what process was due to the plaintiff and whether he was afforded it. Id.; see also Mathews v. Eldridge, 424 U.S. 319, 96 S.Ct. 893, 47 L.Ed.2d 18 (1976)." *Wayfield v Town of Tisbury*, 925 F Supp at 882.

B. Furthermore, the government's deprivation action involved a specific liberty or property interest. The "ability to use a public library implicates important First Amendment rights." The suspension of Wayfield's access to the library was a deprivation of a "liberty or property right." *Id.*

C. The library did not have any procedure or rules either regarding the suspension of library privileges or by which a person could challenge a denial of the First Amendment right of access to the public library. Consequently, the risk of an erroneous deprivation of Wayfield's interest through the procedures used by the library was significantly evident. Wayfield was not afforded either pre-deprivation or post-deprivation due process sufficient to satisfy the mandate of the Fourteenth Amendment.

D. Considering the town's interest and the library's function, there were a number of procedures that the library could have implemented to protect the due process rights of its patrons and without significant fiscal or administrative burdens on the library. "For example, the library could send a letter to patrons who were threatened with potential suspensions, notifying them of the action pending against them and inviting them to argue their cases, in writing or in person." *Id.*

2. Amount of Process Due. The town's failure to take any pre-deprivation action deprived Wayfield of a due process right.

Once legally granted, the right to exercise library privileges vested, and a government action to deprive Wayfield of that right was subject to due process principles. The minimum amount of process due to Wayfield was adequate notice and an opportunity to present argument. *Id.*

§ 11.9. Standards of Judicial Review in Due Process Actions. In a judicial review of a due process proceeding, a court weighs the government's interests against an individual's constitutional right to be relatively free of law and reasonably free from government placing of undue and unnecessary impediments to a person's liberty and property rights.

1. A judicial standard of review is the level of legal scrutiny applied by a reviewing court in evaluating a due process action that challenges an administrative action.

2. Three levels of judicial scrutiny, the strict scrutiny judicial standard, the intermediate scrutiny judicial standard, and the rational scrutiny judicial standard, are used in an appellant review to determine if a government regulatory action violates a Fourteen Amendment guaranty.

3. Selection of Judicial Standard of Review. The choice of an appropriate standard of review is the initial issue before an appellate court in the resolution of a due process question in an article 78 appeal of an administrative determination. The selection of a level of judicial scrutiny is situational; the process is factually dependent on a resolution of three factors:

A. The character of the interest at issue, whether the agency action involves a fundamental or non-fundamental right.

B. The public significance of the interest involved, whether the agency action includes a compelling government interest.

C. The appropriateness of the procedure used to acquire the government interest.

§ 11.10. Application of Standards of Judicial Review in Due Process Actions.

1. Strict Scrutiny Standard of Judicial Review. Constitutional and fundamental rights form the epicenter of the strict scrutiny standard of judicial review.

A. The highest standard of judicial scrutiny, strict scrutiny judicial standard, is used in the judiciary review of a governmental action (1) that deprives a person of a constitutional or fundamental substantive right, or (2) that discriminates against a suspect classification, such as race, religion, national origin, classifications of fundamental rights, denial or dilution of the vote, access to the court, interstate migration, and alienage.

B. The strict scrutiny Judicial standard considers three elements of proof. The administrative action serves an existing, legitimate, substantial, government interest; the agency limits the administrative action to that reasonably needed to achieve the substantial interest; and the method selected by the agency to implement the action complies with constitutional safeguards and is the least restrictive means necessary to accomplish the agency's objective.

(1). The administrative action must serve an existing essential public need. An essential, substantial, compelling, or urgent government interest is an equivalent vital public need. Government interests determined judicially to be vital public interests include the following functions:

(a). National Security. The US Supreme Court decided that

the national security of the United States during World War II was a vital government interest (*Korematsu v United States*, 323 US 214, 65 S Ct 193 [1944]). In *Korematsu,* the US Supreme Court upheld the constitutionality of Executive Order 9066 that ordered Americans of Japanese ancestry into American internment camps for the duration of the war. It was in vital government interest to restricting in America the freedoms of Americans of Japanese descent. The executive order violated the rights of a stated racial classification and historicized de jure discrimination by government.

(b). The Judiciary. The State has a substantial interest in preventing political bias or corruption or the appearance of political bias or corruption in the judiciary. *Matter of Raab*, 100 NY2d 305, 763 NYS2d 213 (2003).

(c). Augmentation of Public Life. Government has an urgent interest in conserving public park property. *Clark v Community for Creative Non-Violence,* 468 US 288 (1984).

(d). Protection of Health and Safety. A sovereign's power is the power to govern people and property within the legal constraints of the sovereign's domain. The power to govern empowers the state to legislate and to regulate. The state's power to regulate commerce and to enact health laws is absolute, except insofar as the state is constrained by the United States Constitution (*Nebbia v New York*, 291 US 502, 54 S Ct 505 [1934]). Regulations impose health and safety protections (*Schulman v. NY City Health and Hospitals Corp.*, 38 NY2d 235 [1975]) and building codes (Department of State, Office of Planning and Development, Division of Building Standards and Codes).

(e). Electoral Process. A State has a vital interest in maintaining the integrity and reliability of its election process and in protecting voters from confusion and undue influence. *Burson v Freeman*, 594 US 91 (1992).

(2). An agency must verify that the administrative process used by the agency to achieve a substantial interest has a close or substantial relationship to that interest. *Supreme Court of New Hampshire v Piper*, 470 US 274, 105 S Ct 1272 (1985).

(a). New York has a substantial interest in monitoring gun licensees, and the state's restriction of weapon licenses (i) to New York State residents and (ii) to persons working primarily in New York State is sufficiently related to that interest. *Bach v Pataki*, 408 F3d 75 (2nd Cir 2005), *cert denied*, 546 US 1174 (2006).

(b). In *Matter of Gordon,* 48 NY2d 266, 422 NYS2d 641 (1979), the Court of Appeals held that "New York has a constitutionally permissible interest to assure that those admitted to the Bar possess knowledge of the law as well as the character and fitness requisite for an attorney (citations omitted)." New York's exclusion of persons from membership in the Bar "based solely on residency" is insufficient to establish a substantial relationship with that interest. The state tried to enforce a legitimate interest with an illegal action.

(2). The state limits its action to that reasonably needed to achieve the objective. The government action selected to fulfill the government's specific goal must be concise, comprehensive, and essential to accomplishing an existing substantial, or compelling, or urgent government interest, or public need. *Clark v Community for Creative Non-Violence, supra.*

(3). The action selected by an agency to fulfill a substantial interest must be "sufficiently tailored." The action selected is the least restrictive method necessary to attain an existing, urgent agency interest. *Burson v Freeman*, 594 US 91 (1992).

(a). In *Burson v Freeman, supra,* a Tennessee state statute survived strict judicial scrutiny. The statute prohibited the solicitation of votes and the display or distribution of campaign materials within 100 feet of the entrance to a polling place. The Supreme Court stated that the law ". . . could not be upheld unless (i) the burden placed on free speech rights is justified by a compelling state interest and (ii) the means chosen bear a substantial relation to that interest and are the least intrusive to achieve the State's goals." Tennessee has a compelling interest in preventing voter intimidation and election fraud. The question was how large a restricted zone around a polling place was necessary to serve the compelling interest, and what size of a restricted zone was required to be considered "sufficiently tailored" to be the least intrusive to achieve the state's goal. The Court ruled the statute constitutional. The law was a reasonable regulation of a nonpublic forum, and the speech restrictions stated in the statute "need not be subjected to 'exacting scrutiny' analysis." *Id.*

(b). Although "a state has a legitimate interest in regulating the attorneys who practice law in its courts, that obligation . . . may not be fulfilled at the expense of constitutionally protected rights . . . by denying otherwise qualified applicants their right to practice their chosen occupation based solely on their State of residence . . . . A number of less drastic, and constitutionally permissible, alternatives are readily available to protect the interest of the State in supervising those who practice in its courts . . . ." *Matter of Gordon*, 48 NY2d, at 275.

(c). The two issues, (i) limitation of state action to a concise and comprehensive act reasonably needed to achieve an existing, substantial, compelling or urgent government interest and (ii) use by the state of the least restrictive method to fulfill a compelling interest within constitutional safeguards are inter-reliant factually but are adjudged individually.

2. Intermediate Scrutiny Standard of Judicial Review. The intermediate scrutiny standard of judicial review is as it is named; it is the level of judicial scrutiny between a strict standard of review and a rational standard of review.

A. The intermediate scrutiny judicial standard is used predominantly in evaluating if an administrative proceeding violates the equal protection clause of the Fourteenth Amendment, specifically in resolving issues of quasi-suspect classifications, such as distinctions based on gender.

B. Intermediate scrutiny judicial standard examines an administrative act to determine two factors: (1) Whether the administrative action furthers a significant or substantial government interest, and (2) whether the method chosen to implement the law is substantially related to the achievement of that interest. *Craig v. Boren*, 429 US 190, 97 S Ct 451 (1976).

C. In cases decided subsequently to *Craig*, the Supreme Court refers to the intermediate scrutiny level of review as "exceedingly persuasive justification."

(1). "Parties who seek to defend gender-based government action must demonstrate an 'exceedingly persuasive justification' . . . ." *United States v Virginia*, 518 US 515 (1996). In that case, the State of Virginia failed to prove an "exceedingly persuasive justification" for excluding all women from the citizen-soldier training program at Virginia Military Institute.

(2). A party seeking to uphold a statute that classifies individuals based on gender must establish an "exceedingly persuasive justification" for the classification. The classification must serve an "important governmental objective," and the means employed must "substantially relate to the achievement of the objective." (*Glenn v Brumby*, 724 F Supp2d 1284 (ND Ga 2010), *affd* 663 F3d 1312 [11th Cir 2011]). Glenn, hired as a Georgia State Assembly Legislative Editor when a man, was terminated as a woman because of the transgender status. The Court held that state's termination of Glenn violated the Equal Protection Clause because the state did not prove a substantial relationship between the transition of gender and a sufficiently significant government interest.

3. Rational Scrutiny Standard of Judicial Review. Judicial reviews of actions involving statutory non-fundamental liberty interests apply the rational scrutiny judicial standard. A logical connection must exist between the state action and a legitimate governmental purpose. An example of a legal correlation between an agency law and a valid government function is Vehicle and Traffic Law § 502 (1).

A. The requirement of a recipient of a driver's license to be photographed for identification (Vehicle and Traffic Law § 502 (1); 15 NYCRR 3.8) is based on legitimate state goals of security and law enforcement, regardless of whether a licensee does or does not smile when being photographed, a rational connection not existing between law enforcement and a licensee's smile.

B. The US Supreme Court applied a rational standard of judicial review in *Foley v Connelie*, 435 US 291 (1978) in an analysis of Executive Law § 215 (3), a New York statute that limited the appointment of members of state police force to citizens of the United States. The Court held that the statute was not in violation of the Equal Protection Clause of the Fourteenth Amendment. "Strict equal protection scrutiny is not required to justify classifications applicable to such positions; a State need only show some rational relationship between the interest sought to be protected and the limiting classification. In deciding what level of scrutiny is to be applied, each position in question must be examined to determine whether it involves discretionary decisionmaking, or execution of policy, which substantially affects members of the political community." [39]

§ 11.11. Limited Application of Due Process in Administrative Law. Constitutional and judicial limitations restrict the application of due process principles in administrative law.

1. Constitutional protection of liberty and property rights guards against government's capriciousness but does not prohibit government regulation. Judicial judiciousness concludes that neither constitution nor legislation gives unlimited or indefeasible rights to a person. Judicial philosophy sanctions government order.

2. State regulatory law balances due process principles with the public welfare. The state may abridge a statutory right. In the public interest, government may restrict, modify, or forfeit a statutory right in time, class and value.

3. The state regulates liberty and property rights at the time and in the manner that the state considers necessary and appropriate for proficient government function. In the public welfare, agencies regulate the exercise of the liberty to contract or to work by restricting the obtaining of permits, licenses, and other privileges. In the public interest, agencies confine private property rights to building codes, sanitation rules, zoning regulations, rent regulations, and other controlling procedures.

---

[39] See Waldman, Lauri, *Erosion of the Strict Scrutiny Standard*, 10 U. Miami Inter-Am. L. Rev. 1049 (1978).

A. State Price Regulation in the Public Welfare. The state manipulates markets with regulation. The state sets prices at retail in markets on commodities and products considered essential or critical to public health, safety, welfare, or economic stability. A state law judicially noticed as reasonably related to a proper legislative purpose and not to be arbitrary or discriminatory satisfies due process demands. *Nebba v New York*, 291 US 502, 54 S Ct 505 (1934).

(1). *Nebba* involved a state price regulation. Nebbia, the owner of a grocery store, sold two quarts of milk and a 5-cent loaf of bread for 18 cents. Under Agriculture and Markets law, New York State, Milk Control Board held Nebbia guilty of violating the Board's minimum price regulation of 9 cents for a quart of milk and fined him five dollars. Nebbia appealed contending that the statute and order violated both the Fifth Amendment and the Fourteenth Amendment. The Court ruled that neither the Fifth nor the Fourteenth Amendment prohibits government from enacting regulations in the public interest and welfare. By appropriate legislation, a state may adopt and enforce an economic policy that reasonably promotes the public well-being. Courts lack the authority and competency either to create government policy or to strike it down. *Id.*

(2). Currently, agency regulations and final marketing orders of the Commissioner of Agriculture and Markets that fix prices for milk are exempt from SAPA. SAPA 102 (2) (b); Agriculture and Markets Law § 258-m.

B. State Regulation of Business Practices. A state law that prohibits a business practice is valid unless the law conflicts with a federal or state constitutional or statutory provision (*Ferguson v Skrupa*, 372 US 726, 83 S Ct 1028 [1963]). At issue in *Ferguson* was a Kansas statute that classified as a misdemeanor the engagement by any person in the business of debt adjusting, except as an incident to the lawful practice of law. Ferguson, who was not an attorney, adjusted debtors' payments to debtors' creditors as contracted in written agreements (the making of a contract). Ferguson argued that an absolute prohibition of the business by the state would violate Fourteenth Amendment due process rights. The Court disagreed: The Kansas statute bore a rational relationship to a constitutionally permissible objective.

C. State Limitations of Liberty of Contract. One is not free to contract unconditionally as one chooses. *West Coast Hotel v Parrish,* 300 US 379, 57 S Ct 578 (1937), discussed the limitation of the application of due process of law in contract adjudications. Questioned was whether minimum wage regulation for women was a deprivation of freedom of contract. The Court stated, "The Constitution does not speak of freedom of contract. It speaks of liberty and prohibits the deprivation of liberty without due process of law. In prohibiting that deprivation, the Constitution does not recognize absolute and uncontrollable liberty. The guaranty of liberty does not withdraw from legislative supervision that wide department of activity which consists of the making of contracts or deny to government the power to provide restrictive safeguards. Liberty implies the absence of arbitrary restraint, not immunity from reasonable regulations and prohibitions imposed in the interests of the community."

§ 11.12. Due Process Protected Liberty Interests in Administrative Law. The state legislature and courts create due process protected liberty interests in administrative law.

1. Due Process Protected Liberty Interest Created Legislatively. Legislatively created liberty interests often arise from laws regulating relationships between the state and persons deprived lawfully of personal freedom, such as relationships

between the state and prison inmates. Prisoners may acquire state-created liberty rights through legislation and agency directives. *Sandin v Conner*, 515 US 472, 115 S Ct 2293 (1995).

A. State statutes may establish liberty interests entitled to Fourteenth Amendment procedural due process protections. "There is no 'constitutional or inherent right' to parole, but once a State grants a prisoner the conditional liberty properly dependent on the observance of special parole restrictions, due process protections attach to the decision to revoke parole." *Vitek v Jones,* 445 US 480, 100 S Ct 1254 (1980).

B. The legal reasoning applied judicially to issues of parole extends to solitary confinement. A decision to impose solitary confinement " 'represents a major change in the conditions of confinement and is typically imposed only when it is claimed and proved that there has been a major act of misconduct.' Once a State has granted prisoners a liberty interest, we held that due process protections are necessary 'to insure that the state-created right is not arbitrarily abrogated.' " *Id.*

C. State legislation that institutes visitation privileges for inmates in New York State correctional facilities initiates a liberty interest protected by the due process clause of the Fourteenth Amendment. *Kozlowski v Coughlin*, 539 F Supp 852 (SDNY 1982).

D. In *Austin v. Wilkinson*, 189 F Supp2d 719, 732 (ND Ohio 2002), *affd in part, revd in part* 372 F3d 246 (6th Cir 2004), *revd* 125 S Ct 2384 (2005), the Court stated the three-factor judicial standard used by reviewing courts to determine if a government procedure meets due process requisites (see *Mathews* v. *Eldridge*, 424 US 319, 96 S Ct 893 [1976]). A due process evaluation of a prison procedure requires consideration of: "(1) the private interest that will be affected by the official action; (2)

the risk of an erroneous deprivation of such interest through the procedures used, and the probable value, if any, of additional or substitute procedural safeguards; and (3) the government's interest, including the function involved and the fiscal and administrative burdens that additional or substitute procedural requirement would entail."

2. Due Process Protected Liberty Interests Created Judicially. Dismissal from government employment joined with defaming public statements by an employer and without notice, and a name-clearing hearing may constitute a deprivation of a liberty interest. Defamation (damage to reputation) combined with the termination of some other legal right or status raises a due process issue. *O'Neill v City of Auburn*, 23 F3d 685, 691 n. 2 (2nd Cir 1994).

A. Governmental allegations that an employee's termination is based on professional incompetence will not support a cause of action for a name-clearing hearing unless the allegations extend " 'to the very heart of (the employee's) professional competence,' Huntley, 543 F.2d at 985, and threaten to 'damage his professional reputation,' . . . significantly impeding his ability to 'practice his profession.' " *Id.*

B. The purpose of a pre-deprivation name-clearing hearing is to give an allegedly stigmatized government employee an opportunity to refute the government's stigmatizing charges. "If the truth of the (government) statements is not contested, there is nothing to have a hearing about . . . " *Id.* In a situation where the truth of the government statements is not contested, the lack of a pre-deprivation name-clearing hearing is not a deprivation of a due process protected liberty interest in employment.

§ 11.13. Due Process Protected Property Interests in Administrative Law. Due process rights in property and liberty interests are recognized legislatively and judicially in administrative law.

1. Due Process Protected Property Interests Created Statutorily. Property rights are ownership rights of a person or entity over things, are not confined to land, tangible personal property, money, and other material assets, and are enforceable by the owner against all other persons. Due process principles protect a vested property interest (an existing legal benefit to which a person is legally entitled). State statutes grant economic benefits are

2. Due Process Protected Property Interests Judicially Determined. State statutes that grant economic benefits are judicially recognized as providing due process protected interests to persons lawfully entitled to receive those benefits.

A. Property Interests in Awarded Welfare Benefits. The US Supreme Court ruled in *Goldberg v Kelly*, 397 US 254, 90 S Ct 1011 (1970), that the due process procedural guarantees of the Fourteenth Amendment apply to government actions to deprive a welfare recipient of benefits. The value of the interest that the person may lose through the administrative process, the loss of welfare benefits, entitle the person (1) to an oral hearing before an impartial decision-maker, (2) to the right to confront and cross-examine witnesses, and (3) to the right to a written opinion setting out the evidence relied upon and the legal basis for the decision. Further, the court stated that New York City violated the Fourteenth Amendment by terminating welfare benefits without a prior hearing. The recipient had a "property interest" in the conferred benefits, and an action by the state to terminate or modify those benefits is an effort to deprive the person of a constitutionally recognized property interest.

B. Property Interests in Employment. A person possessing a

legitimate claim of entitlement to property under state law possesses a due process of law, protected, property interest in employment.

(1). Tenured Employment in Education. A tenured teacher has a protected property interest in employment, and a threat of termination of the employment raises due process considerations. *Matter of Elmore v Plainview-Old Bethpage Central School District, Board of Education,* 273 AD2d 307, 708 NYS2d 713 (2nd Dept 2012).

(2). Untenured Employment. Ordinarily, untenured employment is not considered a legal interest in property.

(a). In *Board of Regents v Roth*, 408 US 564, (1972), a public college refused to renew the contract of an untenured professor. The court held that an untenured professor did not have a liberty interest in any particular job, and the professor did not have a property interest in his job because of lack of "a legitimate claim of entitlement" under state law. The absence of tenure equals the lack of a right to entitlement, and the college was not required to present evidence of poor work performance to sustain a dismissal of the untenured professor.

(b). In addition to a determination of a liberty right, the decision in *O'Neill v City of Auburn*, 23 F3d 685, 691 n. 2 (2nd Cir 1994), also resolved a property interest claim. The Court denied O'Neill's claim that his termination without a pre-termination hearing deprived him of a due process protected property interest. The Court reasoned: "Property interests in employment 'are not created by the Constitution, they are created and their dimensions are defined by existing rules or understandings that stem from an independent source such as state law.' " O'Neill was an independent officer not covered by Civil Service Law § 75 (1) (c), and thus had no property interest in retaining his employment position; the city did not violate his right to due process of law by terminating him from the employment position without notice and a hearing.

(c). Untenured public employees may be terminated from employment without a hearing. However, where an untenured employee has been stigmatized during the termination of employment, the terminated, untenured employee is entitled to a name-clearing hearing. A name-clearing hearing does not prevent termination; the hearing is provided solely " 'to provide the person an opportunity to clear his name.' If he does not challenge the substantial truth (citation omitted) of the material in question, no hearing would afford a promise of achieving that result for him." (*Codd v Velger*, 429 US 624, 97 S Ct 882 [1977]). The only purpose of a name-clearing hearing is to give the former employee an opportunity to clear his or her name.

C. Property Interest in Public Education. A state may adopt regulations providing for fair suspension procedures that synchronize the educational goals, characteristics, and locality of its schools. A state's law providing free education to residents between certain ages (a "group" or "class") with a compulsory-attendance requirement confers a property right to every member of that group or class. That property interest may be taken on the grounds of misconduct in a proceeding providing the minimum legal procedures required by due process of law. *Goss v Lopez*, 419 US 565, 95 S Ct 729 (1975).

D. Property Interest in Wages. Garnishment of a person's wages is a taking of one's property. A prejudgment garnishment procedure lacking notice and a prior hearing violates the fundamental principles of due process of law. *Sniadach v Family Finance Corp.*, 395 US 337, 89 S Ct 1820 (1969).

E. Property Interests in Licenses and Permits. A permit allows the doing of a specific act (permit to build a building). A license approves the continuous engagement in an activity (license to practice a profession, architecture, law, medicine) or to operate a business (real estate office, restaurant).

(1). Property Interest in Liquor License. A licensee has a property interest in a liquor license. A liquor license constitutes property in a debtor's estate. *Go West Entertainment Inc. v NYS Liq. Auth.,* Case No. 08-11420 (ALG), US Bankruptcy Ct (SDNY), May 14, 2008.

(2). Property Interest in Driver's License. *Bell v Burson*, 402 US 535,91 S Ct 1586 (1971), states the general rule. "Once (drivers') licenses are issued . . . their continued possession may become essential in pursuing a livelihood . . . . The licenses are not to be taken away without that procedural due process required by the Fourteenth Amendment."

(3). Property Interest in Building Permit. A property owner may obtain a vested property right in a legally issued building permit. "In New York, a vested right can be acquired when, pursuant to a legally issued permit, the landowner demonstrates a commitment to the purpose for which the permit was granted by effecting substantial changes and incurring substantial expenses to further the development (citations omitted). Neither the issuance of a permit (citations omitted) nor the landowner's substantial improvements and expenditures, standing alone, will establish the right. The landowner's actions relying on a valid permit must be so substantial that the municipal action results in serious loss rendering the improvements essentially valueless *Town of Orangetown v Magee*, 88 NY2d 41, 643 NYS2nd 21 (1996).

(4). Property Interest in Trade Name. The lawful owner of a trade name registration has a qualified property interest in the trade name; the name receives the same protection as a common law distinctive trademark. *Lincoln Restaurant Corp. v Wolfies Restaurant Corp.*, 291 F2d 302 (2nd Cir 1961), *cert denied* 368 US 889 (1961).

F. Property Interest in Entitlements. "Suspension of issued licenses . . . involves state action that adjudicates important interests of the licensees . . . the licenses are not to be taken away without that procedural due process required by the Fourteenth Amendment . . . whether the entitlement is denominated a 'right' or a 'privilege.' Sherbert v Verner, 374 U.S. 398 (1963) (disqualification for unemployment compensation); Slochower v. Board of Education, 350 U.S. 551 (1956) (discharge from public employment); Speiser v. Randall, 357 U.S. 513 (1958) (denial of a tax exemption) . . . ." *Bell v Burson*, 402 US 535, 91 S Ct 1586 (1971).

§ **11.14. Commonality of Due Process Protected Interests in Administrative Law.** A substantive due process protected interest in administrative law adjudications, whether determined a liberty or a property interest, usually derives from a state statute or administrative rule granting a privilege with adjunct vested interests. [40]

---

[40] See Chapter XIII § 13.4. Legal Defense Arguments (traditional legal defenses of affirmative, equitable, jurisdictional, and privilege).

CHAPTER XII. QUASI-JUDICIAL ADMINISTRATIVE HEARING PROCEDURE.

§ 12.1. Beginning of Formal Hearing. The filing of a pleading with an agency's quasi-judicial, administrative law tribunal initiates a formal administrative hearing. The category of the proceeding (regulatory, entitlement, or enforcement action) dictates which documents are filed where and when.

§ 12.2. Reasonable-Time Opportunity for Hearing. The pace of administrative justice at any given time is directly proportionate to the lapse of time between the date of the filing of the complaint and the date of the final decision in a quasi-judicial proceeding.

1. SAPA 301 (1) imposes an affirmative duty upon state executive agencies to conduct adjudicatory proceedings within a reasonable time and nullifies the common-law view that laches may not be interposed as a defense against the State when it acts in a governmental capacity and the public interest. *Cf Cortlandt Nursing Home v Axelrod,* 66 NY2d 169, 495 NYS2d 827 (1985). [41]

A. The statutory, reasonable-time requisite for the opportunity for a hearing is mandatory, not discretionary. *Maxwell v Commissioner of Motor Vehicles,* 109 Misc2d 62, 437 NYS2d 554 (Sup Ct, Erie County 1981); *NY St. Dept. of St., Div. of Lic. Servs. v*

[41]The state acts in a governmental capacity when implementing governmental functions, such as health, police, fire or engaging in legislative dictates. See Chapter XIII §13.7.3 (Agency Performing Governmental Function) and §13.7.4 (Agency Performing Proprietary Function).

Logan, 269 DOS 96 (1996).

B. The statutory right to a hearing within a reasonable time is a vested threshold right. If raised in an administrative action, a reasonable-time issue must be initially determined before a full hearing is held on any other issue.

2. What constitutes a reasonable time is a matter of fact, not law. SAPA 301 (1) does not define "reasonable time" and fails to provide or to indicate an enforcement procedure in the event of a violation of the statute. Judicial decisions ascribe descriptions of case law to the statute.

A. A factual finding only of a lapse of time in rendering an administrative determination does not constitute prejudice as a matter of law. *Louis Harris and Assocs., Inc. v DeLeon,* 84 NY2d 698 (1994).

B. An egregious time delay in conducting a hearing that prejudices a party may constitute an abuse of an agency's discretion. A case in point is *NY St. Dept. of Labor v NY St. Div. of Human Rights,* 71 AD3d 1234 (2010). New York State, Division of Human Rights (SDHR) took 12 years between the filing of the complaint and the commencement of the hearing, incongruent with provisions of Executive Law § 297. "SDHR then spent an inexcusable three years conducting the hearing and rendering its determination . . . (a process that Executive Law § 297 [4] [c] directs to be completed in 180 days). Even if inadequate funding and understaffing contributed to these delays, they were an abuse of SDHR's discretion that prejudiced all parties."

3. To determine reasonable-time issues within the requisites of SAPA 301(1), "an administrative body in the first instance, and the judiciary sitting in review, must . . . (consider four, critical) factors . . . (1) the nature of the private interest allegedly

compromised by the delay; (2) the actual prejudice to the private party; (3) the causal connection between the conduct of the parties and the delay; and (4) the underlying public policy advanced by governmental regulation." *Cortlandt Nursing Home v Axelrod,* 66 NY2d at 178.

A. The aspect of the interest compromised by the delay of hearing. A hearing delay is deemed unreasonable if a party's vested or contingent legal right or interest is lost or infringed because of the hearing delay.

(1). A vested legal right is an existing benefit to which a party (a right-holder) is lawfully entitled. [42] Also, a legal right may be a value assigned to fact by legal definition and institutionalized by usage (for example, substantive due process rights that are instituted by judicial descriptions). [43]

(2). A contingent legal right is an interest to which a party is entitled conditionally. When the specified condition is fulfilled, the contingent interest vests as a legal right.

B. The prejudice endured by the private party. A determination of the reasonableness of an administrative delay considers the critical question, "Has the administrative delay of hearing caused a party to suffer substantial prejudice?"

(1). A party is substantially prejudiced by a delay of hearing that results in the unavailability of a witness or documents that are vital to a defense or that severely compromises the ability of a crucial defense witness to present a clear and detailed recollection of material events. *Reid v Axelrod*, 164 AD2d 972,

---

[42] Campbell, Kenneth, "Legal Rights," *The Stanford Encyclopedia of Philosophy* (Fall 2013 ed.), Edward N. Zalta (ed.).
[43] Chapter XI § 11.5.4. Substantive Due Process.

559 NYS2d 417 (4th Dept 1990); *NY St. Dept. of St., Div. of Lic. Servs. v Bernstein,* 1570 DOS 08 (2008); *Gillette v NY St. Liquor Authority,* 149 AD2d 927, 540 NYS2d 61 (1989).

(2). Unreasonable delay occurs where an administrative delay significantly and irreparably impedes a private party in the preparation of a defense in an administrative proceeding. *Cortlandt Nursing Home v Axelrod, supra; NY St. Dept. of Envtl. Conservation, Matter of Manor Maintenance Corp.,* Order of the Commissioner, February 12, 1996.

C. The causal relationship between the conduct of the parties and the administrative delay.

(1). An agency's failure to act is not unreasonable if the administrative delay is attributable (a) to a lack of agency resources, (b) to the complexity of the issues to be resolved, (c) to a protracted available remedy, or (d) in whole or in part, to the conduct of the involved private party.

(2). Repetitive, purposeless, and oppressive agency proceedings and an agency's failure to follow its procedural regulations are judged unreasonable administrative delays. *Cortlandt Nursing Home v Axelrod, supra; NY St. Dept. of Envtl. Conservation, Matter of Manor Maintenance Corp., supra.*

D. The underlying public policy advanced by the governmental regulation. A public interest underlying a governmental regulation or action may be a determinant factor in resolving an issue of administrative delay. For example, New York has a defined public policy to recover improperly awarded public funds. "The public policy underlying recoupment of Medicaid overpayments, or adjustment of rates based upon past overpayments, must be balanced in conjunction with the nature of the right sought to be protected, prejudice to petitioners, and cause of administrative delay, when assessing whether administrative delay is reasonable." *Cortlandt Nursing Home v Axelrod, supra.*

4. Ordinarily, a court will not consider the reasonableness of an agency's administrative delay until after an administrative hearing and a decision of the issue by the agency; otherwise, a reviewing court's ruling is limited to the granting of mandamus to compel a hearing.

5. Agency regulations fix time limitations (either jurisdictional time-limitations or directional time-limitations) for an adjournment, continuance, or completion of adjudicatory proceedings.

A. A jurisdictional time-limitation is prerogative, and an agency's failure to adhere to its time regulation is reviewable in an article 78 proceeding. A rule of New York State, Department of State, 19 NYCRR 400.13, expresses a standard rule. "A failure of the Secretary of State to observe the time limitations established . . . or the failure of an administrative law judge to make the determination required shall be reviewable under article 78 of the Civil Practice Law and Rules in a proceeding in the nature of mandamus."

B. An agency's failure to observe its directional, time-limitation hearing rule in an administrative action does not impair the validity of the adjudicatory proceeding held or of the decision rendered in the matter by the agency.

6. A decision of an unreasonable delay does not divest an agency of its jurisdiction to convene a license revocation hearing. *Geary v Commissioner of Motor Vehicles*, 92 AD2d 38, 459 NYS2d 494, *affd* 59 NY2d 950, 466 NYS2d 304 (1983).

§ 12.3. Representation in Administrative Proceedings. Enabling statutes, SAPA, CPLR, and agency-specific rules in NYCRR outline the right of parties and nonparties to have representation in agency procedures.

1. Statutory Right of Parties and Nonparties to Representation. Any person obligated to appear or who voluntarily appears in a proceeding before an agency has the right of self-representation or to be accompanied, represented, and advised by an attorney or by another person. SAPA 501.

A. In prehearing deposition proceedings, parties and nonparty witnesses are entitled to have counsel present during depositions. *Sciara v Surgical Associates of Western New York, PC*, 32 Misc3d 904, 927 NYS2d 770 (Sup Ct, Erie County 2011), *aff'd in part, mod in part, motion denied* 104 AD3d 1256, 961 NYS2d 640 (4th Dept), *leave to appeal granted* 107 AD3d 1503, *appeal dismissed in part* 22 NY3d 951 (2013). "The Court has located one decision from a federal district court which recognized that a person being deposed generally is entitled to have counsel present at the deposition (Women in City Government United v The City of New York, 112 F.R.D. 29, 32 [S.D.N.Y.1986]). 'As a general rule, a person being deposed, whether a party or a nonparty witness, is entitled to have counsel present at his deposition. This rule allows a deponent to intelligently exercise testimonial privileges, chief among them being the privilege against compulsory self-incrimination. Counsel is not present to keep the deponent from making a statement against his interest in the absence of a testimonial privilege . . . (or) object on evidentiary grounds.' "

(1). Participation in a pretrial deposition by counsel for a party-deponent is limited to cross-examination, to speaking objections (as to the form of a question and the claiming of a testimonial privilege), and to move to suspend the deposition pending the resolution of a motion for a protective order (CPLR 3103). *Id.*

(2). " 'A nonparty witness' counsel is . . . (prohibited from participating) generally in a deposition by cross-examination or otherwise.' The above quote describes the accepted practice for depositions of nonparties in New York courts. Nonparties are allowed routinely to be represented by counsel during their depositions." *Id.*

(3). A pending bill, S.6656-A, would amend CPLR 3113 to provide, "a non-party deponent's counsel may participate in the deposition and make objections on behalf of his or her client in the same manner as counsel for a party." The bill would legislatively overrule *Thompson v Mather*, 70 AD3d 1436, 894 NYS2d 671 (4th Dept. 2010).

B. An agency may be statutorily required to notify parties of the right to representation in an administrative proceeding. [44]

2. Due Process Right to Counsel. An administrative action that involves a due process, protected property or liberty interest raises the issue of a due process right to representation. A tenured teacher has a due process, protected, property interest and a due process right to be represented by counsel at a hearing to deprive the teacher of that protected property

---

[44] Social Service Law § 22.12 states a procedural mandate: "Every applicant or recipient of public assistance and care shall be informed in writing . . .at the time of application and at the time of any action affecting his receipt of assistance or care . . . of his right to representation by legal counsel, or by a relative, friend, or other spokesmen, or that he may represent himself (or) . . . of the availability of community legal services to assist him in the appeal or fair hearings process."

interest. *Matter of Elmore v Plainview-Old Bethpage Cent. Sch. Dist., Bd. of Educ.*, 273 AD2d 307, 708 NYS2d 713 (2012).

3. Exceptions to Right to Representation. Two agency functions that do not evoke a right to representation are investigations and informal disciplinary proceedings.

A. In an agency, fact-finding, non-adjudicative investigation, the right to counsel exists only where expressly provided by statute or rule. Persons summoned to appear before administrative, investigative proceedings may obtain advice of counsel, but counsel may not participate in the investigative proceeding. Any right of counsel to object and to argue objections in an administrative, investigative process would be a statutory, not a constitutional, right. *Federal Communications Commission v Schreiber and MCA Inc.*, 329 F2d 517 (CA 9th Cir 1964).

B. An informal disciplinary action by a university does not raise a due process right to legal representation. *Mary M v Clark*, 100 AD2d 41, 460 NYS2d 424 (3rd Dept 1984).

4. Record of Appearance of Representatives. Executive Law § 166 directs every state regulatory agency (as defined in the statute) to maintain a record of appearances of attorneys, agents and representatives appearing for a fee to represent any person, firm, corporation or association subject to the agency's jurisdiction.

5. The Right to Representation versus Right to Appointment of Counsel. Economically, a due process right to counsel is often meaningless without the right to appointment of counsel. Right to appointment of counsel is the corresponding need of those who are economically unable to hire an advocate. A statute or rule conferring a right of representation in an administrative

hearing involving a due process protected interest should include the right to both the aid of and the appointment of counsel. Contemporaneously, enactment of due process procedural law and resolution of procedural insufficiencies of due process rights lie with the legislature (adoption of laws) and the people (constitutional amendment).

§ 12.4. Agency Preliminary Pleadings. The initial pleadings of an agency consist of a notice of hearing, a statement of the allegations (complaint), exhibits (if any), and copies of applicable laws and rules. The preliminary pleadings identify the hearing officer assigned to conduct the hearing and the attorney or other advocate assigned to represent the agency. The initial pleadings of an agency must adequately enable the recipient to determine what the agency proposes to do and what the recipient must do to oppose the agency's proposed deprivation of the recipient's interest. SAPA 301; *NY St. Dept. of St., Div. of Lic. Servs. v Sarkissian,* 68 DOS 88 (1988).

1. Notice of Hearing. An agency must give reasonable notice of a proceeding to the party charged in the proceeding. The notice of hearing states the date, time, and place of the hearing and a description of the allegations, the proceeding, and of the law and rules granting the agency the authority and the jurisdiction to conduct the hearing.

2. Statement of Allegations (Complaint). An agency must state the allegations of a complaint in concise and plain-language that definitively informs the party charged of the factual transactions upon which the allegations are founded and the laws and rules allegedly violated. SAPA 301 (2).

3. Summary of Applicable Laws. The initial pleadings of an agency must include a summary of the laws, rules, and orders governing the adjudication and the appellant procedures. SAPA

301 (3); *NY St. Dept. of St., Div. of Lic. Servs. v Sarkissian, supra.*

§ 12.5. Pleadings of Party Charged with Violation. An agency may either require or forego a formal response (an answer or plea) by a party to an agency's complaint.

1. Answer not Required. Unless prescribed by rule, the filing of a formal answer or the entering of a plea to an agency's complaint is not mandatory, and in the absence of a formal response by a party, all allegations of the complaint are deemed denied, and all rights of the party charged are reserved. Apropos is a rule of the Department of State that gives a party accused in a disciplinary action the option to serve an answer denying the allegations and to interpose affirmative defenses. "Absent an answer, all charges are deemed denied and all rights are reserved." 19 NYCRR 400.4 (a).

2. Answer Required by Rule. An agency may demand a response to a pleading and impose a penalty for noncompliance. A rule of the State Liquor Authority provides, "After a disciplinary proceeding has been commenced, the licensee shall be afforded an opportunity to plead either 'not guilty' or 'no contest' to the charges on or before a scheduled date . . . . Failure of a licensee to plead on or before the pleading date shall be deemed a plea of 'no contest,' and no further hearing shall be held." 9 NYCRR 54.2.

3. Objections to Adequacy of Notice and Complaint. Objections to the insufficiency of a complaint must be made before the objecting party participates in the hearing, or the objection is waived, and the complaint is considered in compliance with due process requirements. Failure of a party to object timely to the adequacy of a notice of hearing waives any claim of insufficiency of the notice. *NY St. Dept. of St., Div. of Lic. Servs., Application of Alexander*, 9 DOS 92 (1992); *NY St. Dept. of St., Div. of Lic. Servs.*

v Sarkissian, 68 DOS 88 (1988).

§ 12.6. Service of Pleadings. Judicial decisions and an agency's laws and rules prescribe methods for the service of pleadings in agency adjudications. (CPLR, SAPA, NYCRR, GBL, and RPL).

1. Methods commonly prescribed in various statutes and rules for the service of the pleadings by an agency are the delivery of the pleadings by personal service or by certified mail (return receipt requested) or in any manner authorized by CPLR, to the regulated party's address last listed in the agency's records. *Cf Hill v Jones*, 113 AD2d 874, 493 NYS2d 60 (1985).

2. Service of process in an administrative proceeding fulfills the constitutional guarantee of due process of law if the pleadings are timely delivered and received by the party required by law to be served. (US Const amend XIV; NY Const art I, § 6) "[W]here there is actual notice, procedural irregularities are overlooked since the object of the procedural requirement has been achieved albeit in a technically improper manner." *Drolet v NY St. Racing and Wagering Bd.*, 115 Misc2d 7, 453 NYS2d 361(1982).

3. Specific statutes and rules fix an agency's time limitations for the completion of service of process.

§ 12.7. Amendment and Supplement of Pleadings. Usually, an agency allows an amendment or supplement of a pleading as a matter of right. An amended or supplemented pleading may be filed at any time with permission of the administrative law tribunal or by stipulation of the parties. (CPLR 3025).

1. An amendment pleading supersedes and replaces a prior pleading. An amendment pleading may correct, add, delete or otherwise change the pleas of a prior pleading. The filing date of

an amended pleading is the date on which the amended pleading is submitted to the administrative law tribunal.

2. A supplemental pleading presents additions to or continuations of (does not replace) a previous pleading. A supplemental pleading pleads transactions or events that occurred after the filing date of the preceding pleading. The matters alleged in a supplemental pleading are filed as of the filing date of the supplemental pleading.

3. An amendment or supplemental pleading is served as if it were an original pleading. *NY St. Dept. of St., Div. of Lic. Servs. v Gooding,* 35 DOS 95 (1959).

§ 12.8. Conformity of Pleadings to Proof. On motion or in an ALJ's discretion, a pleading may be amended to conform to the evidence admitted in adjudication. CPLR 3025 (c); *NY St. Dept. of St., Div. of Lic. Servs. v DeMaso,* 40 DOS 91 (1991). Allowing an amendment of pleadings to conform to proof on motion of any party at any time promotes congruency among the pleadings, the proof, and the decision in an administrative action.

1. A pleading to amend a complaint to conform with proof admitted in a hearing may raise issues not stated in the complaint where the evidence reveals clearly (A) had those issues been stated in the complaint, additional evidence would not have been divergent; (B) those issues were fully litigated by the parties; and (C) those issues are within the broad context of the original pleading.

2. Issues not raised by pleadings but fully litigated in an action by express or implied consent of the parties are treated as if the issues were raised in the pleadings. A party may move at any time, even after judgment, to amend the pleadings to conform to the evidence admitted in a hearing. *Cf NY St. Dept. of St., Div. of*

Lic. Servs. v Vuksanaj, 128 DOS 93 (1993).

§ 12.9. Pleas. Specific agency rules in NYCRR outline the procedures that control the filing of pleas in administrative adjudications. SAPA 301 (5) allows the disposition of any adjudicatory proceeding by stipulation, agreed settlement, consent order, default, or another informational method unless precluded by statute. Traditional pleas are:

1. Not Guilty. A plea of not guilty is a denial of culpability, raises the issue of a person's factual guilt, forces a fact-finding hearing, and compels the agency to prove the allegations of the complaint by substantial evidence.

2. No Contest. In an administrative proceeding, a plea of no contest is the equivalent of the common law plea of "*nolo contendere*" or "*non-vault*" and has the same legal effect as a plea of guilty. *Scranton Volunteer Fire Co. v Ball*, 377 AD2d 757 (4th Dept 1971), *affd* 30 NY2d 589.

A. A no-contest plea neither denies nor admits the facts alleged in the complaint. A no-contest plea sanctions the same conclusions of law and penalty as those approved by a tribunal's finding of the truth of the charges after an evidentiary hearing. *NY St. Dept. of St., Div. of Lic. Servs. v D'Elia,* 165 DOS 95 (1995).

B. An administrative decision based on a no-contest plea does not have the preclusive effect of res judicata in a subsequent civil action. *NY St. Dept. of St., Div. of Lic. Servs. v Rexee Realty Inc.,* 55 DOS 88 (1988).

3. Ignorance or Mistake-of-Law. A plea of ignorance or mistake-of-law is unacceptable as a defense for a violation of agency law. A regulated party is presumed to know the law governing the licensed business activities in which the licensee engages.

..A Normally, proof of a party's knowledge of a statutory obligation is not necessary to establish a violation of a regulatory statute. *NY St. Dept. of St., Div. of Lic. Servs. v Itzler,* 21 DOS 87 (1987).

B. An Ignorance or mistake-of-law plea claims inadvertence (negligence) as an extenuating circumstance and asks that the plea be considered to negate issues of unlawful intent, motive, common scheme, or plan. *NY St. Dept. of St., Div. of Lic. Servs. v Cincotta,* 10 DOS 88 (1988).

4. Guilty. Unless barred by statute from pleading guilty to specific charges, a party may plead guilty to an agency's complaint as a matter of right.

A. A plea of guilty may be accepted despite a claim of innocence. *NY St. Dept. of St., Div. of Lic. Servs. v Gooding,* 35 DOS 95 (1995).

B. A plea of guilty admits culpability, eliminates the issue of a party's factual guilt, avoids the need for a fact-finding hearing, and relieves the agency from the requirement of proving by substantial evidence the allegations of the complaint. *Gramatan Avenue Associates v Division of Human Rights,* 45 NY2d 176, 408 NYS2d 54 (1978); *NY St. Dept. of St., Div. of Lic. Servs. v Century 21 Champion Realty Inc.,* 76 DOS 88 (1988).

C. A plea of guilty does not waive any jurisdictional defects in an administrative proceeding involving a due process protected liberty or property interest (*NY St. Dept. of St., Div. of Lic. Servs. v Gooding,* 35 DOS 95 [1995]), and a party's failure to object to a jurisdictional defect does not waive the defect (*Gardner v Coxsackie-Athens Cent. School Dist. Bd. of Educ.,* 92 AD3d 1093, 939 NYS2d 149 [2012]).

§ 12.10. Motions in Administrative Actions. A motion is an application by a party before an administrative tribunal for an order or ruling on a specific demand for a determination of a legal right, of a legal status, of an issue, or of a fact.

1. Legal Bases for Motions. An agency permit motion practice through enactment of rules. Agency-specific hearing procedures structure the form and state when, where, and how motions are made in an administrative action. [45]

2. Motion Forms and Practice. A motion may be oral or written and may be made before, during, and after a hearing.

(A) Before a hearing to decide procedural and primary issues;

(B) during a hearing to resolve dispositive or nondispositive issues arising after the beginning of the hearing;

(C) after a hearing or after a final order or ruling for reconsideration, enforcement, or modification of a final order or ruling.

3. Oral Motions. An oral motion is a verbal application by a party made to a tribunal during a prehearing conference or during a hearing.

A. An oral prehearing motion is made in an administrative hearing before the hearing is convened on the record. The prehearing motion may raise any issue that can be determined by the tribunal without a hearing on the merits of the action. Prehearing motions may or may not be dispositive and argue to

---

[45] An example: "A motion to dismiss the complaint or statement of charges for failure of proof may be made at the conclusion of the direct case presented by the complaining division of the Department of State." 19 NYCRR 400 6 (a).

either limit or end a hearing.

B. Oral motion made during a hearing applies for an order or a ruling to resolve dispositive or non-dispositive issues that arise after starting the hearing.

4. Written Motions. A written motion begins with the filing of motion papers with the administrative law tribunal.

A. Initial motion papers include:

(1). The motion. A motion must state definitively the reasons for the motion, the relief sought, and the supporting legal arguments.

(2). Notice of motion. A notice of motion identifies the parties, states the date and time of the motion, the name and the address of the tribunal in which the motion is scheduled for hearing, the time-limit in which to respond to the motion, and a description of the motion.

(3). Supporting affidavit. In support of the motion, the movant files a notarized statement of only factual information appropriate to establish alleged facts. The affidavit affirms the relevant facts of the case essential to prove to the administrative law tribunal why the pending motion should be granted, and if the request made in the motion has been previously requested in a prior proceeding.

(4). Exhibits. Copies of all documentary and other physical items referred to in the supporting affidavit are attached to the notice of motion as exhibits. A motion requesting substantive relief should include a copy of the underlying administrative order or determination as a separate exhibit.

(5). Affidavit of service. The person who serves the motion papers completes an affidavit that avows by whom, how, when, where, and to whom a copy of the motion papers was delivered.

(6). Memorandum of law (brief). A memorandum of law supports the motion by outlining in writing the movant's perception of the material facts of a case, the decisive questions of law, and the sustaining legal arguments and authorities (agency statutes, rules, and judicial and administrative law decisions).

B. Response to Motion. Papers filed in opposition to a written motion compose the response to a motion and consists of:

(1). Opposing affidavit. In opposition to a motion, the opposing party makes a written notarized statement of factual information appropriate to establish facts. An opposing affidavit states fact relevant to verify to the administrative law tribunal why the contested motion should be denied.

(2). Exhibits. Copies of all documentary and other physical items referred to in the opposing affidavit are attached to the notice of motion as exhibits. A motion requesting substantive relief should include a copy of the underlying administrative order or determination as a separate exhibit.

(3). Affidavit of service. The person who serves the papers opposing the motion completes an affidavit affirming by whom, how, when, where, and to whom a copy of the opposing motion papers was delivered.

(4). Memorandum of law (brief). The opposing brief outlines the opposing party's perception of the pertinent facts of a case, the decisive questions of law, and the supporting legal arguments and authorities (statutes, rules, and decisions) that advocate the opposing party's legal position.

C. Cross-Motion or Request for Affirmative Relief. A party opposing a written motion may also make a written cross-motion. The opposing party asks the tribunal to grant specific relief against the original movant.

D. Reply to Response. A reply to a response may address only matters raised in the response.

5. Service of Motion Papers. Agency-specific rules outline the procedure for the service of documents in an agency's administrative proceeding.

6. Defensive Motions. A defensive motion both challenges the validity of the pleadings and asserts affirmative and equitable defenses.

A. Pleading Defects. A motion may be made during an action at any time to dismiss a pleading or to terminate an action for any of following three defects in a pleading: (1) Lack of subject matter jurisdiction; (2). failure to state a cause of action; or (3) failure to join a necessary party.

B. Affirmative and Equitable Defenses. A motion made within statutorily defined time limitations may demand any of the following actions:

(1). More explicit statement of charges;

(2). dismissal of a complaint or of specific charges for failure of proof;

(3). amendment or supplement to a complaint or an answer;

(4). an extension of time in which to answer or in which to respond to a pleading;

(5). permission to file a document out of time (after the due date);

(6). dismissal of an action based on a claim of qualified immunity;

(7). dismissal of an action based on a statute of limitations claim where permitted by law or rule in an administrative proceeding;

(8). stay of enforcement of a decision pending an appeal;

(9). consideration of other affirmative and equitable defenses.

7. Motion Decision. A motion decision may or may not dispose entirely of an administrative action, may or may not be a final decision, and may or may not be appealable.

A. Non-appealable Interlocutory Determinations of Motions. Typically, a decision of a motion that does not dispose entirely of an administrative action on its merits is an interlocutory decision and is not appealable, not having determined all the rights of all the parties to the proceeding. An interlocutory determination may be part of an appeal of an agency's final decision.

B. Appealable Motion Decisions. Motions deciding dispositive issues of law separate from the merits of a case are immediately appealable. Appealable decisions of motions include:

(1). Motions to Quash a Nonjudicial Subpoena. A decision that resolves a motion to quash a nonjudicial subpoena is appealable immediately in a CPLR article 78 proceeding.

(2). Motions Claiming Immunity. A motion asserting immunity claims as a defense, either absolute or qualified immunity rights, are "too important and too independent" of the cause of action to be denied review until after adjudication of the entire case. *Mitchell v Forsyth*, 472 US 511, 105 S Ct 2806 (1985).

(a). Absolute Immunity Defenses. Absolute immunity is protection from and defense against legal actions. A determination denying a claim of absolute immunity is immediately appealable. In an administrative proceeding, a denial of an absolute immunity claim conclusively determines the question of immunity and is an issue of law separable from the merits of the case. A denial of a claim of absolute immunity is not preserved as part of the appellate review of an appeal of a final determination of an administrative action An immunity claim denied is a privilege lost unless the decision of denial is reversed on appeal. *Cf Nixon v Fitzgerald*, 457 US 731, 102 S Ct 2690 (1982).

(b). Qualified Immunity Demand. A decision denying a qualified immunity claim is a conclusion of law based on a question of law and is immediately appealable. Qualified immunity shields a person from and is a defense against litigation. A legal denial of a qualified immunity claim determines rights separable from and collateral to rights alleged in an adjudication. A claim of qualified immunity legally denied is not preserved as part of an appellate review of a final quasi-judicial administrative decision. A decision denying a motion for qualified immunity bars the claim forever, unless and until that decision is overturned on appellate review.

§ 12.11. Evidentiary Objections in Administrative Actions. A valid evidentiary objection is a formal oral protest made to the presiding officer during an administrative hearing to dispute the acceptance into evidence of written or oral information.

1. In administrative hearings, executive agencies are not required to abide strictly by rules of evidence, and hearsay evidence is admissible. Correspondingly, executive agencies deny license applications and penalize violators with reprimands, fines, suspensions, and revocations. Consequently, administrative proceedings of executive agencies must comply with legislative mandates and with due process criteria.

2. Although evidentiary rules are not strictly applicable in quasi-judicial adjudications, the proper making of evidentiary objections is crucial in administrative proceedings to preserve the rights of parties. An evidentiary objection aims to prevent the acceptance of information in evidence in violation of a law of evidence. Valid evidentiary objections protect both the rights of a party and the record of the hearing by identifying the admission of irrelevant, untrustworthy, or otherwise objectionable evidence in the hearing record. An ALJ's ruling on the admissibility of evidence is a matter of law, except where a statute or rule makes an evidentiary ruling a matter of discretion (for example, expert testimony).

3. During adjudication, rulings made on evidentiary objections chronicle the decisional efficacy of the tribunal in controlling the presentation of information within the rules of evidence and other procedural law. Proper objections preserve issues and clarify occurrences in the hearing record in the event of appellate review.

4. The hearing record must verify that a statement of objection meets the criteria of timeliness, identity, and specificity to preserve the objection as an issue for review on appeal.

A. An objection must be made timely in a hearing. Timeliness is critical in the making of an objection in a hearing. Failure to object timely in an administrative action waives the right to assert prejudicial error in an appellate review of the administrative decision. The failure of a party to object either to an improper question when asked or to inadmissible information when offered permanently waives the objection, allowing the question and the information to be admitted into the record as evidence for consideration by the tribunal.

B. A statement of objection identifies the specific information to which the objection is made, whether to a question, to an answer, or to an exhibit.

C. A statement of objection must enumerate three factors: (1) State the distinct reasons on which the evidentiary inadmissibility objection is based; (2) explain in unambiguous terms on the record (and thereby to a reviewing court) why the information offered into evidence is unreliable or untrustworthy; and (3) properly identify the objecting party.

5. Objections as Part of Record. Once made definitively on the record, an administrative hearing officer's ruling on an objection becomes part of the hearing record and subject to appellate review.

§ 12.12. Categories of Objections in Administrative Actions. Objections challenge points of law, form of questions, and substance of testimony. [46]

---

[46] Jurisdictional Defenses, Affirmative Defenses, Equitable Defenses, and privileges as Defenses, Chapter XII, §§ 13.6-13.8, and 13.10

§ 12.13. Objections in Point of Law. An objection in point of law admits the facts presented in testimony and argues that the facts presented do not form a valid legal claim because of a legal defense.

§ 12.14. Objections to Form of Questions. An objection to the form of a question protests the way in which the question is asked a witness during an examination or a cross-examination. Common objections made to the formation of a question include:

1. Argumentative. The question asserts a conclusion and attempts to influence a particular answer rather than to obtain factual information. An example, "You could not really see anything, could you?"

2. Assumes Facts Not in Evidence. The question contains data not admitted into evidence, and the existence of the information stated in the question is disputed. An example is a pre-suppositional question, "When interviewed by the agency during its investigation, what were you shown in the written complaint?" Information concerning questioning of the witness by the agency is not in evidence.

3. Cumulative. Proof of one issue is repeatedly introduced with the testimony of a succession of witnesses that replicate testimony already given or is repeatedly introduced by a sequence of exhibits that duplicate exhibits already admitted into evidence.

4. Compound Question. A compound question contains two or more separate questions that invoke ambiguity. "Did you go to your office at 2 pm, just after lunch?" A witness's categorical answer of either "yes" or "no" is confusing and ambiguous. A "yes" or "no" may be the answer to one or every question.

5. Confusing, Misleading, Ambiguous, Vague, Unintelligible. The question lacks specification. There are references in the question to an unidentified person ("he" or "she), or to an unspecified place ("an apartment"), or to an uncertain time ("Thursday afternoon"), or to other undefined particulars. To attempt to answer the question, the witness would have to guess as to the identity of the undefined variables.

6. Conclusion. The question calls for the witness to make a legal conclusion of fact: "Was he acting negligently?"

7. Harassing/Oppressive. A questioner asks insulting, scandalous humiliating, offensive, argumentative, or abusive questions to harass or to oppress a witness, usually, in overly-aggressive cross-examinations.

8. Hearsay. A witness is asked to testify about statements made to the witness by another person who is not available for cross-examination, and the witness's testimony is offered to prove the truth of the content of the unsworn statements.

A. An objection made to the admission of hearsay evidence in an administrative hearing requires specificity to protect both the rights of a party and the hearing record. Hearsay evidence is admissible in an administrative proceeding and given weight within the tribunal's discretion. However, the tribunal's ruling is reviewable on appeal. Admission of hearsay evidence in an agency hearing must violate a substantial right of a party to be regarded as an error in appellate review.

B. An objection to hearsay: "Objection, hearsay. The person who purportedly made the statement is not available for cross-examination; there has not been any previous opportunity to cross-examine the declarant, and the information offered impinges on substantial rights of (the objecting party)."

9. Improper Characterization. The question includes a conclusive portrayal of a person's character, for example, "How much did that phony, electronic genius charge you to trash your computer?" Characterization is an issue for the ALJ.

10. Incomplete Hypothetical. An objection to an incomplete hypothesis disputes the appropriateness of the form or foundation of the hypothetical question. The objection asserts that the witness is being asked to give an opinion based on an incomplete hypothetical question. The hypothetical question omits information the witness needs to know to present an accurate opinion. The objection is frequently made in entitlement actions. The objection contends that the hypothetical question posed fails to describe a claimant's limitations or impairments completely. In a disability benefits hearing, an expert's valid opinion must be based on a hypothetical question that factually contains all of a claimant's evidentiary supported impairments and limitations.

11. Improper Impeachment. Impeachment is an attempt to use a witness's prior written or oral statement to reveal an inconsistency in the current testimony of the witness. Impeaching material may be written or oral, cannot contain collateral matter, and must be materially consistent. Written statements or transcript questions and answers are read verbatim and not taken out of context. All relevant portion of an impeaching statement must be offered into evidence.

12. Immaterial. The question asks for an answer containing information inconsequential to any relevant issue in the hearing.

13. Irrelevant. The question asks for information insignificant to any fact material to the determination of the action. In a motor vehicle action alleging only "driving while under the influence,"

an irrelevant question is, "At the time of the accident, were you insured?"

14. Lacks Foundation. The question assumes facts not proven to be within the witness's knowledge. Without proof that the witness is cognizant of a medical prescription, the question asks: "What medications did the prescription order?"

15. Leading Question. A leading question is worded to suggest the answer, and the answer often suggested is a one-word answer of "yes" or "no." An example is a "tag" question with an interrogative fragment (such as "right?" or "correct?"). "Before he entered the property, he shouted that he was a state inspector, correct?" Leading questions are not usually permitted in direct examination and redirect examination. Leading questions are allowed in direct examination to refresh a person's collection, in the questioning of a very young person, and to obtain undisputed, preliminary information such as name, address, occupation or location of a witness. Leading questions are proper when establishing a foundation for an exhibit. Leading questions are allowed in cross-examination.

16. Narrative Answer. A narrative answer is a lengthy response to a question that allows a witness to include inadmissible evidence without giving an attorney a reasonable opportunity to make timely objections. The question calls for a narrative answer by asking for generalities. "Describe what happened and what was said at the meeting with the unemployment insurance claims examiner."

17. Opinion. The question seeks a witness's opinion about an issue in a field or area in which the witness is not an expert and of which the witness has little or no knowledge. Frequently, the question relates to speed, distance, sobriety, design – how fast, how far, how drunk, how loud, how dangerous.

18. Inadmissible Parol Evidence. A rule of substantive law forbids the use of extrinsic evidence to contradict the terms of a written contract. Standard exceptions to the parol evidence rule are claims that attack the existence (not the terms) of the document (fraud, illegality, accident, and mistake).

19. Privileged Communication. Privileged communications include oral and written exchanges between parties in formalized relationships that are protected legally to encourage open and candid communications, for example, exchanges of information between attorney-client, physician-patient, priest-penitent, husband-wife, government employees entrusted with government secrets.

20. Repetitive. Asked and Answered. Repetitive questioning asks the same question repeatedly to emphasize an issue, the question, or in an attempt to obtain additional or conflicting answers to the question.

21. Misstates Evidence. The question contains a misstatement, a misquotation or a distortion of a witness's testimony.

22. Beyond Scope of Direct Examination. Questions asked during cross-examination introduce issues of fact not raised in the direct examination of the witness.

23. Redirect Beyond Scope of Cross-Examination. Questions asked in redirect examination contain issues of fact that were not raised during the cross-examination of a witness.

24. Beyond Scope of Proper Voir Dire. A voir dire examination challenges the admissibility into evidence of an exhibit offered by a party. A proper voir dire examines both the competency of the qualifying witness (testimonial qualifications, such as insanity, infancy, expertise) and the admissibility of evidence

(does the tribunal have discretion).

§ 12.15. Objections to Substance of Testimony. Objections to the content of testimony protest the character or the materiality of a witness's testimony during an examination or cross-examination. The objection does not challenge the form of the question. A validly worded question may call for testimony that violates rules of evidence. The following are common objections made to the substance of testimony.

1. Best Evidence Rule – Original Document Rule (See Chapter XII § 12.11 (5) (C) (1). Best Evidence Rule). The best evidence rule applies to both real evidence and documentary evidence used in a hearing as proof. The best evidence rule requires that original objects and documents be submitted as evidence in a hearing.

A. The best evidence rule prohibits admission of secondary evidence to prove the contents of a written document unless the unavailability of the original document is satisfactorily explained to the tribunal. If other than original evidence is admitted in a hearing, the opposing party should argue that minimal (if any) weight should be given to the evidence

B. The best evidence rule is not applicable in an action in which substantial evidence supports a quasi-judicial determination. *Matter of Barrett v D'Elia,* 102 AD2d 890, 477 NYS2d 62 (2nd Dept 1984).

2. Conclusion. The witness states a legal conclusion of fact in the testimony, such as, "They were very, very intoxicated." The decision-maker determines legal findings of fact in quasi-judicial administrative adjudications.

3. Confusing or misleading.

4. The document speaks for itself. A witness questioned to establish a foundation for a document offered into evidence may describe the document. The witness constructing the foundation may not read from or repeat the text of the offered document.

5. Hearsay. The two elements of hearsay evidence are (A) The witness testifies to prove the truth of what the witness was told in unsworn statements by a person outside of the tribunal; and (B) the unsworn statements relate to matters not perceived by the witness through direct evidence, not obtained directly through sight, hearing, touch, feel or taste. (See Chapter XIII § 13.2.3 (C). Direct Evidence).

6. Immaterial. The testimony is immaterial; it neither proves nor disproves any fact material to the determination of the proceeding.

7. Improper characterization. In testimony, the witness improperly labels a person. "John, a high school dropout called a technical representative, did little to answer my call for help."

8. Inadmissible opinion of a lay witness. A lay witness gives an opinion in an area that requires testimony by a qualified expert. Testimony by a non-expert witness as an opinion is restricted to direct evidence.

9. Irrelevant. The testimony does not have probative value. It neither proves nor disproves any fact relevant to the determination of the proceeding.

10. Narrative. To a specific question that calls for a limited answer, the witness's answer is an editorial that includes information unnecessary to respond to the question posed.

11. Opinion. The witness's answer evaluates an issue in a discipline in which the witness is not qualified as an expert (does not have special education, knowledge, training, or experience), and the witness's answer is not based on direct evidence.

12. Prejudice outweighs probative value. This objection usually protests the submission of an exhibit into evidence. When directed to testimony, the objection contends that the witness's answer contains inadmissible material, for example, without valid legal reason, the testimony refers to insurance, previous criminal convictions, or prior administrative proceedings.

13. Privileged communication. Evidence submitted discloses a confidential communication protected by law, such as a communication between attorney-client physician-patient, priest-penitent, husband-wife, and government employees entrusted with government secrets.

14. Speculation. The question requires a witness to guess or to speculate about an event, what could happen or what is possible to have occurred. Examples: "What do you think happened?" Or "Is it conceivable?"

15. Unresponsive/Volunteered. A witness's testimony does not directly respond to the question asked and may offer information not posed by the question. The attorney who called the witness may also make this objection.

16. Violates parol evidence rule. The testimony modifies or contradicts the contents of a recording, photograph, or of a contractual document facially complete and freely executed by competent parties.

§ 12.16. Objections to Exhibits. Tactically, a document should be marked for identification before being offered into evidence as an exhibit. A request to ALJ to have a document marked for identification is not subject to objection by the opposing party. A document marked for identification and subsequently excluded from evidence in response to an objection may be appended to the record of the hearing as part of an appellate review. Classic objections to the admission of a document into evidence as an exhibit include:

1. Lack of authentication. Proof is insufficient to establish the validity of a written or an oral statement offered into evidence. Signatures on a document offered into evidence must be verified as those of the parties who purportedly executed the document. Analogously, if a witness testifies about statements made in a telephone conversation between a witness and another person, the identity of the other person must be verified by evidence.

2. Cumulative. Evidence is offered repetitively as proof of one issue. Proof of an issue is repeatedly introduced through the testimony of a succession of witnesses that replicate testimony already given or through duplicate exhibits of exhibits already admitted into evidence.

3. Discovery Demand Disobeyed. In violation of mandatory disclosure rules, a party fails to disclose discoverable information requested in a valid disclosure demand.

4. Limited Purpose. A privileged document is admitted only for a limited or restricted purpose, for example, produced for inspection. A privileged document disclosed for a limited purpose does not constitute a general waiver of a privilege.

5. Lack of Foundation. Information offered fails to prove the three prerequisites for admission of information into evidence: (A) the competency of the qualifying witness; (B) the relevance

of the exhibit (it proves or disproves some fact at issue in the proceeding); and (C) the authentication of the exhibit.

6. Hearsay. See Chapter XII § 15.5 (5). Hearsay.

7. Irrelevant. The document does not relate to any issue relevant or material to a determination of the action.

8. Immaterial. The document offered is inconsequential to a determination of any material issue in or to the outcome of the proceeding.

9. Unverified. A public record is not certified or validated.

10. Privileged. The document contains privileged information.

11. Prejudice outweighs probative value. The document depicts pictures or other images that could probably offend feelings and stimulate emotional responses that distract from the accurate evidentiary value of the document.

§ 12.17. Continuing or Running Objections. A continuing or running objection removes the need to object repeatedly to a topic or theme of testimony after an adverse ruling on an objection. A single objection applies to all the questions in the specific area of questioning without need to object each time to every related question asked.

§ 12.18. Non-evidential Objections. Improper conduct of counsel or other non-evidential issues may occur during an administrative hearing. An advocate's opinion on an evidentiary issue and a party's personal attack against a witness or opposing party or counsel are improper and are objectionable non-evidential situations. In *Clarke v NYC Tr. Auth.,* 174 AD2d 268 (1992), the judgment of the lower court was reversed and remanded partly because "counsel committed a number of improper acts, including acting as an unsworn witness, vouching for the credibility of his own witnesses, accusing defense witnesses of lying, and accusing a defense medical expert of lying for pay. It is well-settled law that a trial counsel improperly acts as an unsworn witness when he interjects unsworn statements of personal knowledge of the facts of the case (see Code of Professional Responsibility, DR 7-106 [C)] [3])."

§ 12.19. Objections and Appeals. An ALJ's sustaining of an objection to an offer of evidence excludes the information from admission in the hearing.

1. Preserving Excluded Evidence Ruling as Issue for Appeal. An offer of proof made at the time of a ruling excluding an exhibit or testimony from acceptance into evidence reserves the issue of exclusion for appeal. The administrative ruling becomes part of the hearing record. A reviewing court examines the administrative decision to determine if the exclusion of the information violates a substantial right of a party or otherwise constitutes reversible error.

A. In reply to an adverse evidentiary ruling, a motion to make an offer of proof may be presented to the hearing officer in a quasi-judicial, administrative adjudication to demonstrate the materiality or relevancy of the information as evidence of a determinant issue in the action.

B. An offer of testimonial information may take the form of a statement of the content of the excluded testimony, as to what the witness would have testified and why that information is relevant.

C. An offer of proof may be made orally, through examination or cross-examination of a witness, or in a written notarized statement that summarizes the probable testimony of the witness.

2. Motion to Strike. Immediately after an unsuccessful evidentiary objection in a quasi-judicial hearing, a motion to strike may be made with an alternative statement of why the evidence should not be given any significant weight. An administrative tribunal often refuses to consider a motion to strike. However, the motion to strike promotes the statement of reasons why the secondary evidence should not be given significant weight and emphasizes the evidentiary objection as part of the hearing record for review.

CHAPTER XIII. QUASI-JUDICIAL ADMINISTRATIVE ADJUDICATION ADVOCACY.

§ 13.12. New York Statutory and Common Law Privileges.

§ 13.1. Opening Statement - Just the facts. First impressions persist. The opening statement (when allowed) made in a proceeding is the first opportunity for a party to present the party's version of the case to an administrative law tribunal.

1. An opening statement is a condensed editorial of facts and only facts: Who, what, when, where, why, and how of a case as perceived by the presenter.

2. An opening statement, founded both on the evidence planned to be presented and on the legal issues intended to be proved at the hearing: (A) briefly states the factual theme of the case, (B) concisely states and explains the decisive issues, and (C) succinctly convey the perceived facts of what happened, to whom, when, where, and how.

§ 13.2. Evidence. Evidence forms the character of information used in an administrative proceeding.

1. Law of Evidence. Evidence law consists of the formal rules and procedures that prescribe the admission, the use, and the evaluation of information in administrative hearings. Ordinarily, executive administrative agencies do not follow the technical rules of evidence.

2. Offering of Evidence. An offering of evidence refers to a submission of information for admission as evidence in an administrative hearing. Information is offered as evidence in adjudication to prove or disprove a legal position.

A. Proof. Proof is a product of evidence; proof verifies the truth, accuracy, fallacy, inaccuracy, and erroneousness of information.

B. Evidentiary Proof. Evidentiary proof must consist of relevant information and be based on a proper foundation and in proper form when presented for admission into an administrative hearing.

(1). Relevant Evidence. Relevant evidence is information that assists in developing and deciding any material fact or issue in question in a proceeding. In New York, "Evidence is relevant if it has any tendency in reason to prove the existence of any material fact, i.e., it makes a determination of the action more probable or less probable than it would be without the evidence." (*People v Scarola*, 71 NY2d 769, 530 NYS2d 83 [1988]). The presiding officer in an administrative hearing decides the relevance of evidence.

(2). Proper Foundation. Information that proves sufficiently the authenticity of a document or the competency of a witness to allow admission as evidence in adjudication forms a proper foundation. Four factors determine the adequacy of information needed to establish a foundation for admission of a document into evidence as an exhibit: (a) competence of the witness testifying about the exhibit; (b) identification of the document; (c) authentication of the document; and (d) relevance of the document to material issues in the action.

(3). Proper Form. Questions asked a witness must be correctly phrased and not objectionably worded. [47]

C. Burden of Proof. Burden of proof embodies two duties: The duty of going forward (burden of production), a party's duty to come forward with presentation of proving evidence at different times during a proceeding, and the duty of persuasion.

---

[47] See Chapter XII § 12.11.5 Common Objections to Form of Question.

(1). The burden of proof involves procedural due process; the order of proof (the order in which evidence is presented) does not. The burden to present evidence may relocate from one party to (be imposed upon) another party during a proceeding. The obligation of a burden of proof remains with a party throughout an adjudication.

(2). Typically, the party with the burden of persuasion first presents evidence in a hearing. Unless statutorily demanded, an order of presentation of evidence is not obligatory. An ALJ may allow an out-of-order presentation of evidence for reasonable cause. Availability of a witness and the logical sequence of fact are reasonable causes for an ALJ to allow an out-of-order presentation of evidence. Conversely, a change in the order of the burden of proof may be a violation of due process of law. *Schaffer v Weast*, 546 US 49,126 S Ct 528 (2005).

(3). The burden of proof in administrative hearings may be assigned by statute or by rule. An executive agency with rulemaking authority may allocate by rule the burden of proof in administrative hearings, either in compliance with its enabling law or where the agency's organic statute is silent on the subject.

(a). SAPA 306 (1) provides, "Irrelevant or unduly repetitious evidence or cross-examination may be excluded. Except as otherwise provided by statute, the burden of proof shall be on the party who initiated the proceeding."

(b). Education Law § 4404 (1) (d) (1) illustrates an agency's allocation of the burden of proof by statute. The law provides: In a hearing, the agency responsible for providing education to students with disabilities has the burden of proof, including the burden of persuasion and burden of production, except that persons in parental relations seeking tuition reimbursements for unilateral parental placements have the burden of persuasion and burden of production on the appropriateness of such placement.

(4). The obligation of the burden of proof was a determinant issue in *Schaffer v Weast*, 546 US 49. The US Supreme Court considered the question of the allocation of the burden of proof in a special, education, due process hearing held under the Individuals with Disabilities Education Act. In the initial agency hearing, the hearing officer found the evidence presented by each party (the agency and the disabled child [Schaffer]) to be "equipoise." Correspondingly, the ALJ assigned the burden of proof to Schaffer and decided in favor of the agency. The ALJ reasoned: Where the evidence presented in a hearing by the parties is perfectly balanced, the party with the burden of proof (burden of persuasion) will lose, the burden of persuasion not having been met. The Supreme Court agreed with the determination of the ALJ and upheld the decision of the agency.

§ 13.3. Forms of Evidence. The form of the evidence admitted in an administrative adjudication dictates how a tribunal evaluates that evidence. Forms of evidence include the following.

1. Testimonial Evidence. Testimonial evidence consists of statements made under oath and subjected to examination.

2. Documentary Evidence. Forms of documentary evidence are writings on paper (such as checks, reports, contracts, invoices, wills), and other means of preserving information (photographs, tapes films, printed emails, and computer-generated documents). Computer printouts are admissible as business records, a voluminous-writings exception. *Ed Guth Realty v Gingold*, 34 NY2d 440, 338 NYS2d 367 (1974).

A. A document (writing or another specimen of preserved information) may be considered as documentary evidence or as physical evidence, depending on the reasons why the document is offered as evidence. For example, water damaged, dated invoices introduced into evidence to prove the occurrence of a flood, and not for the contents of the documents, are physical evidence.The same invoices, if offered as proof of the date of the flood, are documentary evidence. The same invoices, if offered as both proof of a flood and proof of the date of the flood, are both physical evidence and documentary evidence.

B. The best evidence rule applies in administrative hearings. If an original document is not produced as an exhibit in a hearing, an explanation legally acceptable by the tribunal must be offered that justifies why the original document is not produced. Application of the best evidence rule is not required in a hearing where substantial evidence supports the decision.

C. Documentary evidence not supported by other (corroborative) evidence may not be considered as conclusive evidence. See Chapter XIII, § 13.3.8. Corroborative Evidence.

3. Direct Evidence: Evidence of the Five Senses. Direct evidence evolves from the experience of a person through personal knowledge, that which a person feels, hears, sees, smells or tastes in a situation.

4. Real Evidence. Real evidence is tangible evidence; it is one of two classifications of evidence that consist of physical objects. Admission of a physical object into evidence requires authentication.

A. A process of authentication of a physical object is verification of the relevance and proof that the physical object is in the same or substantially the same condition when offered into evidence as the physical object was when involved in the events of the case. A method of authentication of a physical object is validation by proof of the "chain of custody."

B. Chain of custody refers to an accurate chronological record of the possession and movement of an object from the time the object is obtained until it is presented for admission as evidence in the administrative proceeding. Chain of custody may be demonstrated through testimonial evidence, including circumstantial evidence (issue of weight rather than admissibility) concerning the time, place, condition, custody, and custodian of the object from the moment of the object's acquisition until the moment of the object's evidentiary offer in the administrative action.

5. Demonstrative Evidence. Demonstrative evidence is the other of the two categories of evidence composed of physical objects. Demonstrative evidence makes information visible through seeing-is-believing demonstrations. Actual items or illustrative items may be used to demonstrate or to clarify information presented in a hearing.

A. Demonstrative evidence may be (1) actual evidence, such as a defective item or a flawed product, or (2) illustrative evidence, such as three-dimensional models and mockups of accident sites or proposed buildings, photographs, or X-rays. A computer-generated video that demonstrated the mechanics of the shaken-baby syndrome was admitted into evidence as illustrative evidence in *People v Yates*, 290 AD2d 888, 736 NYS2d 798 (2nd Dept 2002).

B. Demonstrative illustrative evidence lacks probative value and serves as a visual aid to support a witness's testimony. Illustrative evidence is not actual evidence of the event portrayed. *Kane v Triborough Bridge & Tunnel Authority,* 8 AD3d

239 (2nd Dept 2004).

6. Circumstantial Evidence. Circumstantial evidence is indirect evidence (documentary or testimonial) that formulates an inference of a primary fact. Evidence of circumstances supports indirectly a fact not proved by direct evidence. Direct evidence must support the inference or conclusion created by circumstantial evidence. The direct proves the circumstantial.

A. A concept of circumstantial evidence may be illustrated by an example using the New York subway system. The witness (a subway clerk) testifies that when he walked to the subway station, entered the underground subway booth and started work at 6:00 am, the weather was clear and sunny. Subsequently, at 8:00 am while at work, he observed people who entered the subway station were carrying wet umbrellas and wearing wet outerwear. The reasonable conclusion or inference is that at a time after 6:00 am and by 8:00 am, the weather changed to include rain. To the witness who did not directly see the rain, the evidence (proof) of rain is circumstantial.

B. The witness ascertained the direct evidence through the sense of sight. The witness saw passengers wearing wet clothing, and carrying umbrellas dripping water enter the subway station. From the direct evidence, the water, the only reasonable inference that may be derived is that at the time the passengers entered the subway station, it was raining in that area. The direct evidence of water forms the circumstantial evidence of rain

7. Cumulative Evidence. Information offered to prove further an issue or fact already validated by evidence admitted previously in the adjudication is cumulative evidence. Cumulative evidence is not synonymous with corroborative evidence.

8. Corroborative Evidence. It is additional information offered as supporting evidence to strengthen or confirm other evidence already admitted in support of the same issue. Corroborative evidence is a different character of evidence from the existing evidence that supports an issue. Corroboration may be required statutorily in specific elements of a proceeding, such as the unsown testimony of a child, testimony of an accomplice, testimony of an interested witness, identification of an accused, and information regarding specific offenses (sexual, paternity, treason, and perjury).

9. Competent Evidence. Competent evidence consists of information that is relevant, has probative value, and establishes the truth or falsity of issues of fact raised in administrative adjudication.

10. Substantial Evidence. Essentially, competent evidence sufficient to decide the determinant issues in an administrative proceeding meets the substantial-evidence standard.

A. Substantial evidence is relevant, reasonable, and credible evidence required by law to prove the essential premise of an administrative adjudication. In New York, proof is "relevant if it has any tendency in reason to prove the existence of any material fact . . . it makes determination of the action more or less probable than it would be without the evidence." *People v Scarola,* 71 NY2d 769 (1988).

B. Substantial evidence is the amount and quality of information required to prove a reasonable conclusion that an act did or did not occur in a given situation.

11. Rebuttal Evidence. Rebuttal evidence is a party's reply in evidence that is competent and that directly explains, disproves, or contradicts material evidence presented by an adverse party.

12. Character Evidence. Evidence of general reputation (what the community believes a person's character to be) proves general character (the morality of a person). The three testimonial methods by which character may be proved are testimony about reputation, testimony given as an opinion, and testimony describing explicit conduct.

A. Testimony of Reputation Evidence. A witness testifying about a person's reputation must know the person's reputation in a community (after a criminal conviction if "fitness" to obtain a privilege is at issue).

(1). The testimony of a witness able to know the person's reputation in a community is treated as fact; the witness does not have to be personally acquainted with the person about whom the testimony is given and need not have first-hand knowledge of any facts. *People v Alamo*, 22 NY2d 632 (1969).

(2). Presentation of reputation evidence sufficient to demonstrate a person's good character after a criminal conviction raises a rebuttable inference of reformation in adjudication. *NY St. Dept. of St., Div. of Lic. Servs., Application of Zeher*, 39 DOS 85 (1985).

B. Testimony Based on Opinion. Opinion evidence is a witness's version of the facts of a dispute. A witness's testimony founded on the witness's opinion must be rationally based on the perception of the witness. Proof by opinion is not accepted generally as proof of character.

C. Testimony of Specific Instances. The testimony compares a person's conduct before and after an event, such as the commission of a criminal offense. The witness narrates factually essential elements of an event in which a person was involved, specifically the person's conduct after the occurrence of the event.

(1). If elements of a person's criminal conviction were breaking and entering (burglary or illegal trespass) of residential properties, the testimony regarding the person's reputation after the conviction should include clear evidence of reformation as demonstrated in the person's after-conviction activity. For example, proof by negative evidence may consist of information revealing that after the criminal conviction, the person was employed for the last two years by a real estate firm, was entrusted with keys to numerous properties, including residences, and there is not evidence of any illegal activity by the person.

(2). Applicants for permits, commissions, licensure, and other government privileges often must furnish satisfactory evidence of good character, reputation, and fitness. Applicants with criminal convictions who have obtained requisite certificates of relief from disabilities or certificates of good conduct must also provide evidence of fitness. The relevance of a person's behavior after a criminal conviction was determined in *NY St. Dept. of St., Div. of Lic. Servs., Application of Zeher, supra*. In *Zeher*, the agency based its proposed denial of an application for licensure on the applicant's prior criminal conviction. In an appeal of the proposed denial, the agency's Office of Administrative Hearings held: "To not consider evidence of an applicant's reputation after the criminal conviction would deny the possibility and the hope of reformation, and would punish an individual for past activity without regard for the relevance of a present situation to a licensing regulation."

13. Hearsay Evidence. Hearsay evidence consists of information based on statements of others and not within the direct knowledge of the offeror of the information.

A. Hearsay evidence may be oral or written.

(1). Oral Hearsay. Oral hearsay occurs when a witness testifies about an event in which the witness was not cognizably involved. The testimony expresses what the witness was told in unsworn statements by someone, and the testimony is offered to prove the truth of the contents of the unsworn statement.

(2). Written Hearsay. Written hearsay is a written statement offered into evidence by someone other than the author of the statement to prove the truth of what is written in the unsworn statement.

B. In the receipt and evaluation of hearsay evidence in administrative hearings, "Judge Learned Hand has offered the classic formulation: '[N]o doubt, that does not mean mere rumor will serve to "support" a finding, but hearsay may do so, at least if more is not conveniently available, and if in the end the finding is supported by the kind of evidence on which responsible persons are accustomed to rely in serious affairs.' " Gellhorn, Ernest, *Rules of Evidence and Official Notice in Formal Administrative Hearings*, 1 Duke L J (1971).

14. Prior Acts. Information about previous acts of a party is offered to prove the party's motive, intent, absence of mistake or accident, common scheme or plan, or identity (*People v Molineux*, 168 NY 264 [1901]). To be admitted as evidence, information of prior acts must be relevant and "directly probative" of an issue in the case other than the character of a party (*People v Ventimiglia*, 52 NY2d 350, 438 NYS2d 261 [1981]). The probative value of the evidence of other acts must be weighed against potential, prejudicial effect. Evidence of previous acts should not be admitted supporting an issue already proved by other evidence in an action; if allowed, the evidence could be potentially cumulative and prejudicial.

15. Official Notice. A presiding officer in an administrative action may accept into evidence specific, well-known, publically accepted matters of law and matters of fact documented in available sources of acknowledged trustworthiness.

A. Matters of law officially noticed are federal laws and treaties, state and local government laws and rules, determinations of federal, state, and local government courts and administrative agencies.

B. Matters of fact officially noticed are commonly acknowledged facts, such as time and place of past occurrences (floods, hurricanes, fires); official weather reports; definition of words or phrases as defined in case law, official rules, or traditional dictionaries; "facts within the specialized knowledge of . . . (an) agency." (SAPA 306 [4]). An agency's "specialized knowledge" should include technical and scientific facts that are within an agency's expertise.

C. "When official notice is taken of a material fact not appearing in the evidence in the record and of which judicial notice could not be taken every party shall be given notice thereof and shall on timely request be afforded an opportunity prior to decision to dispute the fact or its materiality." SAPA 306 (4).

16. Conclusive Evidence. Conclusive evidence is a rule of evidence that derives from proof of basic fact. It is evidence that cannot be disputed or contradicted by any other evidence and must be accepted by a tribunal as definitive proof of a fact. As a matter of law, conclusive evidence proves component issues of fact.

A. Evidence proving the registration of a trademark (basic fact) is conclusive evidence. Proof of the registration of a trademark is sufficient to prove concurrently issues of validity (the validity of the mark), of ownership (the registrant's ownership of the mark), and of the right of exclusive use (the registrant's exclusive right to use the mark in commerce). 15 USC § 1115.

B. Evidence verifying a written instrument is conclusive evidence of the written record made between the parties to the instrument, of the truth of the facts recited in the written instrument between the parties or successors in interest by a subsequent title. The conclusive evidence rule does not apply to a recital of consideration in a written instrument.

C. Conclusively proven facts (validity, ownership, and use of the mark or the written record of a contract) cannot be disputed or contradicted. The prime or basic fact (legality of the registration of the mark or the validity of the written instrument) may be challenged. Evidence challenging the basic fact does not vary or contradict the facts proved by the conclusive evidence doctrine.

(1). Evidence disputing the basic fact strives to destroy basic fact, the registration of the trademark. A trademark obtained through fraud is an invalid registration, was never registered, and never existed as a registered mark. Evidence that destroys the basic fact (registration of the trademark) expunges from existence the presumed facts (validity, ownership, and right of exclusive use of the mark).

(2). Evidence, including parol evidence, may overcome the conclusive evidence principle of a written instrument between persons. Fraud, illegality, want of consideration, invalid delivery (unperformed condition) may be shown by parol evidence, "not to contradict or vary but to destroy the written instrument." (*Thomas v Scutt,* 127 NY 133, 27 NE 961 [1891]). Evidence that destroys the written instrument destroys the written record.

D. A conclusive evidence rule may be formulated by policy or by statute. The New York State Division of Housing and Community Renewal, in *Policy Statement 92-3* (August 14, 1992), made the receipt of a DHCR Rent Registration Unit by the agency conclusive evidence of the filing with DHCR of the rent registration of rent regulated housing accommodations. New York Legislative Law § 40 provides that a certificate by the presiding officer of the New York Senate that a bill was passed as required by law "shall be conclusive evidence thereof." *Heimbach v Chu*, 744 F2d 11 (1984).

§ 13.4. Presumptions. A presumption is a law of procedure that guides the application and effect of evidence in an administrative action. A presumption is not evidence. A presumption is either a procedural rule of evidence or a rule of substantive law.

1. Presumption as a Procedural Rule of Evidence. Presumption as a procedural rule of evidence is a factual or real presumption; it is a presumption structured of "basic facts" and "presumed facts." Evidence proving the truth of the primary or basic fact activates the presumption of the existence of the presumed fact.

A. An example of the relationship between a basic fact and a presumed fact is the presumption of mailing (a rule of evidence). The presumption postulates that a letter properly addressed and delivered to a US Postal Service or a common carrier and not returned to the sender was in fact delivered to and received by the addressee. Evidence (such as a properly executed affidavit of mailing) proving the basic fact precipitates the presumed facts that the mailing was delivered to and received by the addressee. A denial of receipt of a mailing is not enough to rebut the presumption raised by the affidavit of mailing. *Engel v Lichterman*, 62 NY2d 943 (1984); *Kihl v Pfeffer and Honda Motor Co.*, 266 AD2d 203 (1999).

B. Presumptions with basic fact are rebuttable presumptions. A rebuttable presumption is a procedural rule that defines the relationship between a basic fact and a presumed fact. Prove the basic fact, and the presumed fact must be accepted as true unless rebutted by factual evidence. The opposing argument presents evidence to rebut the presumption by proving the nonexistence of or the falsity of the presumed fact. Categories of rebuttable presumptions are rebuttable discretionary presumptions and rebuttable mandatory presumptions.

(1). A rebuttable discretionary presumption is a permissive presumption that may constitute prima facie evidence of the basic fact in issue.

(a). A rebuttable discretionary presumption allows, but does not require, the factfinder to infer the existence or nonexistence of a fact from proof of the basic set of facts of the presumption. The presumption does not impose a burden of proof of any kind on the opposing party.

(b). An example of a rebuttable discretionary presumption is the presumption against suicide, applicable only in disputes over life insurance proceeds. "Except in rare cases, a claim of suicide presents a factual issue, not a legal one." *Green v William Penn. Life Ins. Co.*, 74 AD3d 570 (1st Dept 2010). In *Green,* considerable evidence supported the insurer's contention that Mr. Green committed suicide. There was also evidence supporting the wife's contention that suicide was not the cause of death. The Supreme Court found that Mr. Green had committed suicide. In reversing the Supreme Court, the Appellate Division did not exercise its factual review power but held that the evidence failed as a matter of law to overcome the presumption against suicide. The Court of Appeals reversed and remanded the case to the Appellate Division. "We hold that the Appellate Division misconstrued the presumption against suicide. It is a guide for the factfinder, not a rule that compels a result."

(2). A rebuttable mandatory presumption requires the factfinder to infer the presumed fact if the predicate facts of the presumption are proved.

(a). The World Trade Center presumption is a rebuttable mandatory presumption, a presumption bestowed to people who participated in the World Trade Center rescue, recovery, or cleanup efforts. It is presumed that if a person becomes permanently disabled due to certain qualifying conditions (defined in the statute) and cannot perform his or her job (the basic facts), the condition was incurred within the World Trade Center aftermath (the presumed fact). Administrative Code of City of NY § 13-252.1(1) (a).

(b). Once a petitioner proves that he or she worked the requisite number of hours at the site, the World Trade Center presumption puts the burden on the city to show that the petitioner's qualifying injury did not incur in the line of duty. (*Matter of Dement v Kelly*, 97 AD3d 223, 2012 NY Slip Op 04949 [1st Dept 2012]). If New York City fails to present evidence sufficient to rebut the presumption, the factfinder must find the existence of the presumed facts as a matter of law.

2. Presumption as A Rule of Substantive Law. A substantive rule of law presumption is a factitious presumption without basic fact.

A. A presumption without basic fact may arise without proof. The presumption compels a tribunal to make specific determinations in specified situations.

B. Presumptions without basic facts are both rebuttable and

conclusive presumptions.

(1). A rebuttable presumption without basic fact is the presumption of innocence. The presumption is a substantive rule of law judicially determined as protected by the due process of law guarantee of both the Fifth and the Fourteenth Amendments to the US Constitution.

(a). The presumption of innocence sequences the order of the presentation of evidence in administrative proceedings seeking to deprive a regulated entity of an interest protected by due process principles. The presumption of innocence protects an accused from having the preliminary burden of proof, of having to prove innocence as in an assumption of guilt. The presumption of innocence imposes on the state: (i) the burden of proof, the burden of proving the accusations by a standard of evidence (substantial evidence); and (ii) the obligation to first present evidence sufficient to make a prima facie (at first sight) case before an accused has the burden of production. *Taylor v Kentucky*, 436 US 478, 98 S Ct 1930 (1978); *cf People v Patterson*, 78 NY2d 711, 579 NYS2d 617 (1991).

(b). Once the agency presents a prima facie case, an accused has the burden of production; the accused is obligated to produce proving evidence. *Id.*

(2). Evidence proving the existence of the assumed fact produces the conclusive presumption of that fact. When legally invoked, a conclusive presumption is absolute and beyond dispute and cannot be rebutted or contradicted by evidence; it decrees decision; it is a substantive law rule of certainty.

(a). Standard examples of conclusive presumptions without basic fact are age-based presumptions. Age-based presumptions impose binding and determinate directions in actions involving children. Where infancy is pleaded and proved, it is impossible legally to disprove the presumption, and the factfinder's decision is judicially decreed.

(b). Classic age-based presumptions are: (i). A child under seven years of age is presumed to be incapable of committing a felony. (ii). It is conclusively presumed that an infant who has not reached the age of seven is incapable of being guilty of negligence. (iii). An infant is incapable of judging what is or is not in the infant's interest.

3. Statutory Presumptions. New York State statutes codifying presumptions include: Banking Law, § 675; CPLR 211 (b); Estates, Powers & Trusts Law, §§ 2-1.7, 5-1.4; Real Property Actions & Proceedings Law, §§ 991, 1931; Retirement & Social Security Law, §§ 363-d, 363-dd, 363-f; Revised Uniform Probate Code, § 2-804; Surrogate's Law, § 2602; Vehicle and Traffic Law, §§ 1225-c, 1225-d.

§ 13.5. Legal Defense Arguments. A legal defense is a legal argument presented to an administrative agency or tribunal by a party in support of the party's declared legal position.

1. A legal defense may be argued in an oral or a written motion or in an answer that enters a plea, argues dismissal of the charges, denies the truth of the charges or offers reason, excuse, explanation, or justification for the action underlying the charges.

2. Traditional legal defense claims are jurisdictional, affirmative, equitable, and privilege.

§ 13.6. Jurisdictional Defenses. Jurisdiction is the authority of an administrative agency to adjudicate specified cases (potential or subject matter jurisdiction) and to enter valid, enforceable judgments in those cases (active jurisdiction). The jurisdictional authority of an administrative agency is a paired authority – potential (inherent) authority and active authority.

1. Potential or Subject Matter Jurisdiction. Subject matter jurisdiction is authority conferred to an agency through its enabling act. Subject matter jurisdiction is embryonic; it must exist before a tribunal may hear a case. Subject matter jurisdiction refers to the authority of the administrative law tribunal to hear the category of cases brought before it for adjudication. "It is the power to adjudge the general questions involved and is not dependent on a state of facts that might appear in a particular case (citation omitted)." *NY St. Dept. of St., Div. of Lic. Servs. v Carroll*, 113 DOS 94 (1994). It is the authority of a tribunal to hear a specific type of claim (specific subject matter) and to grant the specific relief requested.

2. Active Jurisdiction. Laws that delegate subject matter jurisdiction authority to agencies enumerate factual criteria that must be pled in a party's pleadings to evoke an agency's authority to hear, to decide, and to enter judgment in an administrative proceeding. The legal requirements are mandatory, interpreted literally, and applied rigorously.

3. Jurisdictional Defects. A jurisdictional defect is a deficiency in an agency's authority to hear and to determine an administrative adjudication. A party's noncompliance with a jurisdictional rule may result in a jurisdictional defect that prevents an agency from exerting its jurisdictional authority.

A. Jurisdictional Defects Fatal. In administrative actions involving a due process protected liberty or property interest, a failure in pleadings to fulfill subject-matter jurisdiction criteria is a fatal defect. Three jurisdictional deficiencies in pleadings considered fatal to an action are subject matter, cause of action, indispensable party.

(1). Subject-Matter Jurisdiction. Subject-matter jurisdiction authorizes an agency to hear a statutorily described proceeding involving a stated subject matter. An illustration is the State Liquor Authority's regulation of the alcohol beverage industry (Alcoholic Beverage Control Law).

(a). A party's failure to plead and prove the factors required to incur an agency's subject matter jurisdiction is a jurisdictional defect that cannot be cured by consent, estoppel, stipulation, or waiver and precludes a tribunal from obtaining jurisdiction over the subject matter of an adjudication.

(b). The failure of an agency to designate in writing the hearing officer assigned to a pending hearing as statutorily directed (Civil Service Law §75 [2]) is a fatal jurisdictional defect that bars subject matter jurisdiction. A party's failure to object to a subject matter jurisdictional defect does not waive the defect. *Gardner v Coxsackie-Athens Cent. School Dist. Bd. of Educ.*, 92 AD3d 1093, 939 NYS2d 149 (2012).

(c). A jurisdictional defect may be pleaded at any time, directly or collaterally, and for the first time on appeal. [48] A jurisdictional-defect argument must challenge the basis for subject matter jurisdiction and not relate only to substantive elements in a cause of action (such as a residency requirement). "In sum, the overly stated principle that lack of subject matter jurisdiction makes a final judgment absolutely void is not applicable to cases which, upon analysis, do not involve jurisdiction, but merely substantive elements of a cause for relief. To do so would be to undermine significantly the doctrine

[48] Also see Martineau, Robert J., *Subject Matter Jurisdiction as a New Issue on Appeal*, BYU L Rev 1 (1988).

of *res judicata*, and to eliminate the certainty and finality in the law and in litigation which the doctrine is designed to protect." *Lacks v Lacks*, 41 NY2d 71; 390 NYS2d 875 (1976).

(2). Failure to State a Cause for Relief. The jurisdictional defense of a pleading failing to state a cause upon which relief may be granted is a failure of substance. The ultimate issue is whether the factual allegations of the pleading state any claim upon which relief can be granted.

(a). Technical pleading deficiencies constitute a failure of form in an administrative proceeding.

(b). An agency may by rule narrow an affirmative defense pleading. Department of Environmental Conservation prescribes by rule that failure to state a claim is not pleaded as an affirmative defense but as a motion to dismiss. 6 NYCRR 622. Annotations. Hearing Office Guidance Documents.

(3). Failure to Join Indispensable Party. A legal proceeding fails to include an indispensable party if the action cannot continue without the excluded party's presence; the absence of the party prevents full adjudication of all the issues raised in the case. Where the necessary party is within the jurisdiction of the tribunal, the ALJ should seek joinder to resolve the adjudication.

B. Jurisdictional Defects Not Initially Fatal. Jurisdictional defects waived if not raised by motion or in an answer are a failure of notice, lack of statute citation, and validity of service. In an administrative action, waiver of jurisdictional defects not initially fatal, although legal, may implicate the integrity of both the adjudicatory procedure and due process demands.

(1). Failure of Notice. Failure of notice is a failure in a pleading to give information sufficient for a party to adequately prepare for participation in the pending administrative action.

(2). Lack of Statutory Reference. Failure of statutory citation is a failure in the initial pleadings of an agency to refer to statutes and rules applicable to the causal action and to appellant procedures.

(3). Lack of Personal Jurisdiction. A claim of lack of personal jurisdiction questions the validity of service of pleadings, such as the identity of the party charged or the authority of the agency to charge the party named (party located outside the state, or foreign entity with insufficient contact with the state).

§ 13.7. Affirmative Defenses. An affirmative defense alleges a legal justification for the party's behavior or conduct charged as unlawful in an agency's action. Typical affirmative defenses in administrative actions are:

1. Accord and satisfaction. Obligation was legally discharged.

2. Arbitration and award. The legal issues were resolved through mediation.

3. Authority. The alleged violation was legally sanctioned.

4. Advice of counsel. Acting on the advice of counsel is not considered as engaging in willful misconduct where the statute governing the action defines a "willful act" as an intentional act committed with a wrongful purpose. 49 Ed. Dept. Rep., Decision No. 16,030 (April 5, 2010); *NY St. Dept. of St., Div. of Lic. Servs. v Mole,* 40 DOS 86 (1986).

5. Consent. Permission or approval of an action was obtained.

6. Discharge in bankruptcy. The debts at issue were discharged

in a legal proceeding.

7. Fraud. The alleged unlawful acts were caused proximately by criminal deception committed against the accused.

8. Irresistible impulse. Behavior is non-volitional because of an "impulse control disorder." *Perry v Comm. of Labor*, 283 AD2d 754 (3rd Dept 2010).

9. Payment. The legal obligation owed was legally paid or satisfied.

10. Ratification. The act at issue was intentionally approved subsequently by word, act or deed.

11. Release. A valid and binding document settled all legal liabilities.

12. Statute of frauds. The claim was not evidenced in a legally executed writing.

13. Statute of limitations. The maximum time limit set by law in which to bring a cause of action against a party expired, and the action is barred.

A. Statutes of limitations scheduled in CPLR are not applicable in administrative disciplinary hearings (*Sinha v Ambach*, 91 AD2d 703, 457 NYS2d 603 [3rd Dept 1982]). An administrative agency is not deprived of jurisdiction in disciplinary adjudications by a six-year statutory limitation. CPLR 213 (8); *NY St. Dept. of St., Div. of Lic. Servs. v Bell,* 61 DOS 88 (1988).

B. An agency must begin an action within a reasonable time. SAPA 301 (1).

14. Identity theft. The unlawful act charged was committed by one person's illegal use of the name and personal information of the individual accused in the administrative proceeding.

§ 13.8. Equitable Defenses. Equitable defenses are founded on concepts of "fairness" and "fair dealing" and argue that equity ("Justice") prevents an agency from claiming a legal right in an action arising from the agency's inequitable (unjust) behavior. Equitable defenses are factually dependent.[49]

1. Application of Equitable Defenses to Agency Proceedings. An adjudication involving an equitable defense claim against an agency begins with consideration of a preliminary question: In what capacity was the agency acting? As a sovereign or as a proprietor? Subsequent determinant issues are: Is there an essential public policy involved in the action? If so, does a public interest affect a private right?

2. Agency Function – Governmental or Proprietary. The distinction between governmental and proprietary functions of an agency impacts the applicability of an equitable defense claim in quasi-judicial administrative proceedings.

A. Agency Performing Governmental Function. The state performs as a sovereign when it regulates (not privately participates in) life.

(1). The state performs governmental functions for the public

---

[49] Other equitable doctrines offering equitable relief are equitable adoption, equitable conversion, equitable lien, equitable recoupment, equitable servitude, equity financing, equity in property, and equity of redemption.

benefit and welfare or engages in activities mandated by the legislature or by societal conditions. Providing public advice on health and hygiene issues to citizens is a governmental activity. *Pelaez v Seide*, 2 NY3d 186, 778 NYS2d 111 (2004).

(2). Governmental functions are those "undertaken for the protection and safety of the public under the general police powers" such as crime prevention and traffic regulation. *Balsam v Delma Engineering Corp*, 90 NY2d 966, 665 NYS2d 613 (1997).

(3). Generally, an equitable defense is not available against a governmental agency engaging in the exercise of its governmental functions. (*Daleview Nursing Home v Axelrod*, 62 NY2d 30 [1984]). "We have held many times that estoppel is not available against a governmental agency in the exercise of its governmental functions (citations omitted). And, as was made clear . . . exception as has been made to that rule is of 'very limited application' and . . . unusual factual situation.' " *Id.*

(4). Equity defenses have been applied against state agencies acting in governmental capacities in cases involving due process issues. *Bender v New York City Health and Hospitals Corp.*, 38 NY2d 662, 668 (1976).

B. Agency Performing Proprietary Function. The state operates as a proprietor in fact or in form when the state participates in (not regulates) life. When acting in a proprietary role, government possesses the same rights and is subject to the same liabilities as those of a private citizen.

(1). The state operates proprietarily in fact when offering the same services (in direct competition with) as those provided by the private sector and when participating in activities that are permissive (acting as an employer, landlord, or vendor). *Cf Miller v State of New York*, 62 NY2d 506 (1984). Also see *Lee v*

State of New York, #2001-018-105, Claim No. 100254, Fitzpatrick, D, September 28, 2001.

(2). Governmental, proprietary in-form tasks include upkeep of government-owned buildings and properties, the removal of snow from government building entrances, providing medical and psychiatric care, the operation of compost facilities, landfills, and public parks, and the operation and management of a police training school. *Metz v State of New York,* 27 Misc3d 1209 (A), 2010 NY Slip Op 50635(U), (Ct Cl 2010), *mod in part and affd in part* 86 AD3d 748 (2011), *revd on other grds* 20 NY3d 175 (2012).

3. Agency Actions Implicating Public Policies. The fundamental component of a public policy is the common public welfare. A public policy states a principle that motivates law.

A. The state holds all public interests in trust for the people, for the collective public good. New York epitomizes the State's public policies in state laws, for example, legislation to protect the environment, to guard the elderly and children against abuse, and for open government.

(1). Executive Law § 20 outlines the policy of the state to guide government actions in events of natural and human-made disasters.

(2). Executive Law § 403, New York State Office of General Services Flag Policy, sets forth the rules for the display and use of the American flag on and in public buildings within the state.

B. When the state counterbalances a private interest against a public interest in litigation, the public interest is paramount as a matter of public policy. A private interest is unenforceable if enforcement would defeat an existing public policy or a principal public interest. An equitable defense is unavailing where it would contravene an essential public policy; private rights defer to public needs.

C. If an agency's action involves a public interest, a public official does not have the power or the authority to waive an enforcement of a law to sustain the action. *Eich v Shaffer*, 136 AD2d 973, 523 NYS2d 902 (2nd Dept 1988). The neglect of duty by a government official does not prevent government from subsequently enforcing a public right or a public interest. An equitable defense cannot be used to enable a public officer to do unlawfully by indirect means that which could not be done lawfully by direct methods.

§ 13.9. Categories of Equitable Defenses. Equitable defenses include equitable estoppel, laches, waiver, res judicata (with merger and bar), and collateral estoppel.

1. Equitable Estoppel. The doctrine of equitable estoppel prevents an agency from acting against a party after the party has acted in reasonable reliance on the agency's misconduct (misrepresentation, wrong information), improper action, or erroneous inaction. The doctrine proclaims that equity bars an agency from taking unconscionable advantage of its wrong that causes injustice to a party who acts in reasonable reliance on the agency's error to the party's detriment. The following six factors must be proved by substantial evidence to support an equitable estoppel claim:

A. The agency erroneously made a statement, took action, or failed to take an action that detrimentally affects interests of a party.

B. The affected party reasonably relied on the agency's error.

(1). Reasonable Reliance. A party's reliance on information provided by an agency is reasonable when (a) the information provided by the agency is in writing; (b) the party receiving the information did not know and should not have known the information was erroneous; and (c) the correct information is not contained in a reasonably accessible statute, rule, or other public material.

(2). Unreasonable Reliance. A person must exercise a reasonable level of care and attention (due diligence) in the operation of a privilege. A prudent person is expected (and there is a duty) to acquire knowledge of law relevant to the regulated activities in which the person is licensed to engage (*NY St. Dept. of St., Div. of Lic. Servs. v Cincotta,* 10 DOS 88 [1988]). As a rule, it is unreasonable for a person to rely on an agency's informal opinion or on information given orally by an agency (*United States Environmental Protection Agency v Environmental Waste Control Inc.*, 917 F2d 327 [7th Cir 1990], *cert denied* 499 US 975). Where a reasonably available statute or regulation discloses correct information regarding a topic, a party should know when an agency gives incorrect information about that topic.

C. A party's reliance on the agency's erroneous information directly caused the party significant harm. Proof consisting only that a party has suffered direct, significant detriment does not invoke equitable estoppel (*Matter of Parkview Associates v New York City*, 71 NY2d 274, 279, 525 NYS2d 176 [1988]). In reliance on a building permit erroneously issued by the New York City Building Department to Parkview, construction of a 31-story building started in an area zoned for a maximum of 19 stories. In response to a stop-work order issued after substantial completion of construction above the 19-story height limitation, Parkview claimed equitable estoppel based, in part, on substantial and irreparable harm. The Court held: "We hold in this case involving the height of a building on Park Avenue in

Manhattan, already constructed in excess of the height limitations of applicable zoning provisions, that estoppel is not available to preclude a governmental entity from discharging its statutory duties or to compel ratification of an erroneous issuance of a building permit."

D. Reasonable reliance on the agency's erroneous information caused the party to be deprived of a benefit to which the party is lawfully entitled (reliance-based deprivation).

(1). If a party claiming equitable estoppel received a benefit to which the party was not legally entitled, the benefit was granted unlawfully and is, therefore, invalid. A building permit issued illegally is invalid when issued and does not and cannot confer rights in violation of law. *Id.*

(2). An administrative act that attempts to confer a benefit contrary to law is an unlawful act conferring nothing. As a matter of law, the doctrine of equitable estoppel cannot be claimed as a defense by a party who receives a benefit unlawfully. Lawful deprivation is a pivotal part of the doctrine of equitable estoppel.

E. The doctrine of equitable estoppel does not contravene any function or policy of an agency.

(1). The doctrine of equitable estoppel does not prevent an agency from discharging its statutory duties. The doctrine of equitable estoppel does not compel government's ratification of an erroneous implementation of a regulation (*NY St. Dept. of Environmental Conservation, Matter of Route 52 Property LLC, Decision of the Chief ALJ*, March 14, 2012 [DEC File No. 3-410713]), and does not prevent the revocation of a license issued in error (*NY St. Dept. of St., Div. of Lic. Servs. v Genovese*, 254 DOS 991 [1999]).

(2). Equitable estoppel principles cannot sanction enactment of unauthorized legislation by an agency. An agency engages in illegal legislation when the agency's misinterpretation of or disregard for a statute or rule results in the agency's committing a legislatively unapproved action. An agency may not act in contravention of law and must correct a known administrative error. *Matter of Parkview Associates v New York City, supra.*

F. Equitable estoppel is vital to a manifest-injustice defense. Manifest injustice denotes that the correction of an error or the enforcement of a rule by an agency would result in an action that is evidently unfair or shocking to the conscience, that significantly harms the integrity of the agency, and that imposes an unconscionable consequence on the benefit recipient.

(1). Before a manifest-injustice issue may be considered judicially as a defense in an action, all factors required to be established to sustain an equitable estoppel claim must have been previously proved by substantial evidence

(2). The following two cases considered an issue of manifest injustice:

(a). *Matter of Quigley*, Tax Appeals Tribunal, DTA No. 825906 (June 19, 2014): "Had there been an allegation and proof that the Division confused or misled petitioners at that time, it may have served to prohibit the Division from denying the timeliness of petitioners' protest (see Matter of Eastern Tier, Tax Appeals Tribunal, December 6, 1990, [where a taxpayer essentially relied on confusing letters from the Division to its detriment, and the Tribunal appropriately applied principles of estoppel to prevent the manifest injustice of denial of its right to a conciliation conference.])." The denial of a fixed procedural requirement is also a denial of a right and implicates a due process issue.

(b). Proof of a recipient's inability to repay erroneously paid social benefits (payments not caused by any willful misrepresentation or other violation on the part of the recipient) does not constitute manifest injustice in New York, as it does in some states. [50] Recoupment of an erroneous payment of public funds is consistent with the strong public policy of New York State to recover public funds improperly received. *Matter of Schwartfigure v Hartnett,* 83 NY2d 296, 610 NYS2d 125 (1994).

2. Laches. The doctrine of laches is an equitable defense constructed of three factors: Inexcusable neglect by a party to pursue a known legal right for an unreasonable lapse of time to the detriment of another party.

A. After a party's Inexcusable unreasonable delay in pursuing a legal right, it is unjust and unfair to permit that party to litigate a claim against another party to whom the delay caused a detrimental or a prejudicial change in circumstances. A party claiming laches must prove the three-factor precept to prevail.

B. SAPA 301 (1) modifies the common law rule of laches. The law directs that in an adjudicatory proceeding, all parties shall be given an opportunity for hearing within a reasonable time. *Cortland Nursing Home v Axelrod,* 66 NY2d 169, 495 NYS2d 927 (1985); *Maxwell v Commissioner of Motor Vehicles,* 109 Misc2d 62, 437 NYS2d 554 (Sup Ct, Erie County 1981).

(1). The reasonable-time requirement of SAPA § 301 (1) is mandatory. *NY St. Dept. of St., Div. of Lic. Servs. v Robin,* 254 DOS

---

[50] Evidence of manifest injustice consists of proof of a party's inability to repay benefits that an agency attempts to recoup in an administrative action in the State of Washington. Washington Administrative Code § 182-526-0495. Equitable Estoppel.

97 (1997).

(2). An opportunity for a hearing has not been offered within a reasonable time if the hearing delay is not caused by the injured party and the hearing delay substantially prejudices or significantly and irreparably impedes the aggrieved party's preparation of a defense. *Gillette v NY St. Liquor Authority*, 149 AD2d 927, 540 NYS2d 61 (4th Dept 1989).

(3). A delay of hearing substantially prejudices a party if the delay results in the unavailability of a witness or document crucial to the defense, or severely compromises the ability of a vital defense witness to present a clear and detailed recollection of material events. *Reid v Axelrod*, 164 AD2d 972, 559 NYS2d 417 (4th Dept 1990); *cf Matter of Bonhomme v NY St. Liquor Authority*, 221 AD2d 882, 634 NYS2d 241 (3rd Dept 1995).

3. Waiver. Waiver is the unambiguous and voluntary relinquishment of a legal right made by a person with full knowledge (or the ability to know) of the right relinquished.

A. Proof of Waiver. Intent is a major element of waiver. Evidence proving waiver must verify an intentional relinquishment or abandonment of a known legal right or privilege by the party (or legal agent) entitled to the right or privilege (*Sillman v Twentieth Century-Fox Film Corp.*, 3 NY2d 395, 165 NYS2d 498 [1957]). Negligence of a party does not constitute a waiver of a legal right or of a privilege (*Alsens American Portland Cement Works v Degnon Contracting Co.*, 222 NY 34 [1917]).

B. Waiver of Sovereign Immunity of Public Entities. New York has waived the general rule that administrative agencies are immune from liability for actions by government.

C. Limitations on Waiver of Immunity. The State conditions its waiver of sovereign immunity on compliance with the statute, Court of Claims Act § 8. *Alston v State of New York*, 97 NY2d 159, 737 NYS2d 45 (2010). [51]

(1). "Despite the waiver of sovereign immunity by section 8 of the Court of Claims Act, which made municipalities answerable equally with individuals and private corporations for the wrongs of its officers and employees (Bernardine v. City of New York, 294 N.Y. 361, 365), the 'rule is that, independent of sovereign immunity, a municipality is not liable for failure to supply general police or fire protection.' " *Bass v City of New York*, 38 A.D.2d 407, 330 NYS2d 569 (1972), affd 32 NY2d 894 (1974). [52]

(2). By the enactment of the Court of Claims Act, § 8, "the Legislature intended to put an end to the immunity of the State which derived from its status as a sovereign. In other words, it was the legislative design that, *in respect of its legal status*, the State be treated like any individual or corporation. This is far different from saying, however, that the Court of Claims Act places the State on a parity with private corporations or individuals *in respect of all of its defenses*. Neither the language of the statute nor its tenor supports such a view." *Weiss v. Fote*,

---

[51] Court of Claims Act § 8. The state waives immunity from liability and action, assumes liability, and consents the same actions in the supreme court against individuals or corporations, provided the claimant complies with the limitations of the act.

[52] Senate Bill S 821 (NY 2011) proposes to waive the state's immunity and makes residential facilities controlled by state agencies subject to local site plan review, requiring every state agency to submit a site plan for each residential parcel under its control.

7 NY2d 579 (1960).

4. Res Judicata. Res judicata ("a matter adjudged") prohibits litigation of any claim previously litigated (or that could have been litigated) in a prior proceeding in which a court of competent jurisdiction rendered a final judgment on the merits (*County of Nassau v Public Emp. Rel. Bd.*, 151 AD2d 168, 547 NYS2d 339 [2nd Dept 1989], *affd* 76 NY2d 579, 561 NYS2d 895 [1990]). Res judicata is an equitable defense plea made to prevent or to stop a legal action.

A. Claim-preclusion Doctrine. The doctrine of res judicata is a claim-preclusion concept consisting of the law of merger and bar. A prior judgment on a claim for a party merges with and bars any new action on the same claim by the same party or by any person in privity with that party.

B. Proof of Claim. A party claiming res judicata in a pending action must prove three prerequisites:

(1). The judgment in the first action was decided on the merits and founded on a resolution of the factual and legal issues of the case, not on a procedural defect in the legal process.

(2). The two proceedings have identical claims, evolve from the same transaction, and allege violations of the same rights.

(3). The two actions involve the same parties or parties in privity.

(a). Res judicata precludes a party to an adjudication and all those in privity with that party from subsequently litigating any issue decided in a previous adjudication. *Matter of NY St. Labor Relations Bd. v Holland Laundry*, 294 NY 480 (1993).

(b). "The term privity does not have a technical and well-defined meaning. It denominates a rule." (*Watts v Swiss Bank Corp.*, 27 NY2d 270 [1970]). The term privity refers to a legal relationship between persons, not the legal rights of individuals. Parties are in privity where the legal right of the parties are identical and represented by all the parties.

(c). Legal associations between persons that evoke privity are fiduciary agency relationships.

(i). A fiduciary is a person obligated to discharge faithfully and carefully all duties of a fiduciary agency (a legal relationship created by law based on the actions of the parties in the relationship, regardless of the intent of the parties).

(ii). Customary fiduciary relationships are employee-employer, attorney-client, partner-partner, guardian-ward, and broker-client interactions.

(iii). Privity exists in a guardian-ward relationship. A guardian acts only as guardian when participating alone in a legal proceeding on behalf of the ward. A guardian serves both as guardian and as an individual representing the same legal interests when participating with a ward in a legal proceeding for the ward; the ward and the guardian are in privity.

C. Res Judicata in Administrative Adjudications. In administrative adjudications, the preclusive effect of res judicata is given only to quasi-judicial, administrative decisions. *Taylor v New York City Transit Auth.*, 309 F Supp 785 (EDNY), *affd* 433 F2d 665 (2nd Cir 1970).

(1). "New York has adopted the transactional identity approach to res judicata, under which a claim that could have been asserted under a given set of facts in a concluded action is barred from being asserted under the same set of facts in a subsequent action." (*Heimbach v Chu*, 744 F2d 11 [2nd Cir 1984], *cert denied* 470 US 1084 [1985]). The transaction analysis principle bars a later claim arising out of the same factual grouping as an earlier litigated claim, even if the latter claim is based on different legal theories or seeks different or additional relief (*Smith v Russell Sage College*, 54 NY2d 185, 445 NYS2d 68 [1981]).

(2). Res judicata does not preclude a subsequent legal claim if, in the prior proceeding, a party was not provided a full and fair opportunity to litigate the issue or claim sought to be precluded, or the previous tribunal lacked the power to grant all the relief requested in the later action. *Davidson v Capuano*, 792 F2d 275 (2nd Cir 1986); *Matter of Bernstein v Dept. of St., Div. of Lic. Servs.*, 14 DOS App 09 (2009).

(3). Res Judicata does not preclude an appeal of an agency's decision (a linear extension of the same lawsuit) and does not collaterally attack the validity of an agency's decision.

5. Collateral Estoppel. Collateral estoppel is a form of res judicata.

A. Issue Preclusion Doctrine. A claim of collateral estoppel is limited to issues in the prior litigation and does not apply to an entire controversy. Material facts or essential questions in an issue previously litigated and determined in a previous proceeding may not again be litigated in a subsequent action. *NY St. Dept. of St., Div. of Lic. Servs. v Bell,* 61 DOS 88 (1988). Collateral estoppel prevents repetitive litigation to preclude inconsistent decisions.

B. Essential Factors of Collateral Estoppel. Three essential factors must be proved to support a collateral estoppel claim:

(1). The issues in the previous and the current action are identical and decisive to a determination in both the previous and the current actions.

(2). The identical issues in both the previous and current actions were fully litigated and decided in both the previous and the current actions.

(3). The defending party in the current action had a full and fair opportunity to litigate the issues and to contest the decision rendered in the prior action. *Ryan v New York Tel. Co.*, 62 NY2d 494, 478 NYS2d 823 (1984).

C. The issue, party and litigation factors of collateral estoppel render the doctrine inapplicable to certain legal proceedings.

(1). Collateral estoppel does not apply to proceedings in which occurred a default, a confession of liability, a stipulation or a failure to place a matter in issue by proper pleading. *Kaufman v Eli Lilly and Co.*, 65 NY2d 449, 492 NYS2d 584 (1985); *NY St. Dept. of St., Div. of Lic. Servs. v Marc K Robin and Quail Run Associates*, 80 DOS 97 (1997).

(2). Collateral estoppel does not apply to proceedings in which the relationship between the party in the prior proceeding and the party in the current proceeding is that of assignor and assignee, and the assignor-assignee relationship occurred before the prior proceeding began. *NY St. Dept. of St., Div. of Lic. Servs. v Bell, supra.*

(3). Collateral estoppel does not prevent an administrative agency from conducting a disciplinary hearing regarding a licensee's conduct although there were prior or there are pending civil or criminal actions based on the same behavior of the licensee. *Id*; *Oleshko v NY St. Liquor Authority*, 29 AD2d 84,

285 NYS2d 696 (1986), *affd* 21 NY2d 778, 288 NYS2d 474.

§ 13.10. Privileges as Defenses. Privileges preserve freedoms in associative human relationships.

1. Privileges. A privilege is a legal right developed from a legally proclaimed relationship and conferred constitutionally or statutorily to persons associated in such a relationship. "Privileges simply do not exist in the absence of either constitutional or statutory authority, or, when created as a matter of jurisprudence (common law)." *Matter of 91st St. Crane Collapse Litig.,* 30 Misc3d 521 (Sup Ct, NY County 2010).[53]

2. Law of Privilege. Privilege is a law granting a benefit (a claim of privilege) and providing a procedure by which the benefit may be declared and decided.

3. Privilege as a Rule of Evidence. As a rule of evidence, a privilege protects a person from compulsory disclosure of confidential information (privileged communication). A privilege permits the holder of the privilege to refuse to disclose legally designated information (confidential information) and bars the subsequent disclosure or the use of illegally obtained confidential information.

A. Confidential information is non-public information that if disclosed could prompt criminal or civil liability, or could damage a person's financial status, employability, privacy, or reputation. Confidential information includes any document, writing, recording, transcript of oral testimony, or electronically stored information that contains privileged or competitively

---

[53] Motions subsequently determined in *Matter of 91st St.:* 2014 NY Slip Opinion 30528(U) (Sup Ct, NY County 2014); 2015 NY Slip Opinion 31458(U) (Sup Ct, NY County 2015).

sensitive information, such an individual's social security number, taxpayer identification number, financial account number, credit card or debit card number, driver's license number, state-issued identification number, passport number, date of birth (other than year), and medical records.

B. A privileged communication is a private exchange of information between persons within a confidential relationship. Protection of certain communications serves the public interest. *Liberman v Gelstein*, 80 NY2d 429, 590 NYS2d 857 (1992).

4. Absolute and Qualified Privileges. A Privilege is termed as an absolute (unconditional) or as a qualified (conditional) privilege. "When compelling public policy requires that the speaker be immune from suit, the law affords an absolute privilege, while statements fostering a lesser public interest are only conditionally privileged." *Id.*

A. Absolute Privileges. An absolute privilege entirely shields a person from legal liability either for refusing to disclose information obtained during a legally-designated confidential relationship or for making an immunized statement, regardless of the speaker's or writer's motive. *Park Knoll Assocs. v Schmidt*, 59 NY2d 205, 464 NYS2d 424 (1983).

(1). Absolute privileges develop from public policies. It is in the public interests to have people cooperate and participate in the administrative enforcement and adjudicatory processes of executive agencies. Statements made by parties, attorneys, and witnesses during a quasi-judicial hearing are absolutely privileged if the statements are material and pertinent to a decisive issue in the proceeding. *Rosenberg v Metlife Inc.*, 8 NY3d 359, 834 NYS2d 494 n1 (2nd Cir 2007).

(2). Absolute privilege defenses extend to preliminary and

investigative stages of an administrative process, "especially when compelling public interests are at stake." *Id.*

B. Qualified Privileges. A qualified privilege excludes acts and communications committed without malice (a knowing or reckless disregard of a statement's falsity) in specified relationships from legal liability (*Liberman v Gelstein, supra*). A qualified privilege defends privileged information given by a person to another person regarding a matter in which both persons have a common interest. The person making the statement has a legal, moral, or social duty to make it, and the recipient has a corresponding interest in receiving the information (such as credit reports of potential employees or borrowers to potential employers or lenders).

§ 13.11. Constitutional Privileges. The federal and the New York State constitutions confer a constitutional privilege against self-incrimination. US Const Amend V provides that a person shall not be compelled in any criminal case to be a witness against himself. NY Const art 1, § 6 prescribes that a person shall not be compelled in any criminal case to be a witness against himself or herself. New York State statutorily extends the privilege against self-incrimination. "Self-incrimination. This section does not require a witness to give an answer which will tend to accuse himself of a crime or to expose him to a penalty or forfeiture, nor does it vary any other rule respecting the examination of a witness." CPLR 4501.

1. The privilege against self-incrimination protects a person; it does not protect information that may incriminate the person (*Murphy v Waterfront Comm'n. of New York Harbor*, 378 US 52, 84 S Ct 1594 [1964]). The constitutional privilege against self-incrimination prohibits the government both from using compulsion to obtain self-incriminating information and from the subsequent use of illegally, obtained incriminating

information. A claim of privilege is made in response to specific questions.

2. The privilege against compulsory self-incrimination restricts the power of government to compel testimony in administrative proceedings. The privilege protects against mandatory disclosure of information by a person who reasonably believes that the information demanded would be incriminatory (*Kastigar v United States,* 406 US 441, 92 S Ct 1653 [1972]; *Ronson v Commissioner of Corrections,* 551 F Supp 450 [SDNY 1982]). The constitutional privilege protects individuals from criminal liability, not civil liability. *In re Vitamins Antitrust Litig.,* 120 F Supp 2d 58 (DDC 2000).

3. A corporation (a collective entity) cannot assert the privilege against self-incrimination. The privilege against self-incrimination does not shield corporate records in a corporate officer's custody from disclosure. *Wilson v United States,* 221 US 361, 31 S Ct 538 (1911).

A. The collective entry doctrine applies to corporations and other business entities created by law. "[R]epresentatives of a collective entity act as agents, and the official records of the organization that are held by them in a representative, rather than a personal, capacity cannot be the subject of their personal privilege against self-incrimination, even though production of the papers might tend to incriminate them personally." *Id.*

B. The corporate entity doctrine controls regardless of whether the subpoena is addressed to the corporation or to an individual as the custodian of corporate records. "Any claim of Fifth Amendment privilege asserted by the agent would be tantamount to a claim of privilege by the corporation, which possesses no such privilege." *Braswell v United States,* 487 US 99, 108 S Ct 2284 (1988).

C. A corporate officer or director as an individual may invoke the privilege against self-incrimination if a discovery demand for corporate information compels an officer or director to make self-incriminating statements. *Id.*

D. The privilege forbidding compelled self-incrimination protects the business records of a sole proprietorship. The owner of a sole proprietorship acts in a personal rather than a representative capacity. A sole proprietorship is not a legal entity separate and distinct from the person conducting business as a sole proprietor. A person doing business as a sole proprietor may claim the privilege to challenge the producing of subpoenaed documents. The reason: The act of providing the subpoenaed records would have "communicative aspects of its own." Submission of subpoenaed materials would result in testimonial self-incrimination as to admissions that the records exist, are in the proprietor's possession, and are authentic. *United States v Doe*, 465 US 605, 104 S Ct 1237 (1984); *Braswell v United States, supra*.

4. In *Lefkovitz v Cunningham*, 431 US 801, 97 S Ct 2132 (1997), the US Supreme Court considered a Fifth Amendment challenge to a subpoena issued under New York Election Law § 22. The statute provided: If an officer of a political party refused to answer any question or declined to waive immunity from the use of his testimony against him in a later prosecution, his political party office would immediately terminate, and he would be banned for five years from holding any other political party or public office. Cunningham moved to quash the subpoena claiming that the statute violated his federal constitutional right to be free of compelled self-incrimination. The New York courts denied his motion (*In re Cunningham v Nadjari*, 51 AD2d 927, 383 NYS2d 311, *affd* 39 NY2d 314 [1976]). The US Supreme Court overruled New York and held that the state's enforcement of Election Law § 22 violated the

right against compulsory self-incrimination granted under the Fifth and Fourteenth Amendments to the US Constitution.[54]

§ 13.12. New York Statutory and Common Law Privileges. Statutory and common law privileges develop from and protect societal relationships. Societal relationships protected by privilege include:

1. Attorney-Client Privilege. CPLR 4503 (a) (1) codifies the attorney-client privilege. The attorney-client privilege (a deliberate process privilege) is the oldest of common law evidentiary privileges and applies to the relationship between an attorney and a client.[55] The attorney-client privilege covers communications between an attorney and a client seeking legal advice. Included in the provisions of the privilege are an attorney's employees; professional service corporations that practice law; state, municipal or local governmental agencies; and the legislature or any of its committees or entities.

A. The attorney-client privilege protects the client, and only the client may waive the privilege. Without a client's waiver of the privilege, law prohibits the disclosure of information obtained in a confidential communication between attorney and client during the professional employment of the attorney.

B. The attorney-client privilege is lost if a person entitled to the privilege discloses the privileged information to a third party. Exceptions: Information may be disclosed to third parties under the circumstances of consultation, the common interest

---

[54] See Executive Law § 438 that imposes sanctions for the assertion of privilege against self-incrimination during any hearing, investigation or review authorized by that law.

[55] Chapter XIII § 13.10.5. Deliberative Process Privilege.

doctrine consisting of joint defense and joint client criteria, and the common interest privilege.

C. The attorney-client privilege does not protect the causal facts in the communications between an attorney and a client.

D. A corporation may claim the attorney-client privilege. *Hertzog Calamari & Gleason v Prudential Ins. Co. of America*, 850 F Supp 255 (SDNY 1994).

E. The attorney-client privilege does not protect a client's confidential communication of intent to commit a crime. NY Ct Rules § 1200.19; *People v DePallo*, 96 NY2d 437, 729 NYS2d 649 (2001).

F. The attorney-client privilege applies to data storage of a client's confidential information.

(1). An attorney's storage of a client's confidential information in online storage systems must be reasonably protected from imprudent disclosure.

(2). The New York State Bar Association Committee on Professional Ethics issued *Opinion 842*, September 2010: "A lawyer may use an online data storage system to store and back up client confidential information . . . ." A lawyer must take reasonable care to ensure the confidentiality of client's information and must monitor the law of privilege to ensure that information stored online will not cause the loss or waiver of a client's privilege.

2. Attorney's Work Product Privilege. The work product privilege protects tangible and intangible materials prepared to aid in an anticipated or a pending legal action. Public Officers Law § 96 (2) (d) governs the disclosure of an "attorney's work

product or material prepared for litigation before judicial, quasi-judicial or administrative tribunals."

A. Tangible Work Products. A tangible work product is a physical object, a document, memorandum, record or witness's statement prepared by or for a party or a party's representative to aid in an anticipated or a pending legal action. Ordinarily, a qualified privilege protects a tangible work product from compulsory discovery. A tangible work product is discoverable if the demanding party demonstrates a substantial need for the materials to prepare its case and is unable to obtain the substantial equivalent of the materials by other means without undue hardship.

B. Intangible Work Products. Intangible work product materials express mental impressions, conclusions, opinions, and evaluations of the strengths and weaknesses of the case or legal theories of an attorney or another representative of a party concerning anticipated or existing litigation. Intangible work products have absolute protection from compulsory disclosure. CPLR 3101 (c); *Delta Financial Corporation v Morrison*, 13 Misc 3d 604, 819 NYS2d 908 (2006).

C. Third Party Consultations. Attorney work-product privilege protects experts and consultants retained to assist in or to attain common litigation objectives in a legal action. *Tilberg v Next Management Co.*, 2005 WL 2759860 (SDNY 2005).[56]

(1). The work-product doctrine shields from compulsory discovery confidential communications between an attorney

---

[56] Expert witness. A person qualified by education or experience as an authority in a specific field, an expert witness, expresses an oral or written opinion about an issue of evidence or of fact in the field of the person's expertise.

and a consultant or an expert if the purpose and intent of the communications are to assist the attorney in preparing materials in anticipation of pending or of existing litigation. D*elta Financial Corporation v Morrison, supra.*

(2). In *United States v Aldman*, 134 F3d 1194, 852 F Supp 156 (2nd Cir 1998), the court expanded the work-product protection to safeguard documents created in anticipation of litigation but primarily produced to assist in making a business decision. Aldman contemplated a merger of two wholly-owned subsidiaries that would cause a millions-of-dollars business loss and a tax refund of millions of dollars. Aldman assumed that the Internal Revenue Service was sure to challenge the tax treatment of the merger. In anticipation of the IRS action and to evaluate the risks of the merger, the company hired a lawyer-accountant as a consultant. The company questioned whether in the event of litigation by IRS, would the company have to disclose the consultant's report and expose publicly information that could give competitors a significant marketing advantage. The Court of Appeals held that the work-product protection included the consultant's report; it was prepared to assist in making a business decision that was expected to result in litigation.

3. Clergy-Congregant Privilege. CPLR 4505 created and conferred the confidential communication privilege to the clergy: "Unless the person confessing or confiding waives the privilege, a clergyman, or other minister of any religion or duly accredited Christian Science practitioner, shall not be allowed (to) disclose a confession or confidence made to him in his professional character as spiritual advisor."

4. Common Interest Doctrine. Judicially derived, the common interest doctrine aligns the joint-defense principle with the joint-client criterion. The common interest doctrine is a

doctrine of non-waiver; it permits parties with identical legal interest to share privileged information without waiving the attorney-client privilege. The common interest doctrine extends the protection of the attorney-client privilege by providing an exception to the general rule that a client waives the attorney-client privilege by communicating privileged information to a third party. The common-interest doctrine is not a privilege; it is distinguishable from the common interest privilege. The doctrine does not defend a document or information from compulsory disclosure unless both the document and the information are otherwise legally protected.

A. The rationale for the common interest doctrine is the encouragement and the protection of joint legal efforts of and the exchange of confidential information among parties with identical or common legal interests. [57]

B. The common interest doctrine offers protection in joint legal efforts in which: (1) there is an exchange of confidential information between parties who have a common legal cause or identical legal interest; (2) the purpose and intent of the communications between the parties are to collaborate in a pending or reasonably anticipated litigation; (3) the mutual exchange of information must relate to the pending or reasonably anticipated legal action; and (4) no party to the exchange of confidential information in the joint legal effort has waived the attorney-client privilege. [58]

C. A written agreement between the parties that records the joint legal effort and nonwaiver of the attorney-client privilege

---

[57] See Schaffzin, Katharine Traylor, *An Uncertain Privilege: Why the Common Interest Doctrine Does Not Work and How Uniformity Can Fix It*, Public Interest Journal, 15.1 (2005), 49-90.
[58] Chapter XIII § 13.11.4. Common Interest Privilege.

strongly supports the claim of an exchange of confidential information in a common interest endeavor. *Cf. Ambac Assurance Corp. v Countrywide Home Loans, Inc.*, (Ambac III), N0. 80, slip opinion at 2 NY June 9, 2016).

5. Common Interest Privilege. The common interest privilege is a common law qualified privilege. "A communication made by one person to another upon a subject in which both have an interest is protected by a qualified privilege." *Stillman v Ford*, 22 NY2d 48 (1968).

A. The New York City Bar recommended that CPLR be amended "to expressly incorporate the common interest privilege." New York City Bar, Committee Report, Association of the Bar of the City of New York Council on Judicial Administration, January 28, 1998, *Recommendation that State Civil Courts Adopt the Common Interest Privilege.*

B. The common interest privilege is diverse and distinguishable from the common interest doctrine. The privilege absolves a person from legal liability for making statements (in good faith and without malice) that otherwise could be defamatory. An example, information about an employee's or former employee's work, honesty, efficiency, character, and qualifications given by an employer to any person who has a legitimate interest in the subject matter of the communication, such as a prospective employer. *Loughry v Lincoln Bank*, 67 NY2d 369, 502 NYS2d 965 (1986).

C. "This 'common interest' privilege has been applied . . . to employees of an organization, members of a faculty tenure committee and constituent physicians of a health insurance plan (citations omitted). The rationale for applying the privilege in these circumstances is that so long as the privilege is not abused, the flow of information between persons sharing a common interest should not be impeded." *Liberman v Gelstein*, 80 NY2d 429, 590 NYS2d 857 (1992).

6. Deliberative Process Privilege. The deliberative process privilege originated in common law as a qualified privilege. The deliberative process privilege protects a governmental entity's internal decision-making processes.

A. Purposes of Deliberative Process Privilege. "The privilege has a number of purposes: it serves to assure that subordinates within an agency will feel free to provide the decisionmaker with their uninhibited opinions and recommendations without fear of later being subject to public ridicule or criticism; to protect against premature disclosure of proposed policies before they have been finally formulated or adopted; and to protect against confusing the issues and misleading the public by dissemination of documents suggesting reasons and rationales for a course of action which were not in fact the ultimate reasons for the agency's action." *Coastal States Gas Corp. v Dept. of Energy*, 617 F2d 854 (DC Cir 1980).

B. Scope of Privilege. The deliberative process privilege defends confidential communications of pre-decisional and deliberative information between public officers of the executive branch of government in the performance of official duties. *Matter of Miller v NY St. Dept. of Transp.*, 58 AD3d 981 (2009), *lv denied* 12 NY3d 712 (2009).

(1). The deliberative process privilege applies only to communications that convey information that is concurrently pre-decisional and deliberative. Pre-decisional communications occur before an agency decides the matter deliberated. Deliberative communications are advisory and counseling exchanges that assist an agency's decisionmaker in forming a decision. Deliberative materials in administrative activities, such as advice, recommendations, and opinions, are protected from disclosure by the deliberative process privilege.

(2). New York embodied a deliberative process privilege into provisions of FOIL. An agency's interagency or intra-agency communications are part of the deliberative process of government. "the term 'inter-agency materials' is not defined under the FOIL . . . New York's courts have construed this term to mean 'deliberative material,' i.e., communications exchanged for discussion purposes not . . . final policy decisions." *Russo v Nassau Community College*, 81 NY2d 690, 623 NYS2d 15 (1993).

(3). The deliberative process privilege does not apply to the following -agency communications:(a) Statistical or factual tabulations or data; (b) instructions to staff that affect the public; (c) final agency policy or determinations; and (d) external audits by the state comptroller or by the federal government. Public Officers Law § 87 (2) (g).

(4). The deliberative process privilege is not applicable in actions that challenge an agency's decision-making process. A challenge of an agency's decision directly attacks the agency's decision-making process.

7. Eavesdropping Evidence. CPLR 4506 (1) prohibits any state legislative committee, department, officer, agency, regulatory body, or other authority of the state from receiving in evidence in any proceeding the contents of any overheard or recorded communication, conversation or discussion, or evidence therefrom derived, obtained by conduct constituting the crime of eavesdropping (as defined in Penal Law § 250.05).

8. Fair Report Privilege. The fair report privilege is conditional.

A. The fair report privilege protects one from liability for the publication of information if the publication meets two conditions.

(1). The source of the published information is publicly available government records, official government reports, or statements by government officials on matters of legitimate public concern. Whether a public document or statement implicates a matter of legitimate public concern is determined by examination of the context of the document or statement as a whole, and "not as disembodied words, phrases, or sentences." *Huggins v Moore*, 94 NY2d 296, 704 NYS2d 904 (1999).

(2). The question of what is a fair and accurate interpretation of the source of information in a legal context is an issue separate from the content of the information. If the publication fairly and accurately interprets the source, the fair report privilege prevails whether the published information is true or untrue or was made in bad faith and with actual malice.

B. New York codified the fair report privilege in Civil Rights Law § 74: "A civil action cannot be maintained against any person, firm or corporation, for the publication of a fair and true report of any judicial proceeding, legislative proceeding or other official proceeding, or for any heading of the report which is a fair and true headnote of the statement published."

9. Journalists Privilege. Federal and New York constitutions and a New York State statute express rights of freedom of speech and press.

A. Constitutional Provisions. US Const Amend I and NY Const art I, § 8 declare the liberty of speech and of press.

(1). US Const Amend I: "Congress shall make no law respecting an establishment of religion, or prohibiting the free exercise thereof; or abridging the freedom of speech, or of the press . . . ."

(2). NY Const art I, § 8: "Every citizen may freely speak, write and publish his or her sentiments on all subjects, being responsible for the abuse of that right; and no law shall be passed to restrain or abridge the liberty of speech or of the press." Computer code and programs are "speech" and afforded constitutional protection. *University City Studios v Corley*, 273 F3d 489 (2nd Cir 1984).

(a). The New York Court of Appeals held in *O'Neill v Oakgrove Constr.*, 71 NY2d 521, 528 NYS2d 1 (1988), that freedom-of-press provisions in both the federal and the state constitutions, "provide a reporter's privilege which extends to confidential and nonconfidential materials and which, albeit qualified, is triggered where the material sought for disclosure . . . was prepared or collected in newsgathering."

(b). New York courts recognize a reporter's qualified privilege under the First Amendment guarantee of free press and speech (*United States v Burke*, 700 F2d 70, 77 [2d Cir 1983], *cert denied* 464 US 816, 104 S Ct 72 [1983]). The decision in *Branzburg v Hayes*, 408 US 665, 92 S Ct 2646 (1972), restricting the journalists privilege under the First Amendment in federal courts, does not apply to New York State civil actions or administrative proceedings.

B. Statutory Law. Civil Rights Law § 79-h, (the Press Shield Law) grants to professional journalists and newscasters an absolute privilege that safeguards against compulsory disclosure both identities of confidential press sources and of confidential information. Civil Rights Law § 79-h (b).

(1). The statute also grants a qualified privilege to journalists and newscasters to protect against the compulsory disclosure of non-confidential information. The qualified privilege covers a refusal or a failure to disclose any unpublished news obtained or prepared by a journalist or newscaster during gathering or collecting news where such news was not obtained or received in confidence. To compel disclosure of such information, a qualified privilege notwithstanding, a party must show that the information sought is highly material, is critical to the party's claim, and is not otherwise available to the party. Civil Rights Law 79-h (c).

(2). Civil Rights Law § 79-h (d) prescribes that any evidence obtained in violation of the Press Shield Law is inadmissible in any action or proceeding before any agency.

10. Marital Privilege. Confidential communications between husband and wife during the marriage are privileged. "A husband or wife is not required, or, without consent of the other if living, allowed, to disclose a confidential communication made by one to the other during marriage." (CPLR 4502 [b]). A rush to the altar by parties after engaging in premarital exchanges of private information does not bestow marriage confidentiality on premarital communication.

11. Medical Privilege: Physician, Dentist, Podiatrist, Chiropractor, and Nurse. Not a privilege at common law, CPLR 4504 (a) established the medical privilege. The statute covers the persons and entities engaged in the professions of medicine, nursing, licensed practical nursing, dentistry, podiatry, and chiropractic. The privilege forbids disclosure of any information acquired in the rendering of professional services to a patient in a professional capacity by any person or entity practicing any of the specified professions. A patient may waive the privilege.

12. Parent-Child Privilege. New York courts recognize a parent-child privilege.

A. A parent-child testimonial privilege is founded on constitutionally protected family interests (familial privacy). The privilege bars mandatory disclosure of confidential communications between parent and child, regardless of the age of either (*In re A and M*, 61 AD2d 426, 403 NYS2d 375 [4th Dept 1978]). A parent-child privilege does not protect the "darnest things" that a child might say publically.

B. Usually, disclosure of confidential communications between parent and child requires the joint consent of both (*People v Fitzgerald,* 101 Misc2d 712, 422 NYS2d 309 [Westchester County Ct. 1979]). Antithetically, a parent, seeking a court's aid in the welfare of a child, may waive the parent-child privilege. A child's right to privacy yields to a child's welfare (*In re A and M, supra*).

13. Psychologist-Patient Privilege. Communications between a New York registered psychologist and a patient are confidential, "placed on the same basis as those . . . between attorney and client" and protected against coerced disclosure. CPLR 4507.

14. Quasi-judicial Proceedings. In quasi-judicial proceedings, statements made by parties, attorneys, and witnesses are protected by an absolute privilege, regardless of the motive for making the statements if the statements made are material and pertinent to issues to be resolved in the proceeding. *Cattani v Marfuggi*, 74 AD3d 553 (1st Dept 2010); *Weiner v Weintraub*, 22 NY2d 330 (1968).

A. Statements made in complaints against attorneys filed with a Grievance Committee of a bar association are given absolute immunity. In the investigation of complaints and the conduct of proceedings, a bar association's Grievance Committee acts as a quasi-judicial body. To maintain "the high standards" of the bar and for compelling and vigorous public policy reasons, "all papers * * * upon any complaint, inquiry, investigation or proceeding relating to the conduct or discipline of an attorney * * * shall * * * be deemed private and confidential." *Weiner v Weintraub, supra.*

B. An absolute privilege protects quasi-judicial preliminary and investigative proceedings where compelling public interests are consequential (*Rosenberg v Metlife, Inc,* 8 NY3d 359 (2d Cir 2007).[59] Rosenberg filed a libel claim based on unfavorable statements made by Metlife on a Form U-5, a uniform termination notice of the Securities Industry Registration required by law to be filed with the (then known) National Association of Securities Dealers, NASD (currently, the Financial Industry Regulatory Authority, Inc. [FINRA]). Because of the compulsory nature of the Form U-5 and its role as a preliminary step in NASD's quasi-judicial, regulatory process, the Court of Appeals held that a compelling public policy required that the law bestow an absolute privilege to statements made on the form to assure accurate and forthright responses. In quasi-judicial proceedings, absolute immunity applies to statements material and pertinent to the resolution of determinant questions.

16. Rape Crisis Counselor Privilege. Communications between a client and a rape crisis counselor and any records made or advice given during rape-counseling services are confidential and "shall not" be required to be disclosed. CPLR 4510 (b).

---

[59] Case citations: *Rosenberg v MetLife, Inc.,* 2005 WL 356821, 2005 US Dist LEXIS 2135 (SDNY 2005); *Rosenberg v MetLife, Inc.,* 453 F3d 122 (2nd Cir 2006, certified question); *Rosenberg v Metlife, Inc., et al.,* 8 NY3d 359 (2007, certified question answered); *Rosenberg v MetLife,* 2005 WL 356821, 2005 US Dist LEXIS 2135 (SDNY 2005), *affd* 493 F3d 290 (2007).

17. Social Worker Privilege. A social worker shall not be required to disclose communications held between a client and the social worker during the professional employment. The law prohibits any person working either for the employer of the social worker or for the social worker from disclosing any such communications. CPLR 4508 (a).

18. Trade Secret, Confidential Research, Development or Commercial Information. Common law provisions protect trade secrets in New York. A trade secret is "information, including a formula, pattern, compilation, program, device, method, technique, or process, that derives independent economic value, actual or potential, from not being generally known to or readily ascertainable by appropriate means by other persons who might obtain economic value from its disclosure or use; and is the subject of efforts that are reasonable under the circumstances to maintain its secrecy." (United Trade Secret Act [UTSA]). Trade secret protection exists for as long as the confidentiality of the trade secret is maintained. (*Ashland Management Inc. v Janien,* 82 NY2d 395, 604 NYS2d 912 [1993]). New York has not adopted UTSA.

19. Records Containing Confidential Information. Agencies may delete from any index, decision, determination or order any information that, if disclosed, would constitute an unwarranted invasion of personal privacy. Public Officers Law § 89 (2).

A. At the request of any person, an agency may delete all references to trade secrets that, if disclosed, would cause substantial injury to the competitive position of that person. An agency must delete from any index, decision, determination or order information that would reveal confidential material protected by state or federal statute. SAPA 307 (3) (b).

B. Agencies may deny access to records or portions of records:

(1) Specifically exempted from disclosure by state or federal statute; (2) if disclosed would constitute an invasion of personal privacy under provisions of Public Officers Law § 89; and (3) trade secrets submitted to an agency by a commercial enterprise or derived from information obtained from a commercial enterprise and which if disclosed would cause substantial injury to the competitive position of the enterprise. Public Officers Law § 87.

20. Office of the Airline Consumer Advocate protects confidential information.

A. The Office considers confidential (1) any records, documents, papers, maps, books, tapes, photographs, files, sound recordings or other business material, regardless of form or characteristics, obtained under subpoena by an agency; and (2) any matter determined by the agency, the attorney general, or by a federal or state judicial or administrative body, to be a trade secret or proprietary, confidential business information held at the conclusion of an investigation by either the Office or the attorney general.

B. The agency may use confidential materials in any administrative or judicial proceeding in which the confidentiality and proprietary nature of the materials are maintained. General Business Law § 251-h.

21. Electronic Communications Privacy. The Electronic Communications Privacy Act of 1986 (ECPA), protects wire, oral, and electronic communications when being made, are in transit or stored on computers. The Act applies to email, telephone conversations, and data stored electronically. 18 USC §§ 2510-2522.

22. The Stored Communications Act (SCA). Title II of the ECPA

(18 USC §§ 2701-2712), protects the privacy of the contents of files and records (including a subscriber's name, billing records, and IP addresses) stored by service providers.

A. SCA imposes limitations on discovery proceedings. SCA prohibits a provider of an electronic communication service from knowingly divulging the contents of any communication while in electronic storage by that service to any person other than the addressee or intended recipient. An e-mail message is in "electronic storage" as defined by SCA, before and after the recipient downloads a message.

B. *Theofel v Farey Jones*, 359 F3d 1066 (9th Cir 2004), involved a motion to quash a subpoena for reasons of a violation of SCA. The Court granted the motion and explained: "We interpret federal statutes in light of the common law. *See Beck v Prupis,* 529 U.S. 494, 500-01, 120 S. Ct. 1608, 146 L. Ed.2d 561 (2000). Particularly relevant here is the common law of trespass. Like the tort of trespass, the Stored Communications Act protects individuals' privacy and proprietary interests. The Act reflects Congress's judgment that users have a legitimate interest in the confidentiality of communications in electronic storage at a communications facility. Just as trespass protects those who rent space from a commercial storage facility to hold sensitive documents. . . the Act protects users whose electronic communications are in electronic storage with an ISP or other electronic communications facility."

23. Settlement Offers and Discussions. "As a general rule, offers to compromise are inadmissible at trial (CPLR 4547)." *Soumayah v Minnelli*, 41 AD3d 390, 839 NYS2d 79 (2007).

A. CPLR 4547 codifies and expands the common law rule. The settlement of a disputed claim or an offer to settle a claim is inadmissible in evidence as proof of liability, the amount of damages, or the invalidity of the claim. Evidence of any conduct committed or statements made during compromise negotiations is inadmissible in an ensuing action.

B. CPLR 4547 does not render settlement discussions confidential and does not apply to communications or statements made outside the circumstances of the negotiation of a settlement of a disputed claim. *Alternatives Fed. Credit Union v Olbois LLC*, 14 AD3d 779 (3d Dept 2005).

C. An agency may isolate settlement processes from other agency proceedings. The Division of Human Rights directs, "All materials relating solely to conciliation or settlement discussion shall be placed in a separate folder and shall not form part of the formal evidentiary record. All settlement discussions shall be held in camera." 9 NYCRR 465.12 (e) (10).

24. Materials Containing Public and Protected Information. A disclosure demand may request documents containing both protected and public information.

A. Where agency rules allow, requested materials may be submitted under seal to the presiding ALJ for an in camera review by the ALJ (and staff as necessary) to decide the claim of documents containing protected or privileged information. An in camera review of materials submitted in response to a disclosure demand may result in a restricted discovery order to preserve a privilege or to protect confidential information.

(1). A limited discovery order may form a redacted document. A copy of the requested document is submitted with protected information stricken and with the words "confidential information deleted" inserted in the spaces where the protected information previously appeared.

(2). A restricted discovery order may limit discovery to precise terms of conditions.

B. By rule, an agency may forbid an in camera review of evidence. 9 NYCRR 465.12 (e) (8) proscribes, "Evidence shall not be received in camera." (Division of Human Rights).

CHAPTER XIV. FINAL QUASI-JUDICIAL DECISIONS.

§ 14.1. Final Decision-making Process. A final decision-maker in an administrative proceeding identifies and defines the issues, ascertains and aligns relevant legal criteria, applies pertinent law to finite facts, and renders a conclusive resolution of material, determinant issues.

§ 14.2. Factors of Final Decisions. A final, quasi-judicial decision is an agency's written, conclusive, and last resolution of the legal rights and duties of parties to an adjudication that is not subject to further agency review.

§ 14.3. Scope of Final Decisions. A final determination of an agency binds only the parties subject to the agency's jurisdiction in the causal action. Nonetheless, the general obligations and conditions proclaimed in an agency's final determination apply to the regulated community.

§ 14.4. Precedent and Stare Decisis Constraints on Final Decisions. The principle of precedent and the doctrine of stare decisis endorse coherency among administrative decisions to maintain stability and to permit predictability in the determination of legal disputes. As with rules of evidence, administrative agencies may reasonably and rationally disregard strict adherence to the views of precedent and stare decisis.

1. Principle of Precedent. A precedent characterizes a decision that interprets a provision of a constitution, of a statute, or of a rule of significant legal value with general application and recurrent in adjudication. A decision made in a precedential case is exemplified as an authority to be considered by tribunals when deciding subsequent adjudication with issues or facts significantly similar to the issues or facts in the precedential decision.

A. The purpose of precedent is uniformity in the interpretation of law by agencies. A function of precedent is predictability. Precedent may be used to predict proximate legal consequences of specific acts. Precedent instructs both the regulators and the regulated. Uniformity in an agency's regulatory enforcement both assists the regulated community in the predictability of an agency's conduct and advances the proficiency of an agency's function.

B. A precedent is either binding or persuasive on subsequent determinations in adjudication.

(1). Binding Precedent. A binding precedent in an administrative jurisdiction may be either a judicial precedent or a quasi-judicial precedent.

(a). Binding Judicial Precedent. An unchallenged decision or order of an appellate court disposing of an article 78 review of an administrative action is a binding judicial precedent applicable to the agency. *General Elec. Capital Corp. v NY St. Div.*

of Tax Appeals, Tax Appeals Trib., 2 NY3d 249 (2004).

(i). A binding judicial precedent may be "agency-specific." The precedent applies to a matter over which one agency has primary jurisdiction. "Judicial precedents addressing the application of administrative law doctrines to a given agency tend to rely most heavily on other cases involving the same agency, and use verbal formulations or doctrinal approaches reflected in those cases. Over time, the doctrine often begins to develop its own unique characteristics when applied to that particular agency." Levy, Richard E. and Glickman, Robert L., *Agency-Specific Precedents*, 89 Texas L. Rev. 499 (July 6, 2010).

(ii). The decision of the Court of Appeals in *Roberts Real Estate, Inc. v Dept. of State*, 80 NY2d 116, 589 NYS2d 392 (1992) is a binding judicial precedent that changed an agency's interpretation of a statute. In a disciplinary action against Roberts, the corporate broker's license was suspended under Real Property Law § 442-c. The ALJ held that under the statute, an employee-salesperson's knowledge of a violation of law could be imputed to the representative broker. The Court construed the statute to provide that a suspension or revocation of the corporate broker's license must be based on a representative broker, director, or officer having actual (not imputed) knowledge of a violation of law attributable to the corporation. Imputed knowledge of a violation of law attributable to a corporate broker could support the imposition of a less severe penalty than that of a suspension or a revocation.

(b). Binding Quasi-Judicial Administrative Precedent. A binding, quasi-judicial, administrative precedent is a final quasi-judicial decision to which mandatory deference is given by subsequent administrative actions deciding issues of law and facts significantly similar to material issues of law and facts determined in the precedential case.

(2). Persuasive Precedent. A persuasive precedent refers to a decision that contains legal reasoning and principles of law that are relatable to and may be used as advisory precedent in determining issues and facts in a pending matter. Persuasive precedent is not binding precedent; the administrative law judge may or may not use a persuasive precedent in deciding a current case. Persuasive precedent may include decisions by judges in tribunals of other agencies, legal views presented in legal articles, law reviews, and other legal treatises, and judicial memorandum decisions.

(3). Public Knowledge of Precedent. Public awareness of a precedent is a prerequisite for the use of a precedent in a determination by an agency.

(a). Before being cited by an agency as a precedent, the agency's final order or decision must be reasonably available for discovery in public material. A probable exception is proof of a party's prior actual or constructive knowledge of the final order or determination cited by the agency, such as the party's participation in the action cited as a precedent.

(b). The prerequisite of public knowledge in the use of precedent precludes an agency from using an obscure order or decision unknown by and realistically not available to a party through a reasonable search for precedential information.

2. Doctrine of Stare Decisis. Precedent, binding or persuasive, forms the basis of the theory of stare decisis. Stare decisis is a concept of judicial procedure, not of a quasi-judicial practice.

A. Stare decisis ("bowing to a higher authority" or "not disturb what is settled") directs that legal decisions should follow prior decisions made in actions containing substantively similar or identical issues of facts.

B The procedure of stare decisis is either vertical or horizontal in application. A decisionmaker either applies or does not apply the process of stare decisis when making a determination.

(1). Vertical Stare Decisis. A decisionmaker in an inferior position or inferior jurisdiction follows the precedential decisions of decisionmakers in superior positions or superior jurisdictions in the same or a related legal structure.

(2). Horizontal Stare Decisis. A decisionmaker respects prior decisions of decisionmakers of equivalent authority in the same or equivalent position or jurisdictions in the same or an equivalent legal structure.

C The rule of stare decisis is not strictly applicable operationally in administrative law procedures. The rule of stare decisis requires a relatively coherent environment of consistent, decisional development and predictability. A restrictive procedural environment could stifle the rapidity of change often needed in and among regulatory activities, and additionally, administrative law judges do not determine the constitutionality of legislation.

D. A functional equivalent of stare decisis in administrative law is the general administrative rule that an administrative agency must follow its quasi-judicial precedent or policy unless there is a justification for a change in a rule or policy. *Matter of Terrace Ct., LLC v NY St. Div. of Hous. & Community Renewal*, 18 NY3d 446 2012 NY Slip Op 01100 (Ct App 2010).

§ 14.5. Management of Precedent and Stare Decisis by Executive Agencies. An executive agency must obey laws and policies legislatively prescribed. However, an executive agency may end the precedential use of a decision because of a change in law or policy or for other lawful reasons.

1. An agency's decision may deviate from precedent. When a deviation occurs, the decision must explain the deviation to enable a reviewing court to "determine whether the agency has changed its prior interpretation of the law for valid reasons, or has simply overlooked or ignored its previous decision." (*Matter of Charles A Field Delivery Serv. [Roberts],* 66 NY2d 516, 498 NYS2d 111 [1985]). Failure to justify a change in a prior interpretation of law requires reversal of a decision, even if supported by substantial evidence. "A decision of an . . . agency which neither adheres to its own precedent nor indicates its reason for reaching a different result on essentially the same facts is arbitrary and capricious." *Id.*

2. An agency may abandon a prior administrative posture considered invalid for a lawful reason. The change in position needs only to be reasonable and rational to be legally justified. "when a rule, after it has been duly tested by experience, has been found to be inconsistent with the sense of justice or with the social welfare, there should be less hesitation in frank avowal and full abandonment." (Cardozo, Benjamin N., *The Nature of the Judicial Process* [New Haven and London: Yale University]). An agency's "hasty abandonment of a precedent without adequate explanation" might lead one to conclude that "the agency's decisions are driven by preference rather than by principle." *Cheshire v C.I.R.*, 115 TC 183 (2000), affd 283 F3rd 326 (5th Cir 2000).

§ 14.6. Policy Effects on Final Decisions. A state agency's quasi-judiciary administrative law unit is a unit of the agency and functions as a subordinate of the agency and of the executive branch of state government.

1. Changes in political, economic, and social demands on a state may cause modifications, revisions, or changes in state rules, statutes, policies, or precedents and affect the regulatory acts of

executive administrative agencies.

2. Orders and decisions of an administrative law tribunal must conform to changes to or modifications of an agency's rules and policies and may not adversely affect or contradict any policy of the executive branch, principle of precedent and doctrine of stare decisis notwithstanding.

§ 14.7. Service of Decisions and Orders. As a rule, service of an agency's decision is made by registered or certified mail within statutory time limitations to all parties and attorneys of record in a proceedings. SAPA 307 (1).

§ 14.8. Reconsideration of Agency Decisions. A quasi-judicial, administrative, law tribunal has inherent authority to reconsider and to alter a prior decision or order rendered by the tribunal. *Evan v Monaghan*, 306 NY 312, 118 NE2d 452 (1954).

1. The rebuttable presumption of validity assigned to final orders of an administrative agency imposes upon a petitioner for reconsideration the burden of proving the agency's decision to be invalid.

A. An application to an agency for reconsideration of a quasi-judicial determination must present meritorious evidence that is material to a principal issue decided in the decision.

B. Arguments supporting motions for reconsideration include:

(1). Excusable default. Incarceration is an excusable default for failure to appear in a legal action. *Brown v City of New York,* 105 AD3d 420 (1st Dept. 2013).

(2). Newly-discovered evidence. Evidence newly discovered (a) was in existence but undiscoverable with due diligence at the time of judgment, (b) was found after judgment, and (c) would probably have produced a different decision if the evidence had been submitted into the record at the hearing.

(3). Fraud or other misconduct of an adverse party.

(4). Lack of jurisdiction of the tribunal to decide the matter.

(5). Reversal, modification or vacatur of a prior decision or order underlying the challenged order or decision. *Entes v NY St. Dept. of St., Div. of Lic. Servs.*, 12 DOS 91 (1991).

(6). Excessive or insufficient penalty. The imposition of sanctions by an agency is a discretionary act; the appropriateness of a penalty by an agency is judicially reviewable as a matter of law. *Matter of Pell v Board of Educ.*, 34 NY2d 222, 356 NYS2d 833 (1974).

(7). In the interest of justice. Equity implores relief in an action that does not meet any statutorily prescribed conditions for relief. *Sullivan County Harness Racing Association Inc. v Glasser*, 30 NY2d 269, 332 NYS2d 622 (1972).

2. A filing of a petition for reconsideration of an agency's decision defers the decision's finality; the decision is not the agency's final action Unless statutorily prescribed, the filing of a petition for the rehearing of an agency's decision is not a prerequisite for judicial review of an administrative determination.

CHAPTER XV. APPELLATE REVIEW OF QUASI-JUDICIAL DETERMINATIONS.

§ 15.1. Review of Agency Determinations. Administrative decisions and orders are reviewable strictly by specific, mandatory, statutory standards. The right to appeal an agency's decision is conferred statutorily; it is not a constitutional or an inherent right. SAPA 301 (3) commands agencies to enact and to adopt procedures for adjudicatory proceedings and the executive review of administrative determinations.

§ 15.2. Stay of Agency Action during Review. The stay of an agency's decisional action during an appellate review is not automatic; a petition for a stay must be filed.

1. A petition for a stay is filed with the reviewing body, administrative tribunal, or court, along with or at the time of the filing of the notice of appeal. CPLR 7805.

2. A reviewing body grants a stay within its discretion and after consideration of four determinant factors:

A. There is a reasonable probability of success on the merits of the appeal.

B. Potential harm to the aggrieved party is significant, such as a suspension or revocation of a license, a permit, or a commission.

C. The stay does not pose a probable danger to the public health, safety or welfare.

D. The stay does not compromise a public policy.

§ 15.3. Executive Review. A superior authority of an agency evaluates the legality of a formal determination rendered by an ALJ or another authorized subordinate in the same agency.

1. Procedures for Executive Review. As the decisional authority of hearing officers differs among agencies, so do the executive review procedures of agencies differ. Three standard methods of executive review used by agencies are the following:

A. An ALJ's determination is a report or recommendation to the agency's executive reviewing authority who issues the agency's decision. [60]

---

[60] Department of Agriculture and Markets, 1 NYCRR 200.5; Alcoholic Beverage Control Law, 9 NYCRR 54.4 (g); Department of Environmental Conservation, 6 NYCRR 622.8; Financial Services Law § 305 (b); Corrections and Community Supervision, 7 NYCRR 252.

B. An ALJ's decision is an agency's final decision unless timely appealed by a party (not a unit of the agency). [61]

C. An ALJ's decision is an agency's final decision unless timely appealed by any party to the adjudication (including a subdivision of the agency). [62]

2. Scope of Executive Review. Laws and rules charge agencies to ensure the accuracy of the finding of facts and the just and correct application of legal concepts in administrative adjudications.

A. Law prohibits an agency from combining the two powers of executive review and rulemaking into one function. An agency cannot implement a new policy or a new procedural rule in an executive review determination.

B. In an executive review of an ALJ's order or decision, the agency is not constrained by the ALJ's findings and conclusions. An agency conducts a de novo (over again as if for the first time) review and makes independent determinations of findings of fact and issues of law.

C. Agencies acknowledge an ALJ's findings regarding a witness's testimony, intelligence, state of mind, and demeanor during an administrative hearing.

---

[61] "Appeals from determinations, rules, or orders of the agency go first to the agency's appeal board and thereafter to the courts . . . . (This) shall be the sole and exclusive procedure notwithstanding any other provision of law." Labor Law § 626; Vehicle and Traffic Law § 242; 15 NYCRR 124; Civil Service Commission § 55.2.

[62] New York State Department of State, 19 NYCRR 400.2.

(1). Agencies usually defer to an ALJ's findings in hearings in which contradictory testimony and the credibility of witnesses are decisive decisional issues.

(2). *NY St. Dept. of St., Div. of Lic. Servs. v Santana*, 23 DOS APP 02 (2002) concerned an ALJ's decision appealed by a division of the agency to the agency head. The Secretary of State held: "The ALJ, in assessing . . . (respondent's) testimony, concluded that he acted in good faith . . . Judge Neals was in the best position to weigh . . . (the) testimony and assess his character."

3. Executive Review Determinations. An executive review concludes in a decision or an order that adopts, affirms, reverses and remands, or modifies an ALJ's determination.

A. An executive review does not order a new hearing.

B. A judicial appeal of an executive review decision depends on the finality of the agency action.

§ 15.4. Judicial Review of Administrative Proceedings. Judicial review is a court's power to evaluate and to judge the legality of an administrative action.

1. Judicial Review Prerequisites. A party seeking an article 78 review must prove four factors: The agency determination is final and appealable; all available administrative remedies have been exhausted; the petitioner has standing to appeal, and an actual controversy is in dispute.

A. Agency's Final Determination. An agency's final determination concludes in an official order (1) that states a definite position on the issue disputed, (2) has legal effect, and (3) is invulnerable to further administrative proceedings.

B. Exhaustion of Administrative Remedies. The exhaustion rule compels a party to exhaust all prescribed, available, administrative review procedures before seeking judicial review of an agency's determination.

(1). Exhaustion of administrative remedies is not required in an appeal: (a) that questions the constitutionality of an agency's enabling law or attacks an agency rule as being unconstitutional on its face; (b) in which a clear jurisdictional defect is apparent in the agency's determination; (c) where remedies accessible do not provide opportunity for acceptable relief; and (d) without immediate judicial relief, a party could suffer irreparable injury (*Renegotiation Bd. v Bannercroft Co.*, 415 US 1, 94 S Ct 1028 [1974]). Also see *Walker v. Southern Ry.*, 385 US 196, 87 S Ct 365 (1966), Justices Harlan, Stewart, and White dissent. The potential or actual disclosure of a trade secret may cause irreparable injury. [63]

(2). Where an exception to the exhaustion rule exists, a party may challenge an administrative determination with a petition for a declaratory judgment before exhausting all available administrative remedies. *Cf Xerox Corp. v Dept of Taxation and Fin.*, 140 AD2d 945 (4th Dept), *lv denied* 72 NY2d 809 (1988).

(3). Failure of an agency to timely assert the exhaustion rule waives it. *Custom Topsoil, Inc. v City of Buffalo*, 12 AD3d 1162, 785 NYS2d 634 (2004).

C. Party has Standing to Appeal. A party's interest in an action determines whether the party has standing to appeal a decision.

(1). Individual as Party. A judicial appeal of an administrative

---

[63] Gabby, Edmond, *All The King's Horses-Irreparable Harm In Trade Secret Litigation*, 54 Fordham Law Review 804 (1984).

determination by a party must establish that the party has suffered or will suffer an injury distinct from an injury to the general public. The injury claimed must be within the interests protected by the statute challenged in the appeal. (*Transactive Corporation v NY St. Dept. of Social Services,* 92 NY2d 579, 684 NYS2d 156 [1998]). To maintain an appeal, an individual must have suffered personal damage or injury to a civil, personal, or property right.

(2). Organization as Party. One or more members of an entity must have standing for an organization to bring a CPLR article 78 proceeding (*Cf Matter of Save the Pine Bush, Inc. v Planning Bd. of Town of Clifton Park,* 50 AD3d 1296 [2008], *lv denied* 10 NY3d 716 [2008]). At least one member of the organization (party) must have suffered or will suffer direct harm or injury "that is in some way different from that of the public at large." *Society of Plastics Indus. v County of Suffolk,* 77 NY2d 761 (1991).

(3). Citizen's Constitutional Suit Provision. NY Const art XIV, § 5 (Conservation) grants to the people, or with the consent of the Appellate Division of Supreme Court and on notice to the attorney general, to any citizen the right to sue for any violation of any provision of the article.

(4). Statutory Restraints of Right to Review. A statute may restrain a party's right to review an agency's action. Correction Law § 806.5 provides: "Any action by the commissioner pursuant to this section shall be deemed a judicial function and shall not be reviewable if done in accordance with law." A judicial review under the statute is conditioned on an initial review of the procedure used by the agency in executing the action is found not to have been performed "in accordance with law."

D. An Actual Controversy at Issue. The appeal involves a legal dispute between parties with adverse legal interests and demands a final resolution, unlike a petition either for an advisory opinion or for a declaratory ruling.

2. Judicial Review Proceeding. Judicial review of an administrative action is commenced by an article 78 special proceeding that codifies the common law writs of certiorari, mandamus, and prohibition. CPLR 7801.

3. Scope of Judicial Review. The scope of review of a CPLR article 78 proceeding in the Supreme Court or the Court of Appeals is limited to issues of questions of law (including the measure of the penalty imposed). The reviewing court scrutinizes the administrative or appellate record and decides relevant issues of law by applying the appropriate standard of review.

A. Judicial Deference to Agency Decisions. Judicial deference to an agency's decision is appropriate when the question on review involves the construction of a statute that requires an understanding of the agency's underlying operational practices or includes an evaluation of factual data. Concomitantly, the question of statutory interpretation is left to the specialized expertise of the agency, and the agency's determination is entitled to deference when it is not irrational or unreasonable. *Matter of Jennings v NY St. Off. of Mental Health,* 90 NY2d 227 (1970), 660 NYS2d 352; *Matter of Guido v NY St. Teachers' Retirement Sys.,* 94 NY2d 64 (1999).

B. Appellant courts defer to an agency's interpretation of its regulations if the agency's interpretation is not irrational. The agency's interpretation of its regulation is not irrational just because the regulation may be susceptible to a rational analysis different than that of the agency. An agency's interpretation of its regulations is controlling and "will not be disturbed in the absence of weighty reasons." *Matter of Elgor Health Services, Inc.*

v Novello, 95 AD2d 772, 744 NYS2d 71(2002).

C. An appellant court will usually not defer to administrative law decisions in matters "of pure statutory interpretation" or where the issue is one "of pure statutory reading and analysis, dependent only on accurate apprehension of legislative intent." *Matter of KSLM-Columbus Apts. Inc. v NY St. Div. of Housing & Community Renewal*, 5 NY3d 303 (2005). [64]

4. Standard of Judicial Review. A standard of review expresses the criteria used by a reviewing court to evaluate the validity of a determination being appealed. The rules governing article 78 proceedings are codified into the following four issues that may be raised in an article 78 appeal (CPLR 7803):

A. Was the determination made after an evidential hearing held according to law and supported by substantial evidence on the entire hearing record?

B. Did the agency fail to perform a duty imposed on the agency by law?

C. Was a decision made in violation of lawful procedure, an error of law, or arbitrary, capricious, or an abuse of discretion, including discretion in the measure or mode of penalty or discipline imposed in the determination?

D. Did the agency proceed, is proceeding, or is about to proceed without or in excess of the agency's jurisdiction?

---

[64] Carlisle, Jay, *Getting a Full Bite of the Apple: When Should the Doctrine of Issue Preclusion Make an Administrative or Arbitral Determination Binding in a Court of Law?* 55 Fordham L. Rev. 63 (1986).

5. Application of Standards of Judicial Review. The category of judicial review, whether certiorari, mandamus, or prohibition, dictates the standard of review applicable in evaluating the validity of an administrative determination (CPLR 7803).

A. Certiorari. Fact and law verify the decision. Certiorari is a substantial-evidence review to determine whether an administrative decision made after an evidential hearing held according to law is supported by substantial evidence on the entire hearing record. CPLR 7803 (4). [65]

B. Mandamus to Compel. Discretion is the antithesis of compulsion. A mandamus proceeding raises a question: Did an agency official fail to perform a ministerial act imposed on the agency by law? Mandamus to compel an official to perform a nondiscretionary duty is appropriate where law commands an administrative agent to perform a ministerial duty. The direction by law or rule to act without judgment or discretion constitutes a "clear legal right" to the relief. *Klostermann v Cuomo*, 61 NY2d 525, 475 NYS2d 247 (1984); *Lauer v City of New York*, 95 NY2d 95, 711 NYS2d 112 (2000).

C. Mandamus to Review. Unreasonable and injurious behavior by an agency is at issue. Was the agency's action arbitrary or capricious or an abuse of discretion? Arbitrary administrative determinations are reversed judicially on the law, "even though there is in the record substantial evidence to support the determination made." *Matter of Charles A. Field Delivery Serv. (Roberts), supra*. Also see *Matter of Lipani v NY St. Div. of Human Rights*, 56 AD3d 560 (2nd Dept 2008).

(1). US Constitutional Restraints. Due process principles apply to agency actions. Did the agency decision violate a US

---

[65] Chapter XIII § 13.2.3. (J). Substantial Evidence.

Constitutional provision? An agency's action performed unreasonably and without regard for extant facts is arbitrary (*Matter of Edwards v Oyster Bay-East Norwich Cent. School Dist*, 2010 NY Slip Op 30922 [U] [Supreme Court, Nassau County April 8, 2010]). An administrative determination that exceeds the agency's statutory authority or violates a provision of the US Constitution or the New York State Constitution is arbitrary and capricious. *Matter of NY City Dept. of Envtl. Protection v NY City Civ. Serv. Commn.*, 78 NY2d 318 (1991); *Matter of NY St. Tenants & Neighbors Coalition, Inc. v Nassau County Rent Guidelines Bd.*, 53 AD3d 550 (2008).

(2). Procedural Obligations. Did the agency comply with all applicable procedural requirements? An agency must reasonably and equitably perform required legal processes. The arbitrary-and-capricious standard is used in contract disciplinary actions (*Matter of Edwards v Oyster Bay-East Norwich Cent. School Dist., supra*). Edwards challenged his discharge by the school district on ground that he was not given a Civil Service Law § 75 disciplinary hearing. The collective bargaining agreement under which Edwards was employed incorporated the "protection of Section 75 of the Civil Service Law." The Court held: "It is well settled that when procedural protections are provided by contract, not law, the standard by which an administrative body's decision must be judged is not the 'substantial evidence' standard...but rather the 'arbitrary and capricious' test governs."

D. Prohibition. An enabling law defines an agency's mission. A proceeding in nature of prohibition questions whether an agency's act exceeded the scope of the agency's organic act. An agency must operate within the constraints of its enabling legislation. A court looks to the legal source of the agency's power and examines the statutory language, structure, purpose, and legislative history of the agency's enabling act to determine if the agency acted without statutory authority.

(1). The substantial-evidence standard requires that there be a rational basis in the record to support the determination, an existent, reasonable correlation between facts and decision.

(2). A finding of fact is an evidentiary determination of the existence or occurrence of a phenomenon; the decision is reached without reference to law, for instance, who, when, how fast, what color, how many, how large, how high, or what work performed.

(3). It is axiomatic. In an administrative action in which applicable law applied to verified facts proves the determination, the decision is supported by substantial evidence.

6. Venue of Review Proceedings. A CPLR article 78 special proceeding is brought by petition in the New York State Supreme Court in an appropriate branch located in one of 62 counties, except where otherwise statutorily provided (CPLR 7804 [a]; CPLR 506). There are exceptions to the general venue specification.

A. Article 78 proceedings taken against the following agencies must be begun in Albany County: Agriculture and Markets; Comptroller, Commission of Education; Public Service Commission; Regents of State of New York; Taxation and Finance; Department of Transportation; and the Water Resources Board. CPLR 506 (b) (2).

B. CPLR article 78 proceedings that challenge administrative disciplinary actions involving certain professions governed by Public Health Law § 230-c (5) and Education Law § 6510 (5) must be initiated in the Appellate Division, Third Department.

7. Reviewing Judicial Courts. The Supreme Court is of trial-level with general, original jurisdiction and with appellant jurisdiction in the intermediate appellate court and the lower appellate court. The Appellate Division of the Supreme Court is the intermediate appellate court between the New York Supreme Court and the New York Court of Appeals (New York's highest appellate court). The Appellate Division consists of four judicial departments, one in each judicial district. The lower appellate courts, the two Appellate Terms, are in the 1st and 2nd Judicial Districts. The New York Constitution (NY Const art VI, § 8 [a]) enables an Appellate Division to establish an Appellate Term.

A. The Appellate Term determines if an administrative decision violated lawful procedure, made an error of law, or was arbitrary and capricious or an abuse of discretion (mandamus to review).

(1). The Court reviews the rationality of an agency's conduct, the reason for and the reasonableness of the conduct. CPLR 7803 (3); *Matter of 125 Bar Corp. v St. Liq. Auth. of NY,* 24 NY2d 174 (1969).

(2). If an article 78 proceeding in the Appellate Term raises a substantial evidence question, the Appellate Term must dispose of any objection that could terminate the proceeding (claims of lack of jurisdiction, statute of limitations, and res judicata) without deciding the substantial evidence issue. If the determination by the Appellate Term of an objection does not terminate a proceeding, the matter must be transferred to the Appellate Division for a certiorari review. CPLR 7804 (g).

B. The Appellate Division of the Supreme Court hears appeals from judgments made in article 78 proceedings by the Appellate Term and of matters transferred to the Appellant Division by the

Appellate Term. [66]

(1). The jurisdiction of the Appellate Division is invoked by permission either of the Appellate Term or the Appellate Division. CPLR 5701 (c).

(2). A judgment rendered in an article 78 proceeding against a body or officer is not appealable "as of right" to the Appellate Division. CPLR 5701 (b) (1).

(3). The Appellate Division conducts appellate reviews of any substantial evidence question. Judicial review of an administrative determination made after a hearing required by law is limited to a consideration of whether substantial evidence supports the decision.

C. An appeal from a judgment of the Appellate Division to the Court of Appeals may be taken by permission of the Appellate Division or upon direct application to the Court of Appeals after a refusal by the Appellate Division to grant permission. Normally, the review power of the Court of Appeals is limited to questions of law. NY Const art VI, § 3 (a); CPLR 5602 (a) (1).

§15.5. Judgments of Supreme Court. CPLR article 78 judgments must comply with provisions of CPLR 7806.

1. Scope of Judgment in CPLR article 78 Appeal. A judgment of

---

[66] Jill Paradise Botler, M. Christine DeVita, Stephen John Kallas, and William J. Ruane, *The Appellate Division of the Supreme Court of New York: An Empirical Study of Its Powers and Functions as an Intermediate State Court,* 47 Fordham L. Rev. 929 (1979.

review in an article 78 proceeding annuls, modifies or confirms a determination in whole or in part, or directs or prohibits a specific action, or awards restitution or damages.

2. Forms of Judgment. The Supreme Court issues three types of judgments:

(A). A Regular Judgment. In a regular judgment, the court (1) states the decision, (2) expresses the collective reasoning, rationale, and principles of law underlying the decision, (3) lists the authoring judge, and (4) contains any concurring and dissenting opinions.

(B). A Per Curiam Decision. A per curiam decision is issued by at least a majority of the court anonymously without listing the author. The appropriate judge signs any accompanying dissent or concurring opinion.

(C). A Memorandum Decision. A memorandum decision is rendered in writing and states the judgment of the court without comment or explanation of law. To be an order of the court, it must so state. A memorandum decision should not be cited as precedent for legal argument, but it may be cited as persuasive authority, or in support of the equitable defenses of res judicata, collateral estoppel or the law of the case.

CHAPTER XVI. SOVEREIGNTY OF EXECUTIVE AGENCIES.

§ 16.1. Government by Executive Agency. Executive administrative agencies construct state government's primary and most proficient system of the management of human affairs in the designated governmental functions over which executive agencies have primary jurisdiction. [67]

§ 16.2. Executive Agencies - Virtual Sovereignties. The legal structures of New York State executive agencies fracture the traditional view of state sovereignty.

1. Administrative law fundamentally combines the nature and the power both of natural law and of positive law. Social and political pressures initiate the formation and feed the growth of administrative law. The preamble to administrative authoritarianism is the enablement of government efficiency to protect and to advance the public health, safety, and welfare. Government by executive administrative agencies generates rules and regulations, adjusts rights and privileges, and controls with enforcement. [68]

2. Additionally, State executive agencies are entrusted to act principled and in the public interest when executing delegated

---

[67] Lockwood, Aaron J, *The Primary Jurisdiction Doctrine: Competing Standards of Appellate Review*, 64 Wash. & Lee L. Rev. 707 (2007).
[68] Van Alstyne, William W., *The Demise of the Right-Privilege Distinction in Constitutional Law*, 81 Harv. L. Rev. 1439-1464 (1968).

legislative, judicial, and executive powers. Coupling the power to govern with the duties of legality and ethicality imparts a moral force to the conferred, virtual sovereignty of executive agencies and fabricates the illusion that state, executive, administrative agencies reserve a reverential political distance from state government; the agencies are "of government" but "for the people."

3. State government acquiesces administratively and politically with and encourages public acceptance of the belief that a state, executive, administrative agency that treats both an "urgent government interest" and a "vital, quality-of-life, public need" possesses a moral imperative and a virtuous welfare right to existence. [69]

§ 16.3. The Future: Regulation of Automata. Automata combine theoretical computer science and discrete mathematical structures to develop automatons to perform functions in the daily life of people.

1. Automatons, the application of machines in a self-regulating system, operate without human intervention in many activities and surpass human abilities to perform the same functions. Examples (not all-inclusive) are: (A) Communications systems (satellites, networks, telephone, mailing processes); (B) consumer products (automobile, household appliances); (C) labor (manufacturing, robots); (D) service industry (banking, credit, healthcare, hospital, pharmacy, stock exchange, retail trade, restaurant); (E) robotics; (F) security; and (G) transportation (aircraft, highway, mass transit, rail).

2. Predicted potential effects of automation on society raise fundamental questions concerning dramatic, human, behavioral

---

[69] Chapter X § 10.6.1 (C) (2). Compelling Public Rights.

changes, socioeconomic influences, security issues, and privacy and other legal rights. The speed and constancy in which automata innovation evolves challenge federal and state governments to identify, to implement, and to maintain practical and sufficient regulatory action. As automation of tasks is controlled increasingly through artificial intelligence, automated decisions by AI machines will increasingly directly control human action and raise a multitude of legal and political issues. Examples are the following two, simple automatons.

(A). Lawrence B. Solum's "Artificially Intelligent Traffic Authority (AITA)." [70] AITA units would survey, identify, evaluate, adapt to driver behavior, and control traffic flow. Artificial intelligence would devise, introduce, and operate traffic experiments, and identify and immediately have violators removed from traffic.

(B). Automated compliance consisting of starter-interruption devices. Auto lenders are using starter-interruption devices that allow the lender to remotely disable a car to collect late payments from subprime borrowers.[71] A borrower must make payments timely or lose the use of the vehicle. A lender also uses GPS technology on the starter-interruption devices to track a car's location and movements. Consumers are requesting state and federal authorities to regulate the new technology as "electronic repossession."

3. Progressive automation will repeatedly raise privacy and due

---

[70] Solum, Lawrence B., *Artificial Meaning,* 89 Wash. L. Rev. 69 (2014).

[71] Corkery, Michael and Silver-Greenberg, Jessica, (September 25, 2014), *Miss a Payment? Good Luck Moving That Car,* New York Times, p. A 1.

process issues and revive public policy and political views of deregulation and laissez-faire.

4. Predictably, the standard of life and the health, safety, and welfare of people in future social and economic environments will depend primarily on the human intelligent and reasonable regulation of artificial intelligence technologies. Currently, objective ethics and objective duties govern and regulate human public actions in the interest of human public health, safety, welfare, and advancement.

A. Objective ethics compose a moral code, the moral right and wrong values of a person's actions. Objective ethics assign moral values to a human's actions, regardless of the person's standards and principles.

B. Objective responsibilities focus on rules for governing, regulating, and sanctioning a person's actions as lawful or unlawful regardless of an event or situation or the person's personal opinions. Law imposes public duties on human actors.

5. Futuristically, proficient regulation of automata by state government will demand different and definitive configurations of executive administrative agencies within federal and state constitutional provisions enacted to govern human behavior. In an intra-inter competing society consisting of three populaces (human, artificial intelligences, and human-artificial intelligences), government must concurrently (A) control and advance ever-evolving populaces, and (B) ensure and protect human health, safety, welfare, and freedoms.

TABLE OF AUTHORITIES

I. CASES.

II. CONSTITUTION.

A. United States.

B. New York State.

III. LAWS.

A. Unconsolidated.

B. Consolidated.

IV. DECLARATORY RULINGS.

V. OPINIONS.

VI. BILLS.

VII. POLICIES.

VIII. PROCLAMATIONS.

IX. TREATIES.

INDEX.

B

C

D

E

F

G

H

I

J

L

M

N

O

P

Q

R

S

T

U

V

W

www.ingramcontent.com/pod-product-compliance
Lightning Source LLC
LaVergne TN
LVHW052034200926
848481LV00005B/1676
* 9 7 8 0 6 9 2 3 8 8 0 7 5 *